McDougal Littell
Wordskills

Orange Level

James E. Coomber
Concordia College
Moorhead, Minnesota

Howard D. Peet
North Dakota State University
Fargo, North Dakota

McDougal Littell
A HOUGHTON MIFFLIN COMPANY
Evanston, Illinois • Boston • Dallas

ISBN: 0-395-97983-8

Copyright © 2000 by McDougal, Littell & Company
Box 1667, Evanston, Illinois 60204
All rights reserved. Printed in the United States of America.

5 6 7 8 9 10–HWI–03 02 01

CONTENTS

To the Student

Why study vocabulary? Increasing the number of words that you know helps you read, write, and speak better. You'll understand more of what you read with less reliance on the dictionary, and you'll be able to express yourself more accurately. This doesn't mean using twenty-dollar words to amaze others. It just means using the right words to say exactly what you mean.

How to Use This Book

You may notice something unusual about this vocabulary book. Definitions are not given with the word lists. Instead, you are given something more powerful—strategies for determining the meanings of words yourself. You'll find this information in Strategies for Unlocking Word Meaning (pages 1-12). Then, in the following units, you will master new words using a five-step process:

1. First you will infer the word's meaning through context clues.
2. Second you will refine your understanding by studying the word's use in a reading selection.
3. Then your understanding will be reinforced through a variety of exercises.
4. Next you will relate the word to other words in the same family.
5. Finally you will use the word in writing and speaking.

The words in this book are ones you are likely to encounter in your reading. Some you may already know; others may be completely unfamiliar. As you study these words, try to move them into your "active vocabulary." This means that you understand the words well enough to use them in your speaking and writing.

A Personal Vocabulary-Building Program

You can apply the vocabulary skills in this book to learning any new words that you encounter. Here are several tips that will help you:

1. Keep a vocabulary notebook. Jot down the new words you encounter. Record the essential information for each word: correct spelling, part of speech, pronunciation, definition.
2. Review the words in your notebook. Take a few minutes each day to study them. Set a realistic goal of learning a certain number of new words per week.
3. Study the words actively. Active study means that you use as many senses as possible in studying the word. Say the word. Listen to yourself say it. See the word in your mind's eye. Then make sure you use the word as soon as possible in conversation or in writing. A rule of thumb is that if you use a word twice, it is yours.
4. Invent your own memory devices. Try to associate the word with other similar words you know. Create a mental image that relates to the word and helps you remember its meaning. One student remembered the meaning of the word *pretentious*, "showy, flaunting," by picturing a small boy playing make-believe, *pretending* to be a king.

There is one final reason for studying vocabulary, one that we hope you discover for yourself as you use this book: Words are fascinating! They are as surprising and alive and insightful as the people who use them.

Strategies for Unlocking Word Meaning

What happens when you encounter an unfamiliar word in your reading? If you have a dictionary at hand, you can look up the word. If you don't have a dictionary, you still have two excellent strategies that can help you make sense of the word: **context clues** and **word parts analysis**. You will be using these strategies in every unit of this book. With practice you can master these strategies and improve your reading skills.

Part A   Determining a Word's Meaning from Context

Skilled readers often use context clues to determine a word's meaning. **Context** refers to the words or sentences before or after a certain word that help clarify what the word means. There are several types of context clues you can look for, including **definition and restatement, example, comparison, contrast**, and **cause and effect**.

Definition and Restatement

Sometimes a writer will directly define a word, especially if the word is a technical term that may be unfamiliar to readers. Here is an example:

The scientists studying air pollution were concerned about the concentration of *particulates*, which are solid or liquid particles suspended in the air.

More often, a writer will restate the meaning of a word in a less precise form than a dictionary definition.

The woman was a *philanthropist*, a generous individual who gave thousands of dollars to charity.

The meaning of *philanthropist*—"one who is humane, benevolent"—becomes obvious through the use of the restatement: "a generous individual. . . ." Definition and restatement are often signaled by punctuation (note the commas in the preceding examples) and by certain key words and phrases.

Words Signaling Definition and Restatement		
which is	or	also known as
that is	in other words	also called

Example

The context in which a word appears may include one or more **examples** that unlock the meaning of an unfamiliar word, as in the following sentence.

Our biology class studied various *mollusks* such as clams, oysters, and squid.

The phrase *such as*, followed by a list of examples, helps reveal the meaning of *mollusks*—"a group of animals having soft bodies without backbones, often enclosed in shells." The following words often signal examples:

Words Signaling Examples		
like	for example	other
including	for instance	this
such as	especially	these
		these include

Comparison

Another type of context clue is **comparison.** With this clue the writer compares the word in question with other, more familiar words. By noting the similarities between the things described, you can get an idea of the meaning of the unfamiliar word.

The *herbivorous* cow, like other plant-eating animals, has special, high-crowned teeth suitable for grinding.

The comparison *like other plant-eating animals* clearly conveys the meaning of *herbivorous*—"feeding chiefly on grass." Comparisons are often signaled by these key words:

Words Signaling Comparisons		
like	similar to	similarly
as	resembling	also
in the same way	likewise	identical
		related

Contrast

Context may also help reveal the meaning of a word through **contrast,** as in this example:

The mathematics problem seemed *abstruse* to most of us, but Angie found it quite easy to understand.

In this sentence the word *but* signals a contrast. Therefore, you can assume that *abstruse* means the opposite of *easy to understand*: "incomprehensible, deep." The following key words and phrases signal contrasts:

Words Signaling Contrasts		
but	on the other hand	dissimilar
although	unlike	different
on the contrary	in contrast to	however

Cause and Effect

Another type of context clue is **cause and effect**. The cause of an action or event may be stated using an unfamiliar word. If, however, the effect of that action is stated in familiar terms, it can help you understand the unfamiliar word. Consider the following example:

Because the well water had become *contaminated*, we had to buy bottled water.

In this sentence the cause—contaminated water—leads to the effect—getting bottled water. Therefore, *contaminated* must mean "polluted," or "unsafe to drink." Certain key words and phrases may signal cause and effect:

Words Signaling Cause and Effect		
because	consequently	so
since	therefore	as a result

Inference from General Context

Often the clues to the meaning of an unfamiliar word are not in the same sentence as the word nor are they as obvious as the preceding examples. In such cases you will need to look at the sentences that surround the word and **infer**, or draw a conclusion about, the word's meaning. A single piece of information several sentences away from the unfamiliar word may unlock the meaning. Study the following example:

The *paucity* of rainfall last summer broke a record. The average amount of rainfall in Hobbsville for June, July, and August is 4.1 inches. A summer rainfall of 2 inches is considered to be very low here. However, last year only .5 inches of rain fell during those three months, our driest summer ever.

The clue to the meaning of *paucity* is found near the end of the paragraph. The detail *only .5 inches of rain fell . . . our driest summer* suggests that *paucity* means "scarcity."

Sometimes the supporting details in a paragraph must be examined together to help you infer the meaning of an unfamiliar word. Consider the example below:

When the king was present, his subjects followed a strict *protocol*. They were to stand no closer than ten feet from the king. They were to bow deeply and never look directly at him. They were not to speak until spoken to—and then they were to address him as "Your Highness." They were allowed only one request and were to remain in the court until all the royal officials had left.

A series of descriptive details follows the unfamiliar word *protocol*. The details help you draw a conclusion about what a *protocol* is—"an accepted, proper way of acting in an official setting."

Determining Meaning from Context Each of the sentences and paragraphs on the next page contains an italicized word you may not know. Look for context clues to help you determine the meaning of the word and write the definition in the blank.

1. At first Calvin was *intransigent*, but he finally agreed on a compromise.

   _____

   _____

2. The prisoner was *intractable*, becoming harder to control as time passed.

   _____

3. By the time the state basketball tournament began, Lester was at the *zenith* of his abilities. He was averaging 29 points per game. He led the state in rebounds and assists. He was running faster and jumping higher than ever before. His inspirational playing sparked his team to their third consecutive state championship. In later years Lester could never quite match his performance during that 1979 season.

   _____

4. A *pragmatic* person, Ms. Arnold bought an unstylish car that offered excellent gas mileage and engine performance.

   _____

5. Erica did a *meticulous* job on her homework; in contrast, Sara did careless work.

   _____

6. By wearing a wig, a fake mustache, and glasses, Jeremy traveled through his old hometown *incognito*.

   _____

7. Sherry may think she is perfect, but she is *fallible* like the rest of us.

   _____

8. I knew Greg thought he was superior when I caught him giving me a *disdainful* look.

   _____

9. When the king *abdicated* his throne, the citizens celebrated in the streets for three days. One hundred thousand people paraded to the castle, their mood a mixture of joy, relief, and anticipation. For the king, stepping down was equally joyful. He had never been liked by his subjects, and now he could spend more time with his one true love: auto racing.

   _____

10. Finally it became clear that the newspaper reporter was a *sham*. Her supervisors checked her "sources" for two major articles and were stunned to find that she had made up large parts of the stories. When they called the university listed on the reporter's resume, they were told she had never attended the school.

    _____

11. Like a poisonous snake, the *insidious* disease slithered through the city claiming victims.

    _____

12. After a month in a cast, my right arm had *atrophied*. It was noticeably smaller than my left arm.

_____

13. Mr. Reiff was slowly losing his *composure*. At first he had been the picture of calm. But as the discussion continued, sweat formed on his brow, and his eyes darted around the room nervously. Several times he interrupted the others with strange remarks.

_____

14. The physicist's main area of study was *fusion*, the combining of atoms to release great amounts of energy in a hydrogen bomb.

_____

15. When the explosives were *detonated*, we saw smoke billowing from the windows, and then the building began to crumble.

_____

Number correct _____ (total 15)

Understanding Context Clues Write a sentence for each of the words below, using a different type of context clue for each sentence. After the sentence, label the method you used to define each word in one of the following ways: **definition and restatement, example, comparison, contrast,** and **cause and effect.**

advent   felony   tarnish
conservative   landmark

1. _____

_____

2. _____

_____

3. _____

_____

4. _____

_____

5. _____

_____

Number correct _____ (total 5)

Part B Determining Meaning Through Word Analysis

Word analysis is another way to determine a new word's meaning. If you know what each part of a word means, you can often understand the complete word.

Prefix   a word part that is added to the beginning of another word or word part

Suffix   a word part that is added to the end of another word or word part

Base word   a complete word to which a prefix and/or a suffix may be added

Root   a word part to which a prefix and/or a suffix may be added. A root cannot stand alone.

The word *dysfunctional* is made up of the prefix *dys-*, the base word *function*, and the suffix *-al*. If you know the meanings of these parts, you can determine the meaning of the whole word.

dys ("bad") + function ("operate, work") + al ("relating to")
dysfunctional = relating to something that doesn't work

Now look at a word with a root. *Immutable* is made up of the prefix *im-* ("not"), the Latin root *mut* ("change"), and the suffix *-able* ("inclined to"). *Immutable* means "not inclined to change."

Prefixes

The following chart contains prefixes that have only one meaning.

Prefixes That Have a Single Meaning

Prefix	Meaning	Example
bene-	good	benefit
circum-	around	circumvent
col-, com-	with, together	collapse, compile
con-, cor-		construct, correspond
contra-	opposed	contradict
equi-	equal	equidistant
extra-	outside	extralegal
hemi-	half	hemisphere
hyper-	over, above	hypercritical
inter-	between, among	international
intra-	within	intracellular
intro-	into	introvert
mal-	bad	maltreat
mid-	halfway	midday
mis-	wrong	misspell
non-	not	nonworking
pre-	before	predawn
post-	after in time, space	postpone
retro-	backward, behind	retroactive
sub-	under, below	subzero

Some prefixes have more than one meaning. Study the common prefixes listed in the following chart.

Prefixes That Have More Than One Meaning

Prefix	Meaning	Example
ab-, a-	not	abnormal
	away	absent
	up, out	arise
ad-	motion toward	adopt
	nearness to	adjoin
ante-	before, prior to	antecedent
	in front of	anteroom
anti-	against	anticensorship
	prevents, cures	antidote
	opposite, reverse	antimatter
be-	around, by	beset
	about	bemoan
de-	away from, off	derail
	down	decline
	reverse action of	defrost
dis-	lack of	distrust
	not	dishonest
	away	dispatch
em-, en-	to get into, on	embark
	to make, cause	enfeeble
	in, into	enclose
il, im-, in-, ir-	not	immature
	in, into	investigate
pro-	in favor of	prolabor
	forward, ahead	propel
re-	again	replant
	back	repay
semi-	half	semicircle
	twice in a period	semiannual
	partly	semiconscious
super-	over and above	superhuman
	very large	supertanker
trans-	across	transatlantic
	beyond	transcend
un-	not	unhappy
	reverse of	unfasten

Suffixes

Like a prefix, a suffix has a meaning that can provide a strong clue to the definition of a whole word. Suffixes can also determine the part of speech. Certain suffixes make words into nouns; others create adjectives, verbs, or adverbs.

Once you know suffixes and their meanings, you can form new words by attaching suffixes to base words or to roots. For instance, the suffix *-ist* can be added to the base word *biology* to create the word *biologist*. Notice that the spelling of a base word may change when a suffix is added. In the preceding example, the *y* from *biology* was dropped when the *-ist* was added. For information about spelling rules for adding suffixes, see the **Spelling Handbook**, pages 195–197.

Noun suffixes, when added to a base word or root, form nouns. Become familiar with the following common noun suffixes.

Noun Suffixes That Refer to Someone Who Does Something

Suffix	Examples
-ant	commandant, occupant
-eer	auctioneer
-er	manager
-ier	cavalier
-ist	geologist, somnambulist
-ician	beautician, statistician
-or	counselor

Noun Suffixes That Make Abstract Words

Suffix	Examples
-ance	vigilance
-ancy	vagrancy, vacancy
-ation	imagination
-cy	accuracy
-dom	freedom, kingdom
-ence	independence
-hood	womanhood, brotherhood
-ice	cowardice, prejudice
-ism	realism, federalism
-ity	sincerity
-ization	civilization
-ment	encouragement, commitment
-ness	kindness, fondness
-ship	ownership, worship
-sion	decision
-tude	gratitude, solitude
-ty	frailty

Adjective suffixes, when added to a base word or root, create adjectives—words that are used to modify nouns and pronouns.

Adjective Suffixes		
Suffix	**Meaning**	**Example**
-able	able to	readable
-acious	full of	vivacious
-al	relating to	musical
-ant	relating to	triumphant
-ful	full of	harmful
-ible	able to	convertible
-ic	pertaining to or like	heroic
-ical	pertaining to	economical
-ish	pertaining to or like	waspish
-ive	pertaining to	descriptive
-less	without	senseless
-like	like	lifelike
-ly	like	scholarly
-most	at the extreme	topmost
-ous	full of	furious
-ular	pertaining to	cellular

Verb suffixes change base words to verbs. The following chart lists four common verb suffixes.

Verb Suffixes		
Suffix	**Meaning**	**Example**
-ate	to make	activate
-en	to become	lengthen
-fy	to make	simplify
-ize	to become	crystallize

Adverb Suffixes change base words to adverbs—words that modify verbs, adjectives, and other adverbs. The following chart lists the most common adverb suffixes.

Adverb Suffixes		
Suffix	**Meaning**	**Example**
-ly, -ily	manner	quickly
-ward	toward	skyward
-wise	like	clockwise

Roots and Word Families

A word root cannot stand alone but must be combined with other word parts. A great many roots used in our language originally came from Greek or Latin. These roots generate whole families of English words. A **word family** is a group of words with a common root. For example, all of the words in the following word family are derived from the Latin root *spec*, which means "see."

suspect	speculate	specter
spectacular	circumspect	spectacle
spectrum	inspect	respect

By learning word roots, you develop your vocabulary because you can recognize roots in many related words. The following two charts show some common Greek and Latin roots.

Useful Greek Roots

Root	Meaning	Examples
anthrop	human	anthropology
aster, astr	star	asterisk
auto	self, alone	automobile
bibl	book	bibliography
bi, bio	life	biology
chron	time	chronology
crac, crat	govern	democracy
dem	people	epidemic
gen	birth, race	generation
geo	earth	geoscience
graph	write	paragraph
gram	write	grammar
hydr	water	hydrogen
log	word, reason	dialogue
logy	study of	geology
metr, meter	measure	barometer
neo	new	neophyte
nom, nym	name, word, law	economic
ortho	straight, correct	orthodontist
pan	all, entire	panorama
phil	love	philosopher
phobia	fear	claustrophobia
phon	sound	phonograph
psych	mind, soul	psychology
scope	see	telescope
soph	wise, wisdom	sophisticated
tele	far, distant	television
theo	god	theology
therm	heat	thermometer

Useful Latin Roots

Root	Meaning	Examples
capt	take, hold, seize	capture
cede, ceed, cess	go, yield, give away	recession, proceed
cred	believe	credit, creed
dic, dict	speak, say, tell	dictate, dictionary
duc, duct	lead	induce, conductor
fac, fec, fic	do, make	factory, defect, fiction
fer	carry	transfer, ferry
ject	throw, hurl	eject, inject
junct	join	junction, conjunction
mit, miss	send	admit, dismiss
mov, mot	move	move, motion
par	get ready	prepare, repair
pon, pos, posit	place, put	component, deposit
port	carry	porter, portable
puls	throb, urge	pulsate, compulsory
scrib, script	write	description, scripture
spec, spic	look, see	spectacle, conspicuous
stat	stand, put in a place	statue, stature
ten	stretch, hold	tendon, tenant
tract	pull, move	tractor, retract
ven, vent	come	convention, event
vers, vert	turn	versatile, invert
vid, vis	see	video, vista
voc, vok	call	vocation, invoke
vol	wish	volunteer, malevolent
volv	roll	revolve, involve

Determining Word Meaning through Prefixes and Suffixes Draw lines to separate each of the following words into three parts—prefix, base word, and suffix. Determine the meaning of the prefix and the suffix. Then, by adding the meanings of the prefix and the suffix to the base word, write the meaning of each complete word.

1. unharmonious: _____

2. subtropical: _____

3. interdepartmental: _____

4. inconsiderately: _____

5. semimonthly: _____

6. malodorous: _____

7. enforceable: _____

7/1/02
STUDY!!!

11

8. disquietude: _____

9. hyperacidity: _____

10. immaturity: _____

Number correct _____ (total 10)

Determining Word Meaning through Prefixes, Suffixes, and Roots Each of the following words consists of a Greek or Latin root and a prefix or suffix. Use your knowledge of roots, prefixes, and suffixes to put together the meanings of the word parts and write a definition for each word. You may check your definitions with a dictionary.

1. revoke: _____

2. credible: _____

3. subvert: _____

4. sophist: _____

5. adjunct: _____

6. automation: _____

7. captivate: _____

8. tenacious: _____

9. static: _____

10. remit: _____

Number correct _____ (total 10)

Number correct in unit _____ (total 40)

UNIT 1

Part A   Target Words and Their Meanings

The twenty words below will be the focus of the first unit. You will find them in the reading selection and in the exercises in this unit. By working with these words, you will master their meanings. For a guide to their pronunciations refer to the **Pronunciation Key** on page 220.

1. align (ə līn′) v.
2. aperture (ap′ ər chər) n.
3. appraisal (ə prā′ z'l) n.
4. circumstance (sur′ kəm stans′, -stəns′) n.
5. critically (krit′ i k'lē) adv.
6. determine (di tur′ mən) v.
7. diagonally (dī ag′ ə nə lē) adv.
8. disclose (dis klōz′) v.
9. dissolve (di zälv′, -zôlv′) v.
10. distinguish (dis tiŋ′ gwish) v.
11. grave (grāv) adj., n.
12. image (im′ ij) n.
13. intent (in tent′) adj., n.
14. intermittently (in′ tər mit′ 'nt lē) adv.
15. intruder (in trood′ ər) n.
16. overtake (ō′ vər tāk′) v.
17. retrieve (ri trēv′) v.
18. suffice (sə fīs′, -fīz′) v.
19. sufficient (sə fish′ 'nt) adj.
20. supple (sup′ 'l) adj.

Inferring Meaning from Context

For each sentence write the letter of the word or phrase that is closest to the meaning of the word or words in italics. Use context clues to help you determine the correct answer. (For information about how context helps you understand vocabulary, see pp. 1-5.)

__B__ 1. The railroad workers who were laying track made sure that the rails were *aligned with* each other; otherwise a train could become derailed.
   a. opposite from   b. lined up with   c. crossing   d. close to

__A__ 2. Because of the size of the *aperture* in my grandmother's birdhouse, no bird that is larger than a wren will be able to use the birdhouse.
   a. opening   b. perch   c. room   d. roof

__D__ 3. Since we wanted to get a fair price for the old car, we had a dealer give us *an appraisal of* its worth.
   a. a guess at   b. a bid on   c. a good price for   d. an estimate of

__D__ 4. *Circumstances* beyond our control caused us to be late.
   a. fears   b. enemies   c. habits   d. conditions

__D__ 5. Mrs. Lu examined the garden *critically* before paying the workers.
   a. quickly   b. poorly   c. finally   d. carefully

_A_ 6. Coach Grinaker told Susan, "You are the one who will *determine* whether or not you will succeed."
a. decide b. discover c. tell about d. understand

_A_ 7. Instead of walking straight across the street, Joe walked *diagonally*.
a. on an angle b. carelessly c. slowly d. blindly

_B_ 8. Carl *disclosed* the location of the treasure—under a rock near the barn.
a. covered up b. told c. guessed d. dug at

_A_ 9. The ice cubes *dissolved* after we dropped them into the cup of hot cider.
a. melted b. broke c. froze d. fizzed

_B_ 10. The twins were so alike that I could not *distinguish* one from the other.
a. describe b. see the difference between c. respect
d. see the similarity between

_B_ 11. Joan's *grave* expression led us to suspect that something was wrong.
a. hopeful b. serious c. deadly d. foolish

_AD_ 12. Standing before the mirror in his new suit, Terry was pleased with the handsome *image* he saw.
a. likeness b. clothes c. stranger d. pictures

_A_ 13. Clyde was so *intent on* his work that he did not hear Jack drive up.
a. absorbed in b. tired of c. confused by d. careless about

_A_ 14. Most telephones ring *intermittently*—on again, off again.
a. at intervals b. clearly c. vaguely d. on pitch

_B_ 15. When Ray arrived at her party uninvited, Jane called him *an intruder*.
a. a great help b. an unwelcome person c. a salesman
d. an interesting surprise

_C_ 16. The sheriff raced to *overtake* the fleeing bank robbers.
a. leave b. spot c. catch d. collect

_D_ 17. Ms. Montez tried to *retrieve* the information that had disappeared from the computer screen.
a. give up b. use c. correct d. get back

_A_ 18. The supplies we brought on the camping trip *sufficed* for three days, but on the fourth day we ran out of food.
a. were enough b. didn't last c. were too much d. were tasty

_C_ 19. Fortunately the lumber is *sufficient* to build the garage.
a. too much b. too little c. enough d. not the right size

_A_ 20. The gymnast was *supple* enough to perform the most difficult routines successfully and with a great deal of grace.
a. flexible b. careless c. surprised d. smart

Number correct _____ (total 20)

14

Part B Target Words in Reading and Literature

You should now have a general idea of the meaning of each target word. Refine your understanding by examining the shades of meaning the words have in the following excerpt.

The Surround

Stewart Edward White

Have you ever experienced a moment when you felt someone might be following you? That is what Andy Burnett suspects in this excerpt from a short story about life in the early American West. Andy knows someone is coming, but he does not know whether that person is friend or foe.

Andy Burnett, splashing slowly upstream in inspection of his beaver traps, was suddenly **overtaken** and passed by an old duck and two full-grown flappers. One of the latter almost brushed his elbow. It is not the nature of wild ducks to lose one fear except in a greater fear. Andy looked around appraisingly, waded **diagonally** to the bank, tossed as gently as he might the long rifle to the cushion of a low bush. Then he reached upward to grasp the overhanging sycamore branch his first **appraisal** of the situation had **disclosed.** It was not strong enough to support his whole weight for long; but it **sufficed,** aided by a quick **supple** twist of his body, to swing Andy several feet across the grass bank. He looked back **critically.** Only a scattering of sprinkled water from the legs of his garments marked where he had broken trail. This might be **sufficient** for sharp eyes. Andy **retrieved** the rifle and slipped back downstream a few rods.[1] He sat on a log, well within the screen of alders, and listened.

5

10

[1] rod: a measure of length equal to 5½ yards or 5.029 meters.

For some time he heard nothing but the rare autumnal half-songs of birds, the rustle of the breeze, and the low chattering voices that always accompany fast water undertone. Then fitfully, **intermittently,** his sharpened senses became aware of occasional breaks in the rhythm. Someone was, indeed, wading up the stream. Andy slipped behind his log. Nearly opposite him a small **aperture** in the foliage looked through to the surface of the water. Here Andy would get a fair sight at the **intruder.**

But while the latter was yet some distance downstream, Andy's **intent** scowl of attention **dissolved** to a **grave** smile of amusement. He reseated himself on the log and laid aside his rifle. His ears had caught one sound that **determined** his action. It was the quick, high chirp of a pine squirrel. Pine squirrels may only rarely be seen in midstream; and in such **circumstances** they never chirp.

Andy waited on the log. Now plainly could be **distinguished** the slow-paced interruptions of the smooth current's flow as the unseen wader made his way upstream against it. Andy's buckskins blended into his background; he held himself still as a graven **image;** the opening in the leaves was small, so that only for the briefest moment could the eyes of one passing **align** themselves with it. Nevertheless he was instantly discovered. He grinned again in appreciation as the young Indian checked, then turned to the shore, thrusting aside the screen of leaves.

"Welcome, Kiasax," the white boy greeted his friend in the Blackfoot tongue. "You have sharp eyes."

"Greetings, I-tam-api," returned the Indian. "But if you will sit in plain view, you must be seen."

Refining Your Understanding

For each of the following items consider how the target word is used in the passage. Write the letter of the word or phrase that best completes each sentence.

_C_ 1. The author's use of *supple* (line 9) to describe Andy's quick move suggests that Andy is   a. clumsy   b. smart   c. well-coordinated.

_B_ 2. The fact that Andy "looked back *critically*" (line 10) at the situation suggests he was being   a. fussy   b. careful   c. terrified.

_A_ 3. The *aperture* (line 18) in the foliage could be   a. the space between tree leaves   b. a tree trunk   c. a completely unobstructed view.

_C B X_ 4. The scowl on Andy's face was *intent* (line 21) because   a. the sun was shining in his eyes   b. he was irritated by the presence of an intruder c. he was worried about who the intruder might be.

_A_ 5. The author describes Andy as "still as a graven *image*" (line 29), words that suggest Andy looked like a   a. statue   b. mirage   c. shadow.

Number correct _____ (total 5)

Part C *Ways to Make New Words Your Own*

By now you are familiar with the target words and their meanings. This section presents reinforcement activities that will help you make the words part of your permanent vocabulary.

Using Language and Thinking Skills

Understanding Multiple Meanings Each box in this exercise contains a boldfaced word with its definitions. Read the definitions and then the sentences that follow. Write the letter of the definition that applies to each sentence.

---

image
a. a representation of a person or thing, drawn or painted (n.)
b. the visual impression of something produced by a mirror or lens (n.)
c. a person or thing much like another; a copy (n.)
d. a mental picture of something; an impression (n.)

C 1. Fred is a perfect *image* of his brother Steve.

A 2. In the center of the priest's garden was a beautiful *image* of St. Francis.

B 3. Their *images* in the funhouse mirror made Max and Sheila appear ten feet tall.

D 4. My *image* of a civil engineer changed when I met Helen.

D 5. The *image* his voice created over the telephone was that of an older man.

---

grave
a. requiring serious thought; weighty (adj.)
b. indicating great danger; threatening in nature (adj.)
c. a hole in the ground in which to bury a dead body (n.)

B 6. After reviewing the patient's test results, the doctors concluded that he had a *grave* illness.

A 7. After two weeks at college, Teresa had *grave* doubts about her choice of schools.

A 8. Throughout history the decision to go to war has been a *grave* one.

C 9. Many music lovers in Germany visit the *grave* of the famous composer Ludwig van Beethoven.

B 10. People living near the volcano were told of the *grave* danger long before the lava began to flow.

Number correct _____ (total 10)

Finding the Unrelated Word Write the letter of the word that is not related in meaning to the other words in the set.

<u>C</u> 1. a. dissolve b. distintegrate c. harden d. melt

<u>D</u> 2. a. characterize b. distinguish c. define d. persuade

<u>C</u> 3. a. find b. recover c. lose d. retrieve

<u>D</u> 4. a. cover b. hide c. conceal d. disclose

<u>A</u> 5. a. lacking b. sufficient c. enough d. ample

<u>D</u> 6. a. continually b. constantly c. intermittently d. carelessly

<u>D</u> 7. a. limber b. flexible c. supple d. rigid

<u>C</u> 8. a. intruder b. invader c. guest d. trespasser

<u>C</u> 9. a. aperture b. opening c. cover d. gap

<u>D</u> 10. a. straighten b. align c. even d. curve

Number correct _____ (total 10)

Practicing for Standardized Tests

Synonyms Write the letter of the word that is closest in meaning to the capitalized word.

<u>B</u> 1. APERTURE: (A) fruit (B) hole (C) change (D) serious (E) image

<u>C</u> 2. SUFFICIENT: (A) undisclosed (B) painful (C) enough (D) healthful (E) known

<u>A</u> 3. GRAVE: (A) serious (B) dead (C) ample (D) unknown (E) spiritual

<u>A</u> 4. DETERMINE: (A) decide (B) complete (C) speculate (D) dissolve (E) demonstrate

<u>E</u> 5. IMAGE: (A) apparel (B) massage (C) fiction (D) ad (E) likeness

<u>D</u> 6. RETRIEVE: (A) hunt (B) apprehend (C) devour (D) recover (E) buy

<u>E</u> 7. DISCLOSE: (A) open (B) lock (C) decide (D) acknowledge (E) reveal

<u>E</u> 8. CIRCUMSTANCE: (A) distance (B) knowledge (C) strategy (D) navigation (E) condition

<u>C</u> 9. APPRAISAL: (A) reward (B) appearance (C) estimate (D) report (E) approval

<u>A</u> 10. INTENT: (A) absorbed (B) nervous (C) undisciplined (D) suspicious (E) overwhelmed

Number correct _____ (total 10)

Spelling and Wordplay

Word Maze All the words in the list below are hidden in the maze. The words are arranged forward, backward, up, down, and diagonally. Put a circle around each word as you find it and cross the word off the list. Different words may overlap and use the same letter.

```
A  P  P  R  A  I  S  A  L  X  O  L  S  Q
J  T  K  E  C  I  F  F  U  S  E  Z  U  Y
K  C  P  D  R  Y  B  M  T  V  F  R  F  L
R  N  D  U  I  I  P  D  A  B  S  E  F  T
M  O  I  R  T  A  C  R  L  H  B  T  I  N
D  I  S  T  I  N  G  U  I  S  H  R  C  E
E  T  C  N  C  Z  X  O  G  I  K  I  I  T
T  C  L  I  A  G  M  U  N  C  A  E  E  T
E  E  O  K  L  P  S  T  E  A  Y  V  N  I
R  P  S  U  L  Q  E  K  P  N  L  E  T  M
M  S  E  S  Y  N  A  E  P  O  Z  L  E  R
I  N  X  P  T  T  R  I  S  L  R  L  Y  E
N  I  K  J  R  T  R  S  G  M  P  O  L  T
E  V  D  E  U  N  I  P  S  P  T  J  L  N
K  N  V  R  L  D  X  P  U  E  G  A  M  I
X  O  E  C  N  A  T  S  M  U  C  R  I  C
Z  B  A  T  R  O  B  X  Y  P  O  F  K  M
```

align
aperture
appraisal
circumstance
critically
determine
diagonally
disclose
dissolve
distinguish
grave
image
intent
intermittently
intruder
overtake
retrieve
suffice
sufficient
supple

Word's Worth: grave

Grave, meaning "serious," comes from the Latin word *gravis*, which means "heavy." Accordingly when you make a weighty decision, you are often grave. Also coming from *gravis* is the word *grief*—being heavy with sorrow. Other related words include *aggravate*—"to make things more troublesome, heavier"—and *gravity*—"the force that weighs us to the earth." Interestingly, the other meaning of *grave*, "a place to bury the dead," which is certainly a cause for heavy seriousness—does not come from the Latin *gravis* at all. It derives from the Old English word *grafan*, meaning "dig."

Part D Related Words

A number of words are closely related to the target words you have studied. Use your knowledge of the target words and of word parts to determine the meaning of these words. (For information about word parts analysis, see pp. 6-12.) If you are unsure of any definitions, use your dictionary. Learning these related words expands your vocabulary and helps you learn the target words more thoroughly.

1. alignment (ə līn′ mənt) n.
2. appraise (ə prāz′) v.
3. circa (sur′ kə) prep.
4. circuitous (sər kyoo′ ə təs) adj.
5. circular (sur′ kyə lər) adj.
6. circulate (sur′ kyə lāt′) v.
7. circulation (sur′ kyə lā′ shən) n.
8. circumference (sər kum′ fər əns, -frəns) n.
9. circumnavigate (sur kəm nav′ ə gāt) v.
10. criticism (krit′ ə siz′m) n.
11. determination (di tur′ mə nā′ shən) n.
12. disclosure (dis klō′ zhər) n.
13. imagination (i maj′ ə nā′ shən) n.
14. intention (in ten′ shən) n.
15. intrusion (in troo′ zhən) n.
16. retriever (ri trēv′ ər) n.

Understanding Related Words

Finding Examples Three situations follow each of the boldfaced words below. Write the letter of the situation that best demonstrates the meaning of each word.

_C_ 1. **intrusion**

  a. a medical student studying for an exam
  b. a coach talking to team members
  c. a stranger interrupting a conversation you are having with a friend

_A_ 2. **imagination**

  a. a child pretending to have a tea party with his or her stuffed animals
  b. a secretary typing a legal document
  c. a witness telling a police officer exactly what happened

_B_ 3. **appraise**

  a. a child nodding off to sleep
  b. a jeweler examining a necklace before deciding what to charge for it
  c. a dog bringing a duck to a hunter

_C_ 4. **disclosure**

  a. a florist watering plants
  b. a parent reminding a child that it is time for bed
  c. a friend telling you a secret

_B_ 5. **retriever**

  a. a car dealer determining how much a car is worth
  b. a deep-sea diver who brings out buried treasure
  c. a sky diver mending his or her parachute

_C_ 6. **alignment**

    a. a burglar entering a home

    b. a plate of spaghetti

    c. two straight lines of students entering an assembly

_C_ 7. **determination**

    a. a collie sleeping in front of a warm stove

    b. a student watching a television sitcom

    c. an athlete training by running ten miles every day

_C_ 8. **intention**

    a. a devastating earthquake

    b. a rose bush sprouting new buds

    c. a New Year's resolution to earn better grades

_B_ 9. **circular**

    a. a basketball court

    b. a drawing of the moon

    c. the pyramids of Egypt

_C_ 10. **criticism**

    a. applauding the candidate you favor for President

    b. going to a movie

    c. stating the strengths and weaknesses of Gandhi's peace strategies

Number correct _____ (total 10)

Analyzing Word Parts

The Suffixes -al and -er Suffixes can often help you figure out the meanings of words. For example, the addition of the suffix -al to a verb forms a noun meaning "the act or process of." If the word _retrieve_ means "to find again," the word _retrieval_ means "the act or process of finding again." Another related word, _retriever,_ is created by adding the suffix -er to the word _retrieve._ If the suffix -er means "a person or thing that," what does _retriever_ mean?

Add -al and -er to _appraise_ and to _betray_ to create four common nouns. Then define each noun.

	Noun	Definition
appraise	1. _____	_____
	2. _____	_____
betray	1. _____	_____
	2. _____	_____

Number correct _____ (total 4)

Turn to **The Final Silent** *e* on pages 197-199 of the **Spelling Handbook.**
Read the rules and complete the exercises provided.

The Latin Root *circ* The word *circumstance* contains the root *circ* and comes from the Latin *circulus,* meaning "circle." Other words with the root *circ*—such as *circa, circuitous, circulate, circulation, circumference* and *circumnavigate*—all involve the idea of "circle" in some way. Using this knowledge, complete the sentences in the following exercise. Write the letter of the sentence that best describes each italicized word. Use a dictionary if needed.

B
1. "I took a *circuitous* route home" has approximately the same meaning as
   a. I walked home quickly.
   b. I went home the long way around.
   c. I got dizzy walking home.

B
2. "We *circumnavigated* the earth" means approximately the same as
   a. The earth revolved with us on it.
   b. We traveled around the earth.
   c. We measured the distance around the earth.

C
3. "Columbus sailed to the New World *circa* 1500" means approximately the same as
   a. Columbus sailed to the New World before A.D. 1500.
   b. Columbus sailed to the New World with around 1,500 men.
   c. Columbus sailed to the New World around A.D. 1500.

A
4. "The scientist determined the *circumference* of the earth" means approximately the same as
   a. The scientist determined the distance around the earth at the equator.
   b. The scientist determined the distance from North Pole to South Pole.
   c. The scientist determined the distance from the earth's surface to its center.

B
5. "The perfect hostess, Joana never failed to *circulate* at her parties" means approximately the same as
   a. Joana told jokes and did impressions.
   b. Joana moved from person to person.
   c. Joana danced.

A
6. "The *circulation* of the air in this room is bad" means approximately the same as
   a. The motion of the air around the room is bad.
   b. The smell of the air in the room is bad.
   c. The humidity of the air in the room is bad.

Number correct _____ (total 6)

Number correct in unit _____ (total 75)

The Last Word

Writing

Use your *imagination* to write a story about a character who one day discovers that he or she has a wonderful and terrifying ability. All the character has to do is *imagine* something happening—and soon after, it will really happen.

Speaking

Most often we think of *criticism* as something negative, but constructive criticism can produce positive results. Prepare a speech in which you critique a book you have read, a painting you have seen, or something else about which you have an opinion. Choose something you have mixed feelings about—both positive and negative things to say. Make sure that your criticism is not only honest but also encouraging and constructive.

Group Discussion

What role does *determination* play in success? Discuss the following questions.

1. What specific examples are there of successful people who showed determination?
2. What obstacles can determination help a person overcome?
3. What can't determination do? What are its limitations?
4. How does a person get determination?

UNIT 2

Part A   Target Words and Their Meanings

1. abundant (ə bun′ dənt) adj.
2. corridor (kôr′ ə dər, kär′-; -dôr′) n.
3. cumbersome (kum′ bər səm) adj.
4. enclosure (in klō′ zhər) n.
5. envision (en vizh′ ən) v.
6. herald (her′ əld) v., n.
7. horde (hôrd) n.
8. magnificent (mag nif′ ə s′nt) adj.
9. mass (mas) adj., n., v.
10. multitude (mul′ tə tood′) n.
11. ominous (äm′ ə nəs) adj.
12. pervade (pər vād′) v.
13. proclaim (prō klām′, prə-) v.
14. resemblance (ri zem′ bləns) n.
15. sheer (shir) adj., v.
16. spectacle (spek′ tə k'l) n.
17. teem (tēm) v.
18. transitional (tran zish′ ə n'l) adj.
19. uncharted (un chär′ tid) adj.
20. venture (ven′ chər) v., n.

Inferring Meaning from Context

For each sentence write the letter of the word or phrase that is closest to the meaning of the word or words in italics. Use context clues to help you determine the correct answer.

__B__   1. Because the supply of pure water near Pritchard Creek was *abundant*, many cattle ranchers settled there.

a. contaminated   b. more than enough   c. not enough   d. cold

__A__   2. Hearing the bell and realizing she was late, Ms. Klein rushed down the *corridor* toward her classroom.

a. hall   b. door   c. street   d. play lot

__C__   3. Martha dragged the *cumbersome* bicycle down the basement stairs.

a. flexible   b. miniature   c. clumsy   d. dainty

__B__   4. The dogs were kept in *enclosures* so that they would not run away.

a. muzzles   b. closed up areas   c. close groups   d. good condition

__D__   5. The commencement speaker told us that when she pictures the future, she *envisions* a peaceful world.

a. proclaims   b. calls for   c. appraises   d. imagines

__A__   6. We knew the sunrise in the marsh was coming. It was *heralded* by the calls of many kinds of birds.

a. announced   b. made noisy   c. disturbed   d. made more beautiful

<u>C</u> 7. *Hordes* of people were patiently waiting in line to buy tickets to the movie; so we knew we would have to come back for the next show.
a. loud groups   b. angry groups   c. large groups   d. small groups

<u>D</u> 8. Jane had never seen anything as *magnificent* as the great cathedral.
a. sufficient   b. cumbersome   c. noisy   d. splendid

<u>C</u> 9. The cake Herb dropped at the picnic was devoured by a *mass* of ants.
a. small group   b. hill   c. large number   d. pair

<u>B</u> 10. Jesse couldn't find her friends in the *multitude* of people at the road race.
a. stands   b. crowd   c. team   d. small group

<u>A</u> 11. The clouds were *an ominous* forewarning of a violent storm.
a. a threatening   b. a perfect   c. a poor   d. a good

<u>C</u> 12. The smell of burning rubber *pervaded* the house, so we called the fire department immediately.
a. dissolved   b. perfumed   c. spread throughout   d. cleared out

<u>D</u> 13. Since the governor *proclaimed* May as Auto Safety Month, the number of traffic accidents has decreased.
a. appraised   b. festively celebrated   c. spoke against
d. officially announced

<u>B</u> 14. Although they were not twins, the *resemblance* between the brothers was remarkable.
a. distance   b. likeness   c. difference   d. distinguishing feature

<u>C</u> 15. Through *sheer* determination, the injured soldier finished the mission.
a. joyous   b. rapid   c. absolute   d. grave

<u>B</u> 16. The colorful decorations and the birthday cake with sixty-five candles made it quite a *spectacle*.
a. an enclosure   b. a display   c. a feast   d. a problem

<u>A</u> 17. We saw more than just a few trout; the stream was *teeming* with them.
a. swarming   b. cumbersome   c. polluted   d. half-full

<u>B</u> 18. "On the other hand" was the *transitional* phrase the writer used between paragraphs.
a. grammatical   b. connecting   c. circumstantial   d. verbal

<u>A</u> 19. Since the new territory was *uncharted*, the explorers had little information to guide them on their journey.
a. unmapped   b. untouched   c. underdeveloped   d. unoccupied

<u>A</u> 20. Although I had always been afraid of Professor Bowden, I finally *ventured* to disagree with him.
a. dared   b. wanted   c. expected   d. refused

Number correct _____ (total 20)

25

You should now have a general idea of the meaning of each target word. Refine your understanding by examining the shades of meaning the words have in the following article.

Trail of the Bison

Larry Roop

Just over a century ago there were millions of buffalos, or bison, roaming the Great Plains of the United States and Canada. Today only a small number remain. The author takes us back in time to the days when these great creatures lived in large herds.

Most of us know the buffalo only by the few that we may have seen in zoos or other **enclosures.** But these are not buffalo—they are in a sense but **cumbersome** cattle that bear pitiful **resemblance** to a once-**magnificent** beast. They hardly bring to mind the animal that at one time ruled a continent by **sheer** numbers.   5

Long before wagon ruts cut across trails carved by hooves, the North American bison was the most **abundant** ruminant[1] on earth. No one knows how many there actually were, but naturalists and historians have **ventured** guesses from 40 to over 100 million.

It staggers the imagination to **envision** the plains and prairies when **teeming**   10
hordes of grazing bison spread to the horizon in every direction, covering several townships or even counties at one time. If it were only possible for us to travel back through the lost pages of time, what a marvelous **spectacle** we could witness. Perhaps . . . in the unlimited powers of the mind's eye . . . we could make such a trip.   15

Passing through the **uncharted corridors** of time and space, we come to a place that will one day be marked on maps as central Kansas. The time is 1540, May 12th, 4:15 A.M. At first we are confused because we cannot see anything, but as a thin, pale line of red begins to form on a treeless horizon, we realize it is just before daybreak.   20

---

[1] ruminant: any of a group of four-footed, hoofed, even-toed, and cud-chewing mammals, such as cattle, sheep, goats, deer, camels

In the predawn darkness, a din of noise **heralds** the new day. This is green-up time on the midgrass prairie, a **transitional** zone between the tall grasses to the east and the shortgrass plains to the west. Everywhere feathered harbingers[2] are giving their ringing melodies, shrill whistles, and bubbling, throaty calls with a cacophony [3] that **pervades** the darkness. 25

In the absence of elevated perches, horned and meadow larks sing on high, ceremonious flights. Every patch of tall, dead grass holds a male dickcissel or bobolink that **proclaims** it as a territory. We become aware of a low, throbbing sound around us, but we cannot pinpoint its source until we make out a group of prairie chickens strutting in the dim light, dancing to an age-old ritual. Hundreds 30 of migrating plovers and curlews[4] probe the soil with their long bills for grubs and worms.

Suddenly, as though a signal has been given, the singing stops. For several minutes there is an **ominous** silence. Then, with calls of alarm, the birds take wing. 35

By this time we notice a solid black line growing along the southeastern skyline. Soon the ground begins to vibrate; we no longer wonder what frightened the birds.

We await the advance of the black **mass**. It is still too dark to make out details, but the approaching **multitude** looks like a huge blanket being pulled across the 40 earth.

---

[2] harbinger: something that comes before to announce what follows
[3] cacophony: harsh, jarring sound; discord
[4] plovers and curlews: two categories of wading and shore birds

Refining Your Understanding

For each of the following items consider how the target word is used in the passage. Write the letter of the word or phrase that best completes the sentence.

A 1. Examples of *enclosures* (line 2) other than zoo cages would be   a. pens   b. movies   c. plains.

B 2. The original buffalo ruled a continent "by *sheer* numbers" (line 4). That is, they ruled because they were   a. not abundant but fierce   b. abundant   c. the smartest ruminants.

C 3. *Uncharted* (line 16) space would be   a. uninhabited   b. unavailable   c. unmapped.

B 4. Many bird sounds *pervade* (line 25) the darkness of the Kansas plain, meaning that the sounds are   a. persuasive   b. everywhere   c. maddening.

A 5. The bobolink *proclaims* a patch of grass as its own territory (line 28). They proclaim by   a. singing   b. fighting   c. gathering food.

Number correct _____ (total 5)

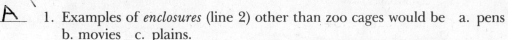

7/8

Part C Ways to Make New Words Your Own

By now you are familiar with the target words and their meanings. This section presents a variety of reinforcement activities that will help you make the words part of your permanent vocabulary.

Using Language and Thinking Skills

Understanding Multiple Meanings Each boldfaced word in this exercise has more than one definition. Read the definitions and the sentences that use the word. Then write the letter of the definition that fits each sentence.

> **corridor**
> a. a passageway or hall (n.)
> b. a strip of land forming a passageway between two parts of a country or between an inland country and a seaport (n.)

__A__ 1. Every floor of the hotel had a long *corridor*.

__B__ 2. The *corridor* between France and Germany was a no-man's land.

> **sheer**
> a. very thin; transparent: said of cloth (adj.)
> b. absolute (adj.)
> c. extremely steep (adj.)
> d. to deviate from a course (v.)

__C__ 3. We gasped at the *sheer* drop into the canyon below.

__D__ 4. The wind was so strong that our boat began to *sheer* off course.

__B__ 5. His approach to the problem was *sheer* nonsense.

__A__ 6. The curtains were so *sheer* that a passerby could see into the house.

> **mass**
> a. a unified body of matter (n.)
> b. a large amount or number (n.)
> c. the largest part of something (n.)

__B__ 7. Inside the fieldhouse was a *mass* of athletes, gathered from many schools.

__A C__ 8. The cliffs of Dover are a *mass* of chalk-like rock rising along the southern
__A__   coast of England.

B   9. The Haymarket Riot began with protests from a *mass* of workers.

X 10. In 1984, Ronald Reagan was re-elected President of the United States
C   because the *mass* of voters favored him.

Number correct _____ (total 10)

Practicing for Standardized Tests

Antonyms An antonym is a word that means the opposite of another word.
(*Good* is an antonym for *bad*.) Write the letter of the word that is the antonym of
the capitalized word in each set.

E 1. ABUNDANT: (A) plentiful (B) soft (C) careful (D) radiant (E) scarce

A 2. MAGNIFICENT: (A) shabby (B) numerous (C) great (D) grave
     (E) sufficient

C 3. PERVADE: (A) spread (B) persuade (C) confine (D) determine
     (E) overtake

E 4. PROCLAIM: (A) declare (B) prevent (C) make known
     (D) dissolve (E) keep secret

A 5. HORDE: (A) individual (B) herd (C) crowd (D) cattle (E) greed

D 6. GRAVE: (A) appraised (B) solemn (C) wise (D) carefree
     (E) deadly

D 7. INTERMITTENTLY: (A) abruptly (B) strongly (C) critically
     (D) constantly (E) occasionally

A 8. RETRIEVE: (A) throw away (B) eat (C) bring back (D) suffice
     (E) value

B 9. CUMBERSOME: (A) bright (B) well-coordinated (C) grave
     (D) intent (E) clumsy

E 10. ENCLOSURE: (A) intruder (B) fence (C) restricted area (D) pen
     (E) open area

Number correct _____ (total 10)

Word's Worth: ominous

Since ancient Roman times, an *omen* has been a sign of something to come,
usually something to fear. The Romans considered such things as thunder
and lightning to be bad omens. The way an animal behaved could also be an
omen—the cry of a hawk was a warning of danger. To form an adjective from
the noun *omen*, the Romans simply added a suffix: *omin+osus*. Accordingly,
when something is frightening, it is omen-like, or *ominous*. Another word
coming from *omen* is *abominate*, meaning "to hate intensely."

Spelling and Wordplay

Crossword Puzzle Read each clue carefully to determine what word will fit into the corresponding squares of the puzzle. Go through the clues to find the words you know. Then go back and determine the rest by working around the letters of the words you have already inserted. There are several target words in this puzzle.

Across

2. A long hall
10. That thing
12. Not mapped
13. Your upper limb
14. Abbr. Bachelor of Science Degree
16. Large crowd
18. The letter "M"
19. Absolute
21. Several male humans
22. Past tense of "run"
23. One of two contractions for "it is"
24. To announce
27. To present
29. Abbr. South America
30. Objective case of "I"
31. A male human
32. Third person singular of "to be"
33. A necessity
35. Compete
36. Sounds made by doves
37. Abbr. avenue
38. Ocean
39. Second person singular of "be"
40. A cover
42. Short for Daniel
44. Spanish "yes"
46. __ __ and behold
47. An undertaking

Down

1. Changing
2. Awkward
3. Not off
4. Abbr. Red Cross
5. Abbr. Right hand
6. Abbr. Iowa
7. Abbr. Doctor
8. Abbr. Old Testament
9. Likeness
11. To swarm
15. See 38 across
17. Word of choice
18. Imagines
20. Abbr. Registered Nurse
24. To spread throughout
25. Abbr. railroad
26. Large quantity
28. Slang for Federal Agents
31. Past participle of "mean"
34. Wicked
41. To act
43. Indefinite article meaning "one"
45. Not out

Part D Related Words

A number of words are closely related to the target words you have studied. Use your knowledge of the target words and of word parts to help you determine the meaning of these words. (For information about word parts analysis, see pages 6-12.)

1. abundance (ə bun′ dəns) n.
2. encumbrance (in kum′ brəns) n.
3. magnanimous (mag nan′ ə məs) adj.
4. magnate (mag′ nāt) n.
5. magnificence (mag nif′ ə s′ns) n.
6. magnitude (mag′ nə tood′, -tyood′) n.
7. multiple (mul′ tə p′l) adj., n.
8. multiplicity (mul′ tə plis′ ə tē) n.
9. pervasive (pər vā′ siv) adj.
10. proclamation (präk′ lə mā′ shən) n.
11. resemble (ri zem′ b′l) v.
12. spectator (spek′ tāt ər, spek tāt′-) n.
13. transcontinental (trans′ kän tə nen′ t′l) adj.
14. transcribe (tran skrīb′) v.
15. transfer (trans fʉr′, trans′ fər) v., n.
16. transform (trans fôrm′) v.
17. transfuse (trans fyooz′) v.
18. transition (tran zish′ ən)n.
19. translate (trans lāt′, trans′ lāt) v.
20. transmission (trans mish′ ən) n.
21. transparent (trans per′ ənt) adj.
22. transplant (trans plant′) v.

Understanding Related Words

Matching Synonyms For each of the following items, write the word from the Related Words list that is closest in meaning to the italicized word or phrase.

abundance 1. Because farmers produce such a *large quantity* of grain, North America can feed millions around the world.

proclamation 2. In 1976 came the *announcement* that Juan Carlos would be King of Spain.

multiplicity 3. The word "interest" has a *variety* of meanings.

transition 4. Junior high school is often thought of as a *link* between elementary school and high school.

magnificence 5. The *splendor* of the Taj Mahal overwhelms many tourists.

spectator 6. The typical American is content to be an *observer* of sports, not a participant.

pervasive 7. The smell of good cooking was *everywhere* in our house.

encumbrance 8. Heavy debts have been a *burden* for many Latin American countries.

resemble 9. Maria and Kirsten *look like* each other, so people sometimes confuse them.

multiple 10. Students discussed the *many* causes of the Vietnam War.

Number correct _____ (total 10)

Analyzing Word Parts

The Latin root *magn* The word *magnificent* contains the root *magn* and comes from the Latin word *magnus*, meaning "great" or "large." Other words with the root *magn* all involve the idea of "large" in some way. Using this knowledge, complete each of the following sentences using one of these words: *magnanimous,* ~~magnate, magnificence, magnify, magnitude~~. Use a dictionary to check your answers.

magnate ~~magnitude~~ 1. Andrew Carnegie was a ? in the steel industry.

magnanimous 2. It was indeed ? of Charlie to let us borrow his car.

magnificence 3. Travelers to Versailles are impressed by the ? of the royal palace.

magnify 4. A microscope can ? objects invisible to the naked eye.

magnitude 5. Most people are amazed at the sheer ? of Sister Theresa's accomplishments in helping the poor.

Number correct _____ (total 5)

Turn to **The Suffix** *-ion* on page 202 of the **Spelling Handbook.** Read the rule and complete the exercises provided.

The Latin root *trans* The target word *transitional* and the related word *transition* come from the Latin word *transire*, meaning "to go over or across." Accordingly, the prefix *trans-* means "over," "across," "through," or "so as to change." Using this knowledge, match the *trans* words in the Related Words list on page 31 to the following definitions. Use a dictionary if needed.

transfer 1. to send or convey from one person or place to another

transform 2. to change the form or outward appearance of

transcontinental 3. crossing or on the other side of a continent

transplant 4. to remove from one place and settle in another

transcribe 5. to write or type out in full

transition 6. a passing from one stage to another

transparent 7. pertaining to something that can be seen through

translate 8. to put into the words of a different language

~~transfuse~~ 9. automobile part that shifts power, as with gears

transfuse 10. to pour in or spread through

Number correct _____ (total 10)

Number correct in unit _____ (total 70)

transmission

The Last Word

Writing

Envision yourself as a participant in a famous historical event. Write the story of how you were the real hero of the event, but the credit went to someone else.

Speaking

Enclosure: In a short speech to the class, describe the pros and cons of keeping animals in *enclosures* such as zoos.

Group Discussion

It is frequently said that the times we live in are *transitional*—that our world is changing rapidly. In small groups, brainstorm to make a list of the changes you have seen in your lifetime. When all group members have contributed to the list, choose the one transition that the group feels is the most significant. Discuss that change, considering such questions as the following.

- What do you think has brought about this transition?
- Do you regard this transition as good or bad—or neither?
- What is the effect of this transition on your life?
- How do you think this change might affect the future?
- Is this transition finished? Or will it continue? If so, how?

Your brainstorming and discussion could be the basis of a composition or a journal entry about change.

UNIT 3

Part A Target Words and Their Meanings

1. clan (klan) n.
2. cleft (kleft) n.
3. complex (kəm pleks′, käm′ pleks) adj., n.
4. conifer (kän′ ə fər, kō′ nə-) n.
5. contour (kän′ toor) n.
6. deplete (di plēt′) v.
7. expanse (ik spans′) n.
8. fierce (firs) adj.
9. finery (fin′ ər ē) n.
10. flounder (floun′ dər) v., n.
11. luminous (loom ə nəs) adj.
12. majestic (mə jes′ tik) adj.
13. mar (mär) v.
14. mythical (mith′ i k'l) adj.
15. outcrop (out′ kräp) n.
16. pristine (pris′ tēn) adj.
17. scuttle (skut′ 'l) v.
18. spontaneous (spän tā′ nē əs) adj.
19. steppe (step) n.
20. stockpile (stäk′ pīl) n.

Inferring Meanings from Context

For each sentence write the letter of the word or phrase that is closest to the meaning of the italicized word. Use context clues to help you determine the answer.

C 1. Eleanor traced her family tree to the MacKinnon *clan* in Scotland.
   a. nation b. castle c. family group d. venture

A 2. The pirates left their treasure in a deep *cleft* in the cliff.
   a. crevice b. rock c. house d. angle

C 3. The causes of emotional illnesses are anything but simple; indeed, they are often so *complex* that they baffle psychiatrists.
   a. sad b. clear c. complicated d. ominous

C 4. If you want to gather pine cones, look under *a conifer*.
   a. a bridge b. a boulder c. an evergreen tree d. an elm tree

A 5. From the space capsule the astronaut could identify Italy's unique *contour*, the shape of a boot.
   a. outline b. aperture c. circumference d. highway

D 6. When the world's reserves of oil are *depleted*, what will we use for fuel?
   a. refilled b. replaced c. disclosed d. used up

D 7. From a peak in Joshua Tree National Monument, visitors can look out over the vast *expanse* of southern California desert.
   a. enclosure b. abundance c. fertile valley d. wide space

34

C 8. Crowds gathered to see the queen in her coronation *finery*. Other members of the royal family were also wearing magnificent costumes.

    a. carriage b. confusion c. elaborate clothing d. costly jewels

B 9. Old legends portray wolves as *fierce*, but in North America wolves rarely attack people.

    a. afraid b. vicious c. supple d. hungry

A 10. When the horse Winged Victory galloped into the deep mud, he *floundered* and nearly threw his rider.

    a. struggled b. raced c. trotted quickly d. disappeared

A 11. To prevent serious night accidents, the town council passed an ordinance requiring *luminous* tape on bicycles.

    a. light-reflecting b. red-and-blue c. dark d. sticky

C 12. Climbers from around the world have scaled *majestic* Fujiyama, Japan's highest mountain.

    a. easy to miss b. relatively unknown c. grand d. uncharted

A 13. His record-setting victory in the marathon was *marred* by his unsportsmanlike attitude.

    a. spoiled b. proclaimed c. distinguished d. helped

B 14. As described in legendary tales, a unicorn is a *mythical* horselike creature with a single horn on its head.

    a. real b. imaginary c. common d. grave

C 15. The coyote leapt up on the *outcrop* of rock and bayed at the moon.

    a. canyon b. multitude c. projection d. aperture

D 16. The Selway-Bitterroot Wilderness in Montana and Idaho consists of over a half million acres of natural, *pristine* land.

    a. suburban b. unnecessary c. populated d. unspoiled

C 17. With our cat Boswell close behind, the mouse *scuttled* across the floor and into a tiny hole in the wall.

    a. looked b. was seen c. scurried d. wandered

C 18. Instead of a carefully prepared speech, Mayor Gibbons decided that informal, *spontaneous* remarks would be more appropriate for the election celebration.

    a. well-thought-out b. victorious c. unplanned d. insulting

B 19. The *stockpile* of steel beams and girders was the first sign that a new factory would soon be built.

    a. building b. accumulation c. hiding d. loss

C 20. *Steppes*, which cover most of the United States from New Mexico north to Montana, are important grain-growing areas in the United States.

    a. Stones b. Valleys c. Plains d. Cities

Number correct _____ (total 20)

Part B Target Words in Reading and Literature

You should now have a general idea of the meaning of each target word. Refine your understanding by examining the shades of meaning the words have in the following excerpt.

7/10

The Clan of the Cave Bear

Jean M. Auel

The following excerpt is from a novel about a clan of prehistoric people. The main character, Ayla, has been banished from her clan; she has found another cave shelter for herself nearby. The first snow of the winter comes, and it impresses her with its beauty. But the second snowstorm makes her realize that she must be resourceful to survive the harsh winter.

The first snow sifted down silently during the night. Ayla exclaimed with delight when she stepped out of her cave in the morning. A **pristine** whiteness softened the **contours** of the familiar landscape creating a magical dreamland of fantastic shapes and **mythical** plants. Bushes had top hats of soft snow, **conifers** were dressed in new gowns of white **finery,** and bare exposed limbs   5
were clothed in shining coats that outlined each twig against the deep blue sky. Ayla looked at her footprints, **marring** the perfect, smooth layer of glistening white, then ran across the snowy blanket, crossing and recrossing her own path to make a **complex** design whose intent was lost in the execution. She started to follow the tracks of a small animal, then **spontaneously** changed her mind   10
and climbed out on the narrow ledge of the rocky **outcrop** swept clean of snow by the wind.

The entire mountain range marching up behind her in a series of **majestic** peaks was covered with white, shadowed in blue. It sparkled in the sun like a gigantic, **luminous** jewel. The vista spread out before her showed the lowest 15 reaches of the snowfall. The blue green sea, whipped to a frothy foam of waves, nestled between the **cleft** of snow-covered hills, but the **steppes** to the east were still bare. Ayla saw tiny figures **scuttling** across the white **expanse** directly below her. It had snowed at the cave of the **clan** too. One of the figures seemed to shuffle with a slow limp. Suddenly the magic left the snowy landscape and 20 she climbed back down.

The second snowfall had no magic at all. The temperature dropped sharply. Whenever she left the cave, **fierce** winds drove sharp needles into her bare face, leaving it raw. The blizzard lasted four days, piling snow so high against the wall, it nearly blocked the entrance to her cave. She tunneled out, using her 25 hands and a flat hipbone of the deer she had killed, and spent the day gathering wood. Drying the meat had **depleted** the supply of fallen wood nearby, and **floundering** through deep snow left her exhausted. She was sure she had food enough to last her, but she hadn't been careful about **stockpiling** wood. She wasn't sure she had enough, and if it snowed much more, her cave would be 30 buried so deep she wouldn't be able to get out.

For the first time since she found herself at her small cave, she feared for her life. The elevation of her meadow was too high. If she got trapped in her cave, she'd never last through the winter. She hadn't had time to prepare for the entire cold season. Ayla returned to her cave in the afternoon and promised 35 herself to get more wood the next day.

Refining Your Understanding

For each of the following items, consider the meaning of the target word as it is used in the passage. Write the letter of the word or phrase that best completes the sentence.

 1. *Mythical* (line 4) suggests that the snow-covered plants looked
   a. cone-shaped   b. scary   c. like something out of a storybook.

 2. The conifers are described as being dressed in *finery* (line 5). This means that the trees looked   a. elegant   b. deathly   c. cold.

 3. The word *expanse* (line 18) suggests that the figures Ayla saw below must have been moving across a   a. mountain peak   b. plain   c. trail.

 4. The author emphasizes that the winds are *fierce* (line 23) by describing
   a. the depleted wood supply   b. the temperature dropping sharply
   c. Ayla's raw face.

 5. Ayla needs to *stockpile* (line 29) wood. This means that she must
   a. build up a supply of wood   b. burn more wood for fires   c. find the right sizes of wood.

Number correct _____ (total 5)

37

Part C Ways to Make Words Your Own

This section will help you make the target words part of your permanent vocabulary.

Using Language and Thinking Skills

Finding the Unrelated Word Write the letter of the word that is not related in meaning to the other words in the set.

_A_ 1. a. individual b. family c. clan d. tribe

_C_ 2. a. plain b. expanse c. outcrop d. plateau

_A_ 3. a. simplicity b. frills c. elegance d. finery

_A_ 4. a. mend b. mangle c. mar d. destroy

_D_ 5. a. brilliant b. radiant c. luminous d. faint

_~~DA~~B_ 6. a. scurry b. scamper c. scuttle d. shuffle

_C_ 7. a. exhaust b. consume c. stockpile d. deplete

_B_ 8. a. steppe b. mountain c. expanse d. prairie

_B_ 9. a. oak b. conifer c. elm d. maple

_D_ 10. a. mythical b. imaginative c. legendary d. real

Number correct _____ (total 10)

Practicing for Standardized Tests

Synonyms Write the letter of the word in each set that is closest in meaning to the capitalized target word.

_D_ 1. CONTOUR: (A) statue (B) dialogue (C) image (D) outline (E) mass

_A_ 2. MYTHICAL: (A) imaginary (B) sad (C) odd (D) pristine (E) unsolved

_D_ 3. SPONTANEOUS: (A) sorry (B) sheer (C) tan (D) unplanned (E) fast

_C_ 4. COMPLEX: (A) kind (B) wise (C) intricate (D) wary (E) simple

_A~~B~~_ ~~X~~ 5. FIERCE: (A) fearful (B) furious (C) strike (D) temper (E) transitional

_B_ 6. STEPPE: (A) mountain (B) plain (C) foothill (D) basin (E) corridor

_A_ 7. FLOUNDER: (A) struggle (B) eat (C) mar (D) teem (E) discover

_E_ 8. CLEFT: (A) cliff (B) hill (C) enclosure (D) altitude (E) aperture

_B_ 9. PRISTINE: (A) icy (B) untouched (C) feminine (D) supple (E) old

_B_ 10. MAJESTIC: (A) odd (B) magnificent (C) magic (D) sheer (E) unknown

Number correct _____ (total 10)

7/10

Turn to **The Prefix *com-*** on pages 191-192 of the **Spelling Handbook.**
Read the rule and complete the exercises provided.

Spelling and Wordplay

Word Maze Find the target words in this maze and circle them.

```
B  E  C  H  N  R  L  F  Z  I  C  K  O
S  T  E  P  P  E  S  C  U  T  T  L  E
T  P  F  B  R  F  I  N  E  R  Y  M  B
O  R  O  X  Z  M  Y  T  H  I  C  A  L
C  I  E  N  F  I  E  R  C  E  O  J  I
K  S  O  X  T  L  C  J  L  G  M  E  S
P  T  A  Z  P  A  O  W  A  O  P  S  P
I  I  M  E  O  A  N  U  N  V  L  T  U
L  N  D  L  R  K  N  E  N  Q  E  I  E
E  E  Z  T  C  D  G  S  O  D  X  C  H
C  L  E  F  T  F  Y  D  E  U  E  H  N
M  A  R  L  U  M  I  N  O  U  S  R  C
C  O  N  T  O  U  R  E  F  I  N  O  C
P  E  F  U  D  C  H  I  L  J  B  Y  M
```

clan
cleft
complex
conifer
contour
deplete
expanse
fierce
finery
flounder
luminous
majestic
mar
mythical
outcrop
pristine
scuttle
spontaneous
steppe
stockpile

Part D   Related Words

The words below are closely related to the target words. Use your knowledge of the target words and of word parts to help you determine the meaning of these words. (For information about word parts analysis, see pages 6-12.) Use your dictionary if necessary.

1. complexity (kəm plek′ sə tē) n.
2. coniferous (kə nif′ ər əs) adj.
3. depletion (di plē′ shən) n.
4. expand (ik spand′) v.
5. expansive (ik span′ siv) adj.
6. ferocity (fə räs′ ə tē) n.
7. illuminate (i lōō′ mə nāt) v.
8. illumination (i lōō′ mə nā′ shən) n.
9. illuminator (i lōō′ mə nā′ tər) n.
10. lumen (lōō′ mən) n.
11. luminary (lōō′ mə ner′ ē) n.
12. majesty (maj′ is tē) n.
13. myth (mith) n.
14. spontaneity (spän′ tə nē′ ə tē) n.

Understanding Related Words

Sentence Completion Write the related word that best completes each sentence.

majesty   1. The finery she wore and the way she carried herself emphasized Queen Elizabeth's ? .

illuminate   2. Sodium streetlights ? many shopping areas at night.

complexity   3. Ms. Cohen's word processing class was amazed by the ? of the computer's interior, with its maze of wires and circuit boards.

depletion   4. The ? of fuels may some day leave people freezing in the dark.

coniferous   5. If you want to gather pine cones, hike through a ? forest.

expansive   6. Alonso has ? ideas for his small corner store: he plans to make it into a magnificent supermarket.

myth   7. According to an ancient ? , a stone bridge appeared out of the sky, and the fleeing clan hurried across it to safety.

spontaneity   8. Always ready with a natural smile and a quick-witted reply, the politician was known for her ? .

ferocity   9. To avoid the dangerous ? of a grizzly bear, avoid surprising it; make noises that will proclaim your presence.

expand   10. With more people moving into the area each year, experts expect the suburbs of Phoenix to ? .

Number correct _____ (total 10)

Analyzing Word Parts

The Latin root *lum* The target word *luminous* contains the root *lum* and comes from the Latin word *lumen*, meaning "light." A number of English words contain the root *lum*—words you are likely to hear in reference to light. Match each of the following words containing *lum* with its appropriate definition. Write the letter of the definition in the blank. Use your dictionary to check your work.

C   1. illuminate   a. a state of being lighted

A   2. illumination   b. a unit of light

E   3. illuminator   c. to light up

D   4. luminary   d. a body that gives light; a famous person

B   5. lumen   e. someone or something that illuminates

Number correct _____ (total 5)

Number correct in unit _____ (total 60)

Part C   Related Words Reinforcement

Using Related Words

Forming Words Write a related word for each target word below. The related word you form should be the part of speech shown in parentheses.

Example   tragedy   (adj.) _____tragic_____

1. abundant   (n.) _____

2. align   (n.) _____

3. appraisal   (v.) _____

4. disclose   (n.) _____

5. luminous   (adv.) _____

6. magnificent   (n.) _____

7. majestic   (n.) _____

8. mythical   (n.) _____

9. proclaim   (n.) _____

10. retrieve   (n.) _____

Number correct _____ (total 10)

Reviewing Word Structures

Roots and Suffixes Complete each sentence below with a word from the Related Words lists. Use a related word that contains one of these roots—*circ, lum, magn, trans*—or one of these suffixes— *-al, -er*.

1. My Irish setter, a good _____ , brought back the ball I threw.

2. The beam from Bill's spotlight will _____ the entire area.

3. Wide vents allow the air to _____ freely.

4. A microscope is used to _____ objects.

5. The diver's _____ of the sunken row boat was remarkable.

6. A _____ cable carries messages across the ocean.

7. Jenny will _____ her roses from their pots to the garden.

8. The _____ of the Rocky Mountains takes your breath away.

9. At the equator the earth's _____ is 24,902 miles.

10. A newspaper's _____ is the number of people who read it.

Number correct _____ (total 10)

Number correct in unit _____ (total 100)

Vocab Lab 1

FOCUS ON: The Arts and Crafts

The words in previous units have been ones of average difficulty that you can use in your own writing, speaking, and reading. Now, in order to expand your vocabulary even further, look at the following words that are used in the fields of arts and crafts.

aesthetic (es thet′ ik) adj. sensitive to art and beauty; artistic. • The *aesthetic* quality of the sculpture made it priceless.

batik (bə tēk′, bat′ ik) n. a process in which color is printed on cloth by using wax and dye; the cloth produced in this process. • The colorful shirt is made from *batik*.

capital (kap′ ə t'l) n. the upper portion of a column or pillar. • The White House entrance consists of four columns with decorative *capitals*.

chalice (chal′ is) n. a decorative cup or goblet. • The table was adorned with a gold *chalice* at each setting.

cloisonné (kloi′ zə nā) n. a process of decorative enameling in which enamel sections form a pattern; the enamel used in this process. • The jeweler used *cloisonné* to create a design on the ring.

collage (kə lazh′) n. a composition made by pasting together bits of various materials, such as newspaper, cloth, and flowers. • Her *collage* contained many materials of diverse textures.

connoisseur (kän′ ə sʉr′, -soor′) n. an expert or especially discriminating critic. • The art critic was considered a *connoisseur* of nineteenth-century French art.

emboss (im bôs′, -bäs′) v. to ornament a surface with a raised design. • Her three initials were *embossed* in white gold onto the surface of the locket.

filigree (fil′ ə grē) n. delicate and intricate metallic ornamentation made of fine wire; any delicate work or design like this. • The *filigree* surrounding the picture frame is as delicate as lace.

fresco (fres′ kō) n. a method of painting with watercolors on fresh plaster. • It took great skill for Michelangelo to complete the *fresco* on the ceiling of the Sistine Chapel.

gargoyle (gär′ goil) n. a carved waterspout, often in the form of a grotesque face. • It was popular to include *gargoyles* on Gothic cathedrals.

hue (hyoo) n. the distinctive characteristics of a color; a particular shade or tint of a given color. • The red *hues* of the sunset made the sky appear on fire.

mosaic (mō zā′ ik) n. a decoration made of small colored pieces of stone or glass set into a background of cement or plaster and forming an intricate design. • The artist created a detailed portrait through the use of tiny stones in her *mosaic*.

relief (ri lēf′) n. in sculpture, figures projecting from a background. • The figures were done in *relief;* they seemed to jump out of the sculpture and come to life.

terra cotta (ter′ ə kät′ ə) adj., n. hard-baked, reddish clay used for pottery and tile. • Plants are often planted in pottery made of *terra cotta*.

Sentence Completion Complete each sentence by writing the appropriate focus word.

_____ 1. An art _?_ was brought in to determine the authenticity of Picasso's signature.

_____ 2. The floor of the courtyard is set in a colorful sunburst _?_, accenting the home's Spanish decor.

_____ 3. Over the altar, figures in _?_ depicting Noah's story emerged from the stone.

_____ 4. The clashing colors violated the observer's _?_ sense.

_____ 5. Photographs, newspaper clippings, and matchbook covers were all used in the _?_ commemorating the past decade.

_____ 6. Pots made of _?_ and filled with dried flowers added color to the hospital waiting room.

_____ 7. In Java, where the process of _?_ originated, tourists can buy many beautifully colored fabrics.

_____ 8. Wine was offered in a silver _?_.

_____ 9. We asked the engraver to _?_ the family crest on each invitation.

_____ 10. The clear _?_ of the primary colors lend a childlike brightness to the painting.

Number correct _____ (total 10)

Precise Word Choice Choose the word in parentheses that best completes each sentence.

_____ 1. (Filigree, Mosaic, Terra Cotta) usually employs intricately worked wires to create a visual design.

_____ 2. If you were to wear jewelry made of (fresco, cloisonné, collage), it would have a shiny, enameled finish that is set in metal.

_____ 3. The (gargoyle, capital, hue) of the pillar was of a simple design.

_____ 4. When creating a (chalice, batik, fresco), it is important to work very fast so that the piece is completed before the plaster dries.

_____ 5. A dragon spewing water from its mouth is an example of a (connoisseur, gargoyle, cloisonné).

Number correct _____ (total 5)

FOCUS ON: *Analogies*

Various activities help build vocabulary skills, such as synonym, antonym, and sentence completion exercises. An analogy exercise is another way to enrich your understanding of words. An **analogy** shows a relationship between words. A typical analogy problem looks like this:

> Choose the lettered pair of words that best expresses a relationship similar to that of the original pair.
>
> _____ ROBIN : BIRD :: (A) frog : pond (B) crow : canary
> (C) auto : van (D) poodle : dog (E) plane : housefly

An analogy can be expressed this way: "A *robin* is to a *bird* as a __?__ is to a __?__."

To answer an analogy problem, first determine the relationship between the original pair of words. State this relationship in a sentence:

"A *robin* is a type of *bird*."

Then decide which other word pair expresses a similar relationship. You can test your choice by substituting that pair for the original pair in the sentence. It becomes apparent that (D) is the best answer when you use the test:

"A *poodle* is a type of *dog*."

Here are the most common types of relationships used in analogies.

Type of Analogy	Example
cause to effect	virus : cold :: carelessness : errors
part to whole	finger : hand :: spoke : wheel
object to purpose	car : transportation :: lamp : illumination
action to object	dribble : basketball :: fly : kite
item to category	salamander : amphibian :: corn : vegetable
age	kitten : cat :: cygnet: swan
type to characteristic	owl : nocturnal :: lion : carnivorous
word to synonym	nice : pleasant :: gratitude : thankfulness
synonym variants	pliant : flexibility :: unruly : disobedience
word to antonym	nice : unpleasant :: lazy : industrious
antonym variants	spotless : filth :: faultless : accuracy
object to its material	shoe : leather :: necklace : gold
product to source	apple : tree :: milk : cow
worker and creation	composer : symphony :: author : novel
worker and tool	carpenter : hammer :: surgeon : scalpel
worker and workplace	mechanic : garage :: judge : courtroom
time sequence	sunrise : sunset :: winter : spring
spatial sequence	mountain top : valley :: engine : caboose
word and derived form	act : action :: image : imagine
degree of intensity	pleased : ecstatic :: drizzle : downpour
manner	shout : speak :: swagger : walk

Analogies Write the letter of the pair of words that best completes each analogy.

_____ 1. EYE : SEE :: (A) sense : smell (B) ear : hear (C) food : taste (D) speech : tell (E) bend : elbow

_____ 2. LAZY : HARD-WORKING :: (A) daring : cautious (B) bold : adventurous (C) industrious : busy (D) characteristic : careless (E) sluggish : slow

_____ 3. GRAPE : VINE :: (A) pear : fruit (B) cherry : tree (C) flower : pot (D) orchard : apple (E) roots : leaves

_____ 4. TUESDAY : WEDNESDAY :: (A) Monday : Wednesday (B) Saturday : Friday (C) yesterday : tomorrow (D) today : tomorrow (E) day : week

_____ 5. STOP : END :: (A) go : finish (B) help : hinder (C) continue : persist (D) start : continue (E) rip : mend

_____ 6. TRIGGER : GUN :: (A) bullet : target (B) ignition : car (C) umbrella : handle (D) crossbow : arrow (E) rifle : bullet

_____ 7. GO : WENT :: (A) walk : amble (B) drive : driven (C) jog : run (D) drink : drank (E) lose : losing

_____ 8. CHEF : MEAL :: (A) banker : loan (B) doctor : medicine (C) ship : anchor (D) food : buffet (E) soldier : officer

_____ 9. READ : BOOK :: (A) type : typewriter (B) spend : store (C) hit : baseball (D) title : chapter (E) swim : dive

_____ 10. ICE : SLIPPERY :: (A) porcupine : quilled (B) smoke : charred (C) west : western (D) explosion : sudden (E) cold : frigid

_____ 11. ELEPHANT : HERD :: (A) colt : stallion (B) bull : cow (C) fish : school (D) invertebrate : vertebrate (E) group : individual

_____ 12. THERMOMETER : TEMPERATURE :: (A) degree : measurement (B) calendar : time (C) Fahrenheit : Celsius (D) freezing point : boiling point (E) herbs : seasonings

_____ 13. MONEY : BANKER :: (A) safe : security (B) chef : waiter (C) doctor : hospital (D) lariat : cowboy (E) oil : resource

_____ 14. LIBRARY : BOOKS :: (A) title : chapter (B) camera : photographer (C) magazine : periodical (D) Dalmation : fire station (E) pharmacy : medicine

_____ 15. DOVE : PEACE :: (A) skull and crossbones : poison (B) state : county (C) democracy : monarchy (D) chalice : cup (E) scarecrow : crow

Number correct _____ (total 15)

Number correct in Vocab Lab _____ (total 30)

UNIT 5

Part A Target Words and Their Meanings

1. assemble (ə sem′ b'l) v.
2. brilliant (bril′ yənt) adj.
3. coincide (kō′ in sīd′) v.
4. compulsion (kəm pul′ shən) n.
5. development (di vel′ əp mənt) n.
6. enact (in akt′) v.
7. froth (frôth, fräth) n.
8. interior (in tir′ ē ər) n., adj.
9. maelstrom (māl′ strəm) n.
10. mature (mə toor′, -choor′, -tyoor′) adj., v.
11. migration (mī grā′ shən) n.
12. mysterious (mis tir′ ē əs) adj.
13. navigate (nav′ ə gāt) v.
14. phenomenon (fi näm′ ə nän′) n.
15. romantic (rō man′ tik) adj.
16. spawn (spön) v.
17. suitable (soot′ ə b'l) adj.
18. tragedy (traj′ ə dē) n.
19. treacherous (trech′ ər əs) adj.
20. unerringly (un ʉr′ iŋ lē, -er′-) adv.

Inferring Meaning from Context

For each sentence write the letter of the word or phrase that is closest to the meaning of the word or words in italics. Use context clues to help you determine the correct answer.

___D___ 1. Reporters from throughout the city *assembled* at the airport to welcome the President of France, who had come to the United States on a mission of good will and friendship.

a. held a party   b. scattered   c. flew   d. gathered

___B___ 2. Venus can be seen as a *brilliant* point shining in the evening sky.

a. large   b. very bright   c. strangely shaped   d. yellowish-green

___C___ 3. If you were born on January 1, your birthday and New Year's Day would *coincide*.

a. make a glorious event   b. accelerate   c. happen at the same time
d. follow each other

___D___ 4. Jacqueline had one *compulsion*—to swim in the lake every day, even in rainy or sub-zero weather. She didn't feel right if she missed her swim.

a. ability   b. stupid idea   c. bet with friends   d. overriding desire

___D___ 5. Benjamin Franklin's experiments with lightning were among the early *developments* in the study of electricity.

a. proclamations   b. magnates   c. setbacks   d. stages

___B___ 6. The law against slavery was *enacted* in 1863, during Lincoln's administration.

a. dissolved   b. passed   c. rejected   d. estimated

C 7. The high winds had caused the *froth* on the waves.
   a. oil b. ice c. foam d. calm

C 8. We entered the house and found that not just the front room, but the whole *interior* had been newly painted.
   a. ceiling b. automobile c. inside d. outside

D 9. Violent crosswinds between the two islands created a *maelstrom* strong enough to pull sailboats underwater.
   a. electrical force b. noise c. wave d. whirlpool

B 10. So that most fish will live to breeding age, only *mature* fish may be taken from the streams in this state.
   a. delicious b. fully grown c. slow-swimming d. a few

D 11. *The Grapes of Wrath* is a novel focusing on the *migration* of a family in the 1930's from Oklahoma to California in search of a better life.
   a. enclosure b. satisfaction c. living d. moving

A 12. Mr. Well's *mysterious* disappearance was finally referred to the air force department handling UFO cases.
   a. unexplained b. expected c. illegal d. magnificent

D 13. It is difficult to *navigate* the Snake River because of the many rocks.
   a. walk across b. assemble c. take pictures of d. travel on

C 14. A cow jumping over the moon would indeed be a *phenomenon*.
   a. possibility b. strong cow c. peculiar event
   d. grave development

B 15. Bonita's favorite painting depicted *a romantic* scene, with great flying ships and a strange mythical bird hovering over a beautiful shore.
   a. a lifelike b. a fanciful c. an unartistic d. an indescribable

A 16. Weather forecasters are always wary of a mass of warm, humid air rising quickly, for such a condition can *spawn* a tornado.
   a. cause b. distinguish c. pervade d. envision

B 17. Casual clothes are *suitable* for picnics.
   a. required b. appropriate c. manufactured d. improper

B 18. The death of so many in the Battle of Gettysburg was indeed a *tragedy*.
   a. celebration b. disaster c. necessity d. surprise

C 19. That river is *treacherous*; no one should swim or boat in it.
   a. deep b. slow-moving c. dangerous d. interesting

A 20. These birds fly *unerringly* to the same spot each winter.
   a. without fail b. without feelings c. helplessly d. unnecessarily

Number correct _____ (total 20)

Part B Target Words in Reading and Literature

You should now have a general idea of the meaning of each target word. Refine your understanding by examining the shades of meaning the words have in the following excerpt.

Salmon Run

Linda Curtis

Spawning, the laying and fertilizing of eggs, is a key stage in the reproductive cycle of most fish. Each year thousands of salmon migrate from the Pacific Ocean back to the streams from which they originated, perhaps hundreds of miles away, to spawn and then die. In this passage writer Linda Curtis describes this annual migration.

7/15

The most **romantic tragedy** of nature is **enacted** every year about mid-October in the Adams and Little Rivers, deep in the **interior** of British Columbia, west of Salmon Arm.

The drama is the **mysterious** return of the sockeye salmon from the far northern expanse of the Pacific Ocean to the sparkling little mountain stream   5
where they were born four years before.

It is a spectacle of joy and sadness, of **brilliant** autumn beauty and the sorrow of death.

The Adams becomes a **frothing maelstrom** of flashing, jumping, twisting red sockeye as thousands of fish arrive to **spawn** and die.   10

It is a **phenomenon** that has never been fully explained by scientists.

Driven by some overwhelming **compulsion,** the fish **assemble** near the Gulf of Alaska after four years of feeding. Now fully **mature,** they head **unerringly** for the mouth of the Fraser River where they wait for several weeks before starting their **treacherous** journey upriver. How they find their way to the river's mouth   15
is unknown. Some experts believe they **navigate** by a highly developed sense of smell. Others think they work out their directions from the stars. In any case, the **migration coincides** with the **development** of **suitable** temperatures, around fifty-eight degrees Fahrenheit in their home streams.

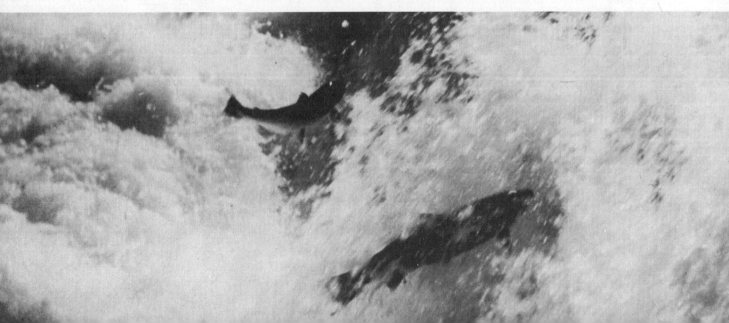

Refining Your Understanding

In each of the following items, consider how the target word is used in the passage. Write the letter of the word or phrase that best completes the sentence.

__C__ 1. This trip that the salmon take is described by the author as a *tragedy* (line 1) because at the end of it the salmon   a. feed   b. lay eggs   c. die.

__C__ 2. The salmon return to rivers in the *interior* (line 2) of British Columbia. The interior is the opposite of   a. the streams   b. the inland   c. the coast.

__B__ 3. For the sockeye salmon to return to their place of birth to *spawn* (line 10) means that they   a. feed   b. lay eggs   c. find a new environment.

__B__ 4. The salmon are driven by a *compulsion* (line 12); that is, they   a. are pushed by ocean currents   b. are driven by instinctive demands   c. remember a place where they are safe.

__C__ 5. Another title that would be *suitable* (line 18) for this selection would be   a. The Fascinating Rivers of British Columbia   b. Facts About Fish   c. A Dramatic Annual Migration.

Number correct _____ (total 5)

Part C   Ways to Make New Words Your Own

By now you are familiar with the target words and their meanings. This section presents a variety of reinforcement activities that will help you make these words part of your permanent vocabulary.

Using Language and Thinking Skills

Understanding Multiple Meanings Each boldfaced word in this exercise has several definitions. Read the definitions and then the sentences that use the word. Write the letter of the definition that applies to each sentence.

> **brilliant**
> a. sparkling (adj.)   c. magnificent (adj.)
> b. vivid (adj.)   d. keenly intelligent (adj.)

__D__ 1. John is *brilliant* in math.

~~B~~ A. ✗ The *brilliant* colors made it a memorable piece of Native American art.

__C__ 3. Her performance of the concerto was *brilliant*.

A ~~B~~ ✗ The reflection of the sun on the water was *brilliant*.

55

7/15

> **assemble**
> a. to gather together into a group (v.)
> b. to put together (v.)

A 5. The students began to *assemble* for the principal's speech.

B 6. Mary found it easy to *assemble* the model car kit.

> **development**
> a. a stage in growth, advancement (n.)
> b. a tract of land with newly built homes (n.)
> c. an event (n.)

A 7. Their stay in Germany was important to the *development* of the Beatles.

C 8. That character's death in Chapter Two is an unexpected *development*.

B 9. The Jabars are moving to that *development* that was built near Wolf Road.

A 10. The newspaper reported the latest *development* in the search for the child.

> **mature**
> a. full-grown; fully developed (adj.)   c. ripe (adj.)
> b. due; payable (said of a note or bond) (adj.)   d. to develop fully (v.)

C 11. The color of the fruit indicated it was *mature*.

A 12. Some people are not *mature* in their thinking.

A **B** 13. The dog's size indicated it was *mature*.

B 14. Terry was happy that his United States savings bond was *mature*.

D 15. It takes many years for a person to *mature*.

Number correct _____ (total 15)

Word's Worth: maelstrom

Maelstrom is the name of a notoriously dangerous current off the northwest coast of Norway. The Maelstrom current whips back and forth between two islands. The word *maelstrom* entered the English language through the fiction of Jules Verne and Edgar Allan Poe. Both writers painted an exaggerated picture of the Maelstrom as a giant whirlpool that engulfed entire vessels.

Synonyms-Antonyms Each of the words below the target word is a synonym or an antonym of the target word. Label the synonyms **S** and the antonyms **A.** Use a dictionary if needed.

1. **assemble**
   - S collect
   - A dismiss
   - A disperse
   - S concentrate
   - S meet
   - A scatter
   - S gather

2. **spawn**
   - A end
   - A expire
   - S teem
   - A destroy
   - S bring forth
   - S produce

3. **tragedy**
   - A good fortune
   - S calamity
   - S setback
   - S disaster
   - A comedy
   - S misfortune
   - A celebration

4. **compulsion**
   - S A pressure
   - S driving force
   - A option
   - S urge
   - A choice
   - S necessity

5. **mature**
   - A childish
   - A youthful
   - S ripe
   - S developed
   - A inexperienced
   - A juvenile
   - S grown
   - A green

6. **mysterious**
   - A understood
   - S hidden
   - S strange
   - A explainable
   - S obscure
   - A straightforward

7. **suitable**
   - S appropriate
   - S apt
   - S fitting
   - S rightful
   - S proper
   - S becoming
   - A unbecoming
   - S correct

8. **maelstrom**
   - A peacefulness
   - A calm
   - S violence
   - S turbulence
   - A serenity
   - S confusion
   - S whirlpool

9. **navigate**
   - S voyage
   - S steer
   - A S follow
   - S pilot
   - A drift
   - A float aimlessly
   - S guide

10. **brilliant**
   - S beaming
   - A murky
   - S radiant
   - S sparkling
   - A gloomy
   - S smart
   - S intense
   - A S subdued
   - A dim

Number correct _____ (total 10)

Analogies Each item below consists of a related pair of words followed by five pairs of words. Write the letter of the pair of words that best expresses a relationship similar to that of the original pair.

B 1. DIM : BRILLIANT :: (A) grave : serious (B) quiet : loud (C) cloudy : stormy (D) glowing : luminous (E) pervasive : abundant

E 2. MIRACLE : PHENOMENON :: (A) joke : laughter (B) spoon : soup (C) fall : winter (D) generosity : stinginess (E) event : occurrence

A 3. COMPASS : NAVIGATE :: (A) pencil : write (B) country : govern (C) car : manufacture (D) pill : dissolve (E) eggs : hatch

E ~~A~~ 4. CORRESPOND : COINCIDE :: (A) win : award (B) train : obey (C) sow : reap (D) teach : learn (E) accumulate : gather

D 5. ANSWER : RESPONSE :: (A) work : vacation (B) state : county (C) sidewalk : cement (D) multitude : crowd (E) river : ocean

E 6. MISTAKEN : UNERRING :: (A) expensive : fashionable (B) immoral : wrong (C) exterior : interior (D) icy : cold (E) intermittent : occasional

E 7. ASSEMBLE : PUZZLE :: (A) sew : tailor (B) navigate : chart (C) build : ruins (D) perform : stage (E) compose : novel

E 8. MIGRATION : TRAVEL :: (A) sonnet : poetry (B) plan : outcome (C) law : court (D) doctor : medicine (E) laughter : humor

B 9. MATURE : IMMATURE :: (A) wintry : autumnal (B) grown : young (C) astonished : surprised (D) cumbersome : clumsy (E) beige : tan

C 10. UNUSUAL : MYSTERIOUS :: (A) tense : intense (B) fierce : mild (C) teeming : crowded (D) supple : tight (E) rectangular : triangle

Number correct _____ (total 10)

> Turn to **Words Ending in y** on pages 195–197 of the **Spelling Handbook**. Read the rule and complete the exercises provided.

Spelling and Wordplay

Proofreading Find the misspelled word in each sentence below. Spell the word correctly in the blank to the left.

brilliant 1. There was a briliant light in the yard.

interior 2. We traveled into the interier of Australia.

romantic 3. The harvest moon truly made the evening romatic.

7/15

spawn   4. Each generation will spown another.

maelstrom   5. The boaters became suddenly aware of the dangerous malestrum downstream.

mysterious   6. Mysterous sounds came from the old house.

unerringly   7. The white mouse ran unerrorly through the maze.

treacherous 8. After the rain the path was slippery and trecherous.

phenomenon 9. Having lightning rip the top off our car was a phenomon we didn't expect.

coincided 10. Steve's lunch break coinsided with Mary's.

Number correct _____ (total 10)

Part D   Related Words

A number of words are closely related to the target words you have studied. Your knowledge of the target words and of word parts will help you determine the meaning of these words. (For information about word parts analysis, see pages 6–12.) If you are unsure of any definitions, use your dictionary. Learning these related words expands your vocabulary and helps you learn the target words more thoroughly.

1. assembly (ə sem′ blē) n.
2. brilliance (bril′ yəns) n.
3. coincidence (kō in′ sə dəns) n.
4. compulsive (kəm pul′ siv) adj.
5. develop (di vel′ əp) v.
6. enactment (in akt′ mənt) n.
7. err (ur, er) v.
8. exterior (ik stir′ ē ər) adj., n.
9. frothy (frôth′ ē, fräth′ ē) adj.
10. immigration (im′ ə grā′ shən) n.
11. maturity (mə toor′ ə tē, -choor′-, -tyoor′-) n.
12. migrate (mī′ grāt) v.
13. mystery (mis′ tə rē) n.
14. mystify (mis′ tə fī′) v.
15. navigation (nav′ ə gā′ shən) n.
16. phenomena (fə näm′ ə nə) n.
17. romanticize (rō man′ tə sīz′) v.
18. suit (soot, syoot) n., v.
19. tragic (traj′ ik) adj.
20. treachery (trech′ ər ē) n.

Understanding Related Words

Matching Definitions Refer to the Related Words list above. Use your knowledge of the meaning of the target words to match the following definitions with the related words. Write the correct related word in the blank.

enactment 1. the act of making into law

phenomena 2. occurrences

assembly 3. a group of people coming together for one purpose

treachery 4. treason; a betrayal of trust

59

maturity 5. the state of being fully developed

coincidence 6. a chance, simultaneous happening of related events

suit 7. to meet the needs of

mystery 8. something that has not or cannot be explained

exterior 9. the outside

navigation 10. the science of charting and steering a course

Number correct _____ (total 10)

True-False Decide whether each statement is true or false. Write **T** for True or **F** for False.

_F_ 1. An act of treachery inspires trust.

_F_ 2. A tragic occurrence always makes us laugh.

_T_ 3. To err is to make a mistake.

_T_ 4. A good magician can mystify an audience.

_T_ 5. The exterior of a building is exposed to sun, wind, and rain.

_F_ 6. Fur coats are frothy.

_T_ 7. Successful navigation means steering a boat down a winding river.

_F_ 8. When thinking about ordinary, everyday happenings, a person is romanticizing.

_T_ 9. A diamond's brilliance is one of its most attractive qualities.

_F_ 10. A compulsive talker is one who likes to be silent.

Number correct _____ (total 10)

Sentence Completion Complete each sentence with a related word from the list on page 59. A word may be used only once.

enactment 1. The _?_ of the legislation will help citizens over sixty-five.

brilliance 2. The _?_ of the lights made them visible for many miles.

develop _romanticize_ 3. Most people tend to _?_ the life of the cowboy.

assembly 4. All high-school students were expected to attend the _?_ yesterday afternoon.

navigation 5. Laws governing _?_ state that a captain must yield to a ship coming from the right, or starboard, side of the ship.

immigration 6. During the 1800's there was a massive _?_ of Europeans into the United States.

develop   7. The diplomats from the two countries worked hard to ⸮ a plan that would bring a lasting peace to the region.

migrate   8. Every winter, whales from the North Pacific ⸮ south toward Hawaii.

compulsive 9. A ⸮ gambler cannot resist making one more bet.

treachery 10. The agent was imprisoned for his ⸮, his selling of top-secret information to a foreign country.

Number correct _____ (total 10)

Analyzing Word Parts

The Plural of *phenomenon* Some English words derived from Greek and Latin have an *a* ending in their plural forms. One of these is the target word *phenomenon*; its plural is *phenomena*. Other English words that normally have the *a* plural ending include *medium* (*media*), *criterion* (*criteria*), *datum* (*data*), and *memorandum* (*memoranda*). Complete each of the following sentences with either the singular form (*phenomenon*) or the plural form (*phenomena*).

1. After maintaining an A average for four years, the student was known as an

   academic _____ .

2. Hurricanes, tornadoes, and earthquakes are only some of the

   natural _____ being studied by scientists.

3. The overnight success experienced by the rock star was a

   _____ no one could explain.

4. On that planet, dust storms and volcanic eruptions were common

   _____ .

5. The unbeaten track team, consisting of only four athletes, was described by a

   local newspaper reporter as a track-and-field _____ .

Number correct _____ (total 5)

Adding Suffixes Spell the related word by filling in the blanks before each suffix. Note that some words have spelling changes when a suffix is added.

1. assemble: _ _ _ _ _ _ _ _ y

2. coincide: _ _ _ _ _ _ _ e n c e

3. compulsion: _ _ _ _ _ _ _ i v e

4. brilliant: _ _ _ _ _ _ _ a n c e

5. enact: _ _ _ _ _ _ m e n t

61

6. mature: _ _ _ _ _ _ _ i t y

7. navigate: _ _ _ _ _ _ _ _ i o n

8. romantic: _ _ _ _ _ _ _ _ _ _ i z e

9. tragedy: _ _ _ _ i c

10. treacherous: _ _ _ _ _ _ _ _ _ y

Number correct _____ (total 10)

Number correct in unit _____ (total 115)

The Last Word

Writing

What are some of the indications that a person has passed from childhood to adulthood? In other words, what are the signs of a person's *maturity*? Think of various behaviors that indicate maturity. Write a paragraph in which you can explain three of these signs.

Speaking

Have you ever had a *brilliant* idea that somehow backfired? Why did it flop? In a speech relate your experience or one that you know about. Also give some suggestions as to why the idea was not a great success.

Group Discussion

Immigration has played a large role in American history. For nearly four hundred years, wave after wave of immigrants have come to America; this process continues today. Discuss several aspects of the immigrant experience.
1. What have been some of the reasons people have come to America? Are these reasons different today from those of immigrants in the 1800's?
2. What hardships do immigrants experience when they first come to America?
3. Give examples of how people try to retain their ethnic identity.
4. Should immigrants try to become completely Americanized? Or should they try to retain as much of their national identity as possible?

UNIT 6

1. advertise (ad′ vər tīz′) v.
2. coarse (kôrs) adj.
3. comic (käm′ ik) adj., n.
4. derision (di rizh′ ən) n.
5. glamorize (glam′ə rīz′) v.
6. heartily (härt′ ′l ē) adv.
7. inevitable (in ev′ ə tə b′l) adj.
8. lawless (lô′ lis) adj.
9. persuade (pər swād′) v.
10. picturesque (pik′ chə resk′) adj.
11. recline (ri klīn′) v.
12. reputation (rep′ yoo tā′ shən) n.
13. seldom (sel′ dəm) adj., adv.
14. taciturn (tas′ ə tʉrn′) adj.
15. thrust (thrust) n., v.
16. typical (tip′ i k'l) adj.
17. undoubtedly (un dout′ id lē) adv.
18. urge (ʉrj) n., v.
19. vanity (van′ ə tē) n.
20. version (vʉr′ zhən) n.

Inferring Meaning from Context

For each sentence write the letter of the word or phrase that is closest to the meaning of the word or words in italics. Use context clues to help you determine the correct answer. (For information about how context can help you understand vocabulary, see pages 1–5.)

__D__ 1. The local department store *advertises* its sales in the news section of the Sunday newspaper.

a. hides   b. never includes   c. carefully writes   d. publicly announces

__A__ 2. Debbie and John showed their typically *coarse* behavior at the dinner table; their lack of manners upset the other guests.

a. crude   b. happy   c. lawless   d. pristine

__D__ 3. Tim's *comic* performance in the play kept the audience laughing for several minutes.

a. quiet   b. hearty   c. ominous   d. funny

__C__ 4. Jenny and Sam felt that the prank played on them was a form of *derision*; their anger was justified.

a. acceptance   b. carelessness   c. mockery   d. persuasion

__C__ 5. By emphasizing the magnificent scenery and including two superstars, Redford and Streep, the film gave a *glamorized* picture of Africa.

a. coarse   b. simple   c. unrealistically attractive   d. negative

__C__ 6. Ben laughed *heartily*, and his voice was heard throughout the building.

a. foolishly   b. faintly   c. vigorously   d. intermittently

63

C 7. People say that only death and taxes are *inevitable*.

a. a privilege   b. a right   c. unavoidable   d. romantic

B 8. The Wild West is usually pictured as a *lawless* place, where bandits roamed at will.

a. without comforts   b. without regulation   c. comic   d. law-abiding

A 9. By showing how the vacuum worked, Janice *persuaded* me to buy one.

a. convinced   b. forced   c. allowed   d. forbade

D 10. The countryside provided a *picturesque* scene, with a beautiful seacoast and a quaint fishing village.

a. lawless   b. frothy   c. treacherous   d. visually pleasing

A 11. Matt was *reclining* on the couch, asleep, when his cat raced into the room and leaped on him.

a. lying down   b. floundering   c. talking   d. maturing

A 12. Julia Ward Howe's *reputation* as a women's rights leader was great; her ideas were read and quoted across the country.

a. fame   b. disgrace   c. advertisement   d. education

B 13. Anna *seldom* cared for the company of others. Except for occasional visits from her sister, Anna was a loner.

a. never   b. rarely   c. repeatedly   d. often

A 14. Francois likes to talk a lot, but his friend Pierre is *taciturn*.

a. quiet   b. spontaneous   c. exotic   d. younger

D 15. With great delight Dan *thrust* his fork into the plate of spaghetti.

a. threw   b. assembled   c. bent   d. plunged

B 16. It was a *typical* day for Don; he went to choir practice after school, did his homework, and then listened to his favorite albums.

a. comic   b. usual   c. spontaneous   d. unusual

C 17. According to the laws of gravity, unsupported objects will *undoubtedly* fall to the earth.

a. occasionally   b. never   c. certainly   d. intermittently

B 18. Ms. Jameson *urged* us to see the movie before it left town, but we simply did not have time to go.

a. called   b. encouraged   c. drove   d. forced

A 19. It was his *vanity* that others could not tolerate; he could talk about little other than his own accomplishments.

a. conceitedness   b. exertion   c. interest in others   d. maturity

B 20. Tara's *version* of the story differed slightly from Mark's telling of it.

a. advertising   b. account   c. setting   d. derision

Number correct _____ (total 20)

Part B   *Target Words in Reading and Literature*

You should now have a general idea of the meaning of each target word.   Refine your vocabulary by examining the shades of meaning the words have in the following excerpt.

Cowhands

Edwin Tunis

Countless TV and film Westerns have portrayed the cowboy as a colorful figure on the American frontier. Fictional portraits aside, what were these people really like? In this passage from Frontier Living, *Edwin Tunis discusses the origin of the word* cowboy *and describes these folk heroes of the West.*

Except in songs, they **seldom** called themselves "cowboys," but then a lot of people are called things they don't call themselves. "Cowpuncher" and "cowpoke," too, they first called each other in **comic derision,** but only after the railroad came west. A cowpuncher, armed with a long pole, **urged** cows up the runways to cattle cars; a cowpoke **thrust** a similar pole between the slats of the car to **persuade reclining** animals to stand up and avoid being killed by their fellows. "Cowhand," and more often, just "hand" was the range word.

5

٦/١٧

"Buckaroo," for cowhand, was the best Wyoming and Montana could do with vaquero.[1]

The **typical** hand was young, bowlegged, easygoing, and cheerful. He was 10 fearless, even reckless, but he was rarely **lawless.** He was healthy and strong; the work quickly weeded out weaklings. His **reputation** for **taciturnity,** like the Indian's, was given him by strangers; with his friends the cowhand was lively, chatty, and **heartily coarse.** He made twenty or twenty-five dollars a month (and keep[2]), paid in gold and silver coins, which he kept in a drawstring "poke" made 15 of leather; he had seen what happened to Confederate paper money, and he wanted no part of it. Some few range men saved their money and in time became ranchers, but most . . . "shot the works" in town as soon as they were paid off. The town welcomed them with crooked gamblers and bad whisky. . . .

The costume of the cowboy, at least a **glamorized version** of it, is as familiar 20 to an American as the clothes he wears himself. Until Buffalo Bill Cody **advertised** the glamor with his Wild West Show—the "Bill Show," the range called it—the simple cowhand didn't realize he was **picturesque.** His clothes were those best suited to his work, though **undoubtedly** they owed something to the Mexicans. 25

His **inevitable** vest may have been a survival of the Mexican's short jacket. The tight, ornamented boots with underslung high heels that all but crippled an early cowboy on the ground had no excuse but **vanity.** The tightness made the foot look trim, and the high heel made the man a little taller. Cutting the heel under, however, did nothing but interfere with walking.

---

[1] vaquero: Spanish word for cowboy; comes from Spanish for *cow, vaca*
[2] keep: food and shelter

Refining Your Understanding

For each of the following items, consider how the target words are used in the passage. Write the letter of the word or phrase that best completes the sentence.

~~B~~ ~~A~~ 1. We would expect that the *comic derision* (line 3) among cowboys would lead to   a. a gunfight   b. a hearty laugh   c. an apology.

B 2. When the author describes the *typical* (line 10) cowboy, he is describing a. all cowboys   b. most cowboys   c. the best cowboys.

B 3. Cowboys had a *reputation* for *taciturnity* (line 12), which suggests that a. cowboys thought themselves to be tough   b. others saw cowboys as unsociable   c. others felt cowboys were boisterous.

C 4. If cowboys were *heartily coarse* (line 14), they would probably not be comfortable   a. in a town saloon   b. around a campfire at night   c. at a formal tea.

B 5. When Buffalo Bill Cody *advertised* (line 22) the cowboy and his clothing, Cody apparently was   a. trying to sell cowboy clothing   b. promoting a romantic view of cowboys   c. adding to the comic derision of cowboys.

Number correct _____ (total 5)

7/17

Part C   Ways to Make New Words Your Own

This section presents a variety of activities reinforcing the target words.

Using Language and Thinking Skills

Finding the Unrelated Word Write the letter of the word that is not related in meaning to the other words in the set.

D 1. a. common b. usual c. typical d. strange

A 2. a. often b. seldom c. rarely d. infrequently

D 3. a. coarse b. rough c. crude d. polite

B 4. a. push b. pull c. thrust d. shove

C 5. a. enthusiastically b. vigorously c. sadly d. heartily

C 6. a. persuade b. urge c. discourage d. coax

D 7. a. derision b. ridicule c. mockery d. praise

C 8. a. advertise b. proclaim c. hide d. announce

A 9. a. stand b. lie down c. rest d. recline

A 10. a. talkative b. taciturn c. unsociable d. uncommunicative

Number correct _____ (total 10)

Homonyms Homonyms, such as *coarse* and *course*, are words that have the same pronunciation but different meanings and different spellings. Look up these two words in your dictionary. Complete the following exercise, inserting the appropriate word in the blank.

course 1. Why, of ? I will help you.

course 2. The ship's ? was due south.

coarse 3. His lack of refinement makes him ? .

course 4. She followed a ? of study in law.

Coarse 5. ? sandpaper is the roughest.

coarse 6. The grain of the wood is ?

course 7. Maturing is the ? of natural development.

coarse 8. The ? piece of furniture began to fall apart.

course 9. He was nicknamed Two-Ton because he enjoyed eating eight- ? meals.

course 10. Jeff was a caddy at a golf ? during the summer.

Number correct _____ (total 10)

Practicing for Standardized Tests

Analogies Write the letter of the pair of words that best expresses a relationship similar to that expressed in the original pair.

_B_ 1. BED : RECLINE ::   (A) tree : grow   (B) chair : sit   (C) car : fix
   (D) bird : migrate   (E) tornado : mar

_A_ 2. USUAL : TYPICAL ::   (A) phenomenal : amazing   (B) brilliant :
   dark   (C) reptilian : cold-blooded   (D) first : last   (E) lawless : legal

_D_ 3. SEEK : AVOID ::   (A) assemble : gather   (B) overtake : overtook
   (C) heat : expand   (D) coincide : separate   (E) grow : mature

_E_ 4. COMET : SELDOM ::   (A) skyscraper : enormous   (B) morning :
   sunny   (C) valley : low   (D) analogy : fun   (E) moon : frequent

_D_ 5. COARSE : COURSE ::   (A) beautiful : painting   (B) adjustable :
   wrench   (C) interior : inside   (D) banned : band   (E) decent : dissent

_C_ 6. UGLY : PICTURESQUE ::   (A) courageous : brave   (B) cumbersome :
   awkward   (C) bad : good   (D) mythical : fictional   (E) treacherous :
   disloyal

_B_ 7. ADVERTISEMENT : ADVERTISE ::   (A) advice : give
   (B) announcement : announce   (C) persuasion : convince   (D) see :
   sail   (E) consciousness : teach

_D_ 8. CRUEL : DERISION ::   (A) bookish : education   (B) aquatic :
   amphibians   (C) capable : capability   (D) kind : support
   (E) ignorant : opinion

_C_ 9. LAUGH : COMIC ::   (A) sleep : sleepy   (B) climb : mountainous
   (C) cry : tragic   (D) argue : argumentative   (E) adapt : adept

_E_ 10. BEAUTIFY : GLAMORIZE ::   (A) lose : win   (B) walk : run
   (C) sky-dive : surf   (D) mumble : enunciate   (E) proclaim : announce

Number correct _____ (total 10)

Word's Worth: glamor

Do you find _grammar_ to be _glamorous_? Long ago, people did. Only a select few scholars knew how to read and write. The language of the literate was Latin. These scholars were often held in awe by the uneducated masses, and Latin and its grammar came to be associated with magic. At some point a second word (with a change in spelling) evolved from the word _grammar_. The new word—_glamor_—retained the association with magic and awe.

Spelling and Wordplay

Crossword Puzzle

Across

1. Praised to promote sales
11. Appears to be
12. Calm; quiet
14. Auto
16. Huge
17. Abbr. Roads
18. A thrust with something pointed; a stab
20. Contraction of "I have"
22. Negative word
23. Abbr. Southeastern
25. Rowboat paddle
26. Damp
29. Abbr. States
31. This and the other
32. Opposite of "down"
33. A bear's home
34. Container for a plant
37. Young male
38. Abbr. State University
39. To keep away from
41. Positive word
42. Without law
43. To pound

Down

1. To attribute to
2. Deceased
3. One side of the story
4. Abbr. Enlisted Man
5. Abbr. Royal Society
6. Third person singular of "to be"
7. Rarely
8. A period of time in history
9. Mockery; ridicule
10. Four-winged, hairy insects
13. Abbr. National Guard
15. Conjunction
18. To convince
19. Not off
21. Abbr. Veterans Administration
24. Abbr. Estimated
27. To follow orders
28. To shove
30. Abbr. Title Page
33. A tiny spot
34. A friend
35. Egg cells in mammals
36. To pull behind
38. Ocean
40. Abbr. Illinois
41. Biblical "you"

Part D   Related Words

A number of words are closely related to the target words you have studied. Your knowledge of the target words and of word parts will help you determine the meaning of these words. (For information about word parts analysis, see pages 6-12.) If you are unsure of any definitions, use your dictionary. Learning these related words expands your vocabulary and helps you learn the target words more thoroughly.

1. comedy (käm′ ə dē) n.
2. decline (di klīn′) n., v.
3. deride (di rīd′) v.
4. derisive (di rī′ siv) adj.
5. glamorous (glam′ ə rəs) adj.
6. hearty (härt′ ē) adj.
7. incline (in′ klīn) n., (in klīn′) v.

8. lawful (lô′ f'l) adj.
9. persuasion (pər swā′ zhən) n.
10. persuasive (pər swā′ siv) adj.
11. reputable (rep′ yōō tə b'l) adj.
12. urgency (ʉr′ jən sē) n.
13. urgent (ʉr′ jənt) adj.
14. vain (vān) adj.

Understanding Related Words

Matching Antonyms Match each word on the left with its antonym on the right. Write the letter of the antonym in the blank at the left.

_D_ 1. vain   a. illegal
_G_ 2. comedy   b. discouragement
_E_ 3. decline   c. unnecessary
_H_ 4. deride   d. humble
_I_ 5. glamorous   e. accept
_F_ 6. hearty   f. unenthusiastic
_C_ 7. urgent   g. tragedy
_A_ 8. lawful   h. praise
_B_ 9. persuasion   i. unattractive
_J_ 10. reputable   j. dishonorable

Number correct _____ (total 10)

Turn to **Words Ending in** *ize* or *ise* on page 201 of the **Spelling Handbook.** Read the rule and complete the exercises provided.

Analyzing Word Parts

The Suffix *-ize* The noun *glamor* is made into the verb *glamorize* by adding the suffix *-ize*. The primary meaning of this suffix is "to cause to become." Many nouns are turned into verbs by adding *-ize*. In each of the following sentences, there is a blank followed by a word in parentheses. Add *-ize* to the word to form the appropriate verb and write it in the blank. Also note that the verb tense may need to be changed.

1. One special part of the news program allowed the anchorperson to
editorialize (editorial) about a particular issue.

2. Next year the teachers will *standardize* (standard) all the exams given in English classes.

3. Who *popularized* (popular) the line "Make my day"?

4. It doesn't take long before our culture *Americanizes* (American) most immigrants.

5. When will this business *computerize* (computer) its operations?

Number correct _____ (total 5)

Number correct in unit _____ (total 70)

The Last Word

Writing

Describe a place that, in your opinion, is *picturesque*. It can be a place that you have visited or that you have seen in photographs. Make sure your description is complete enough to create a clear picture in the reader's mind.

Speaking

Write a radio commercial that *advertises* your favorite food. Read your commercial to the class.

Group Discussion

Derision—What causes a person to make fun of someone else? What is your opinion of a person who does such a thing? Share your opinions with the rest of the class.

71

U N I T 7

Part A Target Words and Their Meanings

1. adapt (ə dapt′) v.
2. constitution (kän′ stə tōō′ shən, -tyōō-) n.
3. convalescence (kän və les′ ′ns) n.
4. exhaust (ig zôst′) n., v.
5. expose (ik spōz′) v.
6. hazard (haz′ ərd) n., v.
7. immoderate (i mäd′ ər it) adj.
8. inured (in yoord′) v.
9. involve (in välv′) v.
10. mechanism (mek′ ə niz′m) n.
11. moderate (mäd′ ər it) adj., n. (-ə rāt′) v.
12. noxious (näk′ shəs) adj.
13. organism (ôr′ gə niz′m) n.
14. potent (pōt′ ′nt) adj.
15. psychological (sī kə läj′ i k′l) adj.
16. repetition (rep′ ə tish′ ən) n.
17. response (ri späns′) n.
18. restorative (ri stôr′ ə tiv) adj.
19. stress (stres) n., v.
20. volume (väl′ yoom, -yəm) n.

Inferring Meaning from Context

For each sentence write the letter of the word or phrase that is closest in meaning to the italicized word or words. Use context clues to help you determine the correct answer. (For information about how context can help you understand vocabulary, see pages 1-5.)

__C__ 1. Tanya is an excellent mountain climber because she can *adapt to* many different situations.

a. drop out of b. run away from c. adjust to d. deplete

__B__ 2. We hope that my grandmother's strong *constitution* will help her recover from her operation.

a. stress b. physical makeup c. house d. reputation

__D__ 3. George's *convalescence* went well following his operation, and he returned to school sooner than expected.

a. glamorization b. compulsion c. payments on his bill
d. gradual recovery

__A__ 4. The soccer players were *exhausted* following the long, hard game.

a. tired out b. excited c. thoroughly happy d. thoroughly saddened

__D__ 5. In the final scene, Sherlock Holmes *exposed* the murderer, and the police took the culprit away.

a. covered up b. forgot c. killed d. made known

__D__ 6. Too much noise is considered a *hazard* to a person's health.

a. complement b. necessity c. development d. danger

A   7. The family's phone bill was quite high due to *an immoderate* number of calls.

   a. an excessive   b. a modest   c. a typical   d. a brilliant

B   8. At first Ella hated the weather in Northern Canada, but after living there for several years, she became *inured to* the harsh conditions.

   a. injured by   b. accustomed to   c. delighted by   d. fearful of

B   9. Julio's job *involved* typing letters and making copies for Mr. Perez; the job required no sales calls.

   a. avoided   b. included   c. exposed   d. adapted to

C   10. A small *mechanism* that could be fixed easily ran Jody's watch.

   a. case   b. set of numbers   c. system of parts   d. button

A   11. Germaine played her trumpet solo with *moderate* speed, neither too fast nor too slow.

   a. regulated   b. careless   c. sheer   d. excessive

B   12. Property owners often destroy such *noxious* weeds as goldenrod, which can cause hay fever and other allergies.

   a. healthful   b. harmful   c. suitable   d. mysterious

B   13. The amoeba is a one-celled *organism*; we studied it under the microscope.

   a. response   b. living thing   c. accelerator   d. event

C   14. The plant food has a *potent* effect on our garden; our vegetables are thriving.

   a. psychological   b. treacherous   c. powerful   d. weak

A   15. Gerry's illness was caused by a *psychological* problem, not a physical one.

   a. mental   b. tragic   c. typical   d. comical

C   16. Ellen found the constant *repetition* of television commercials boring.

   a. variety   b. novelty   c. repeating   d. loudness

C   17. Betty gave Harry a direct *response* to his question.

   a. repetition   b. compliment   c. answer   d. plan

A   18. The witch doctor claimed that his people were healed because of the water's *restorative* powers.

   a. renewing   b. reviewing   c. reclining   d. repeating

D   19. The old bridge cracked under the *stress* of the heavy traffic.

   a. spectacle   b. sound   c. repetition   d. force

C   20. The *volume* of the radio is unbearable. Please turn it down.

   a. arrangement   b. musical format   c. loudness   d. restoration

Number correct _____ (total 20)

Part B Target Words in Reading and Literature

You should now have a general idea of the meaning of each target word. Refine your understanding by examining the shades of meaning the words have in the following excerpt.

The Tyranny of Noise

Robert Alex Baron

A plane roars overhead. Cars honk at a busy intersection. Daily we face a barrage of noise. According to Robert Baron, noise can be harmful to the human body. Stress from excessive noise is a serious health hazard.

People are being **exposed** to increasing amounts of a new and **potent** mix of **stresses**—chemical, physical, and **psychological.**

Noise, at even **moderate** levels, forces a systemic[1] **response** from the total **organism.** It is not only the sense of hearing that is **involved.** What is also involved is what happens after the brain receives the sound signal. The brain places the body on a war footing. The **repetition** of these alerts is **exhausting.** It depletes energy levels; it can cause changes in the chemistry of the blood, in the **volume** of the blood circulation; it places a strain on the heart; it prevents **restorative** sleep and rest; it hinders **convalescence;** it can be a form of torture. It can so weaken the body's defense **mechanisms** that diseases can more readily take hold. The organism does not **adapt** to noise; it becomes **inured** and pays a price. The price . . . is in itself a **hazard** to health.

Noise per se[2] may not be dangerous. But when noise becomes **immoderate,** as with anything else in life, it loses its innocence. It also loses its innocence when it strikes at those whose **constitutions** are weakened by ill health or old age. Noise may yet prove to be as deadly a threat to man as the **noxious** fumes about which we are presently hearing so much.

5

10

15

---

[1] systemic: of a system; in physiology, affecting the body as a whole
[2] per se: by (or in) itself; inherently

7/22

Refining Your Understanding

For each of the following questions, consider how the target word is used in the passage. Write the letter of the word or phrase that best completes the sentence.

_B_ 1. *Psychological* stress (line 2) indicates that noise affects a person's
    a. sense of direction   b. mind   c. respiratory system.

_C_ 2. By *organism* (line 4) the author means   a. crucial organs of the body
    b. the mind   c. the entire body.

_B_ 3. Noise hinders *convalescence* (line 9); this means that with immoderate
    amounts of noise   a. people are more likely to get diseases   b. recovery
    from diseases takes longer   c. various body processes slow down.

_A_ 4. "The organism does not *adapt* to noise" (line 11) means that the body
    does not   a. make changes   b. remain the same   c. break down.

_C_ 5. Since *immoderate* (line 13) amounts of noise are the real problem, we can
    conclude that noise probably will not harm a person as long as it is
    a. low-pitched   b. expected   c. in small amounts.

Number correct _____ (total 5)

Part C   Ways to Make New Words Your Own

Using Language and Thinking Skills

Using Words in Context In the blank write the target word that best completes each sentence in this story. Refer to the list of words on page 72.

A Sound Solution

Dr. Christine Jones, chief of staff at Mercy Hospital, was concerned about the immoderate noise level tolerated by the patients and the staff.

Many people turned the volume of the radio or television too high. This created unnecessary stress on the eardrums. Patients and staff seemed to adapt to this sound because they were constantly expose (ed) to it. However, Dr. Jones felt this high level of sound was a hazard. She also felt that the constant repetition of high noise levels often caused psychological problems.

Dr. Jones came up with a system to decrease the noise hazard. She equipped every radio and television with a mechanism that would allow the volume to be turned up only halfway

The patients and staff soon appreciated the moderate level of sound.

Number correct _____ (total 10)

7/22

Practicing for Standardized Tests

Antonyms Write the letter of the word that is most nearly *opposite* in meaning to the capitalized target word.

_E_ 1. HAZARD: (A) sign (B) danger (C) adventure (D) waste (E) safety

_B_ 2. POTENT: (A) stressful (B) weak (C) taciturn (D) cumbersome (E) powerful

_B_ 3. EXHAUST: (A) devise (B) energize (C) suffice (D) deplete (E) release

_E_ 4. EXPOSE: (A) open (B) proclaim (C) pose (D) permit (E) cover

_A_ 5. INVOLVE: (A) omit (B) mingle (C) enact (D) assemble (E) turn

_E_ 6. STRESS: (A) derision (B) emphasis (C) retrieval (D) maintenance (E) relaxation

_C_ 7. NOXIOUS: (A) anxious (B) unwholesome (C) harmless (D) mysterious (E) transitional

_A_ 8. MODERATE: (A) excessive (B) reasonable (C) new (D) sufficient (E) pristine

_B_ 9. RESPONSE: (A) answer (B) question (C) intrusion (D) compulsion (E) appraisal

_D_ 10. CONVALESCENCE: (A) recovery (B) retirement (C) circumstance (D) decline (E) version

Number correct _____ (total 10)

Spelling and Wordplay

Forming Words Using only the letters found in the word *restorative*, make as many words as you can of four or more letters. Form at least ten words. For example, the words *strive* and *rise* can be formed from *restorative*.

1. _____   6. _____

2. _____   7. _____

3. _____   8. _____

4. _____   9. _____

5. _____   10. _____

Number correct _____ (total 10)

Turn to **The Prefix *in-*** on pages 192–193 of the **Spelling Handbook**. Read the rule and complete the exercises provided.

Part D Related Words

A number of words are closely related to the target words you have studied. Your knowledge of the target words and of word parts will help you determine the meaning of these words. (For information about word parts analysis, see pages 6–12.) If you are unsure of any definitions, use your dictionary. Learning these related words expands your vocabulary and helps you learn the target words more thoroughly.

1. adaptation (ad əp tā′ shən) n.
2. convalesce (kän′ və les′) v.
3. exhaustion (ig zôs′ chən) n.
4. exposure (ik spō′ zhər) n.
5. hazardous (haz′ ərd əs) adj.
6. involvement (in volv′ mənt) n.
7. mechanical (mə kan′ i k′l) adj.
8. mechanics (mə kan′ iks) n.
9. moderation (mäd′ ə rā′ shən) n.
10. organization (ôr′ gə ni zā′ shən, -nī-) n.
11. potential (pə ten′ shəl) adj., n.
12. psychologist (sī käl′ ə jist) n.
13. psychology (sī käl′ ə jē) n.
14. repetitious (rep′ ə tish′ əs) adj.
15. respond (ri spänd′) v.
16. responsive (ri spän′ siv) adj.
17. restore (ri stôr′) v.
18. voluminous (və lōō mə nəs) adj.

Understanding Related Words

Sentence Completion In each blank write the related word that best completes the sentence. Refer to the Related Words list above.

hazardous 1. The winding road is ? to travel by night.

repetitious 2. Listening to the same record every day is very ?.

psychology 3. Susan was interested in the reasons people behave the way they do, so she studied ?.

exposure 4. Too much ? to the sun can result in sunburn.

potential 5. Teachers felt that Sarah had the ? to do well in school if she studied harder.

moderation 6. Tony avoids muscle strain by exercising in ?.

exhaustion 7. ? can result from too much exercise.

restore 8. The workers will try to ? that old building to its former beauty.

adaptation 9. The fish in this dark cave have undergone a fascinating ? to their environment—they have lost their sight.

mechanical 10. Mrs. Jones is quite ?; she has repaired and serviced foreign cars for over twenty years.

Number correct _____ (total 10)

77

Finding Examples Answer the following questions regarding the related words. In the blank write the letter of the best answer.

___C___ 1. Which of the following would most likely be an expert in *mechanics*?
    a. a politician
    b. a psychologist
    c. the person who services your car

___C___ 2. Imagine you are injured in a traffic accident. Which of the following people is being *responsive* to your needs?
    a. the person who called the ambulance
    b. the ambulance driver
    c. both of the above

___A___ 3. What does a *psychologist* do?
    a. studies and works with human behavior
    b. works as a librarian
    c. studies the earth

___C___ 4. Which of the following could be called a *voluminous* amount of water?
    a. a raindrop
    b. the amount of water in your car radiator
    c. an ocean

___C___ 5. Which of the following is an example of *adaptation*?
    a. a person who wears sandals in cold weather
    b. a person who eats great quantities of food
    c. a person who learns sign language to communicate with a friend who is hearing impaired

Number correct _____ (total 5)

Matching Synonyms Match each related word on the left with its synonym on the right. Write the letter of the synonym in the blank.

___B___ 1. convalesce   ✓ a. massive
___G___ 2. exhaustion   ✓ b. recover
___J___ 3. hazardous   ✓ c. restraint
___H___ 4. involvement   ✓ d. rebuild
___C___ 5. moderation   ✓ e. possible
___E___ 6. potential   ✓ f. answer
___I___ 7. organization   ✓ g. fatigue
___F___ 8. respond   ✓ h. inclusion
___D___ 9. restore   ✓ i. group
___A___ 10. voluminous   ✓ j. dangerous

Number correct _____ (total 10)

7/22

Word's Worth: psychological

Psyche was the Greek word for "soul" or "mind." The Greeks had stories for many important human characteristics—and the soul was no exception. According to Greek myth, Psyche was a princess whose beauty was so great it was said to rival that of Venus, the goddess of love. When the goddess's own son, Cupid (Love), fell in love with Psyche, Venus became angry. She punished Psyche by having the girl perform many tasks. Cupid finally rescued Psyche and appealed to Zeus, the head of all the gods, to make peace with Venus. That is how Cupid came to be married to Psyche—and how Love was united with Soul forever.

Analyzing Word Parts

The Greek Root *psyche* English words with the root *psyche* have meanings related to the way the mind works or to the emotional disorders that people suffer. In your dictionary look up the following *psyche* words and write their definitions.

1. psychology: _____

2. psychiatrist: _____

3. psychic: _____

4. psychosomatic: _____

   _____

5. psychopath: _____

Number correct _____ (total 5)

Number correct in unit _____ (total 85)

79

The Last Word

Writing

Choose one item from each of the columns below. Then write a story based on these three items. Let your imagination wander.

Characters	Incidents	Conditions
• a famous *psychologist*	• *depleting* the supply of food	• in a *hazardous* location
• an unidentified *organism*	• experiencing *stress*	• in a *voluminous* cavern
• an *exhausted* musician	• *exposing* film	• in need of *convalescence*
• a *responsive* friend	• *adapting* to new surroundings	• *involved* in a secret plot
• a *mechanical* genius	• *advertising* a product	• with a *moderate* amount of success
• a person with *potential*	• *navigating* through the ocean	• in a *lawless* manner
• the president of an *organization*	• *persuading* others to imitate someone	• with great *maturity*
• a *glamorous* movie star	• talking with *repetition*	
	• reading a *mystery*	

Speaking

Have you ever moved to a new town? In what ways did you have to adapt to your new surroundings? Give a short speech about the ways you had to adapt and the traits that were acquired.

Group Discussion

Discuss the problem of noise pollution. Do you agree that it is a potential *hazard* to our physical and *psychological* health? If so, what should be done about it?

Sentence Completion Complete each sentence by using one of the focus words.

_____ 1. The ? child was raised speaking both English and Spanish.

_____ 2. The ? of *chauvinist* reveals that this word is derived from the name of a French soldier, Nicholas Chauvin, who was fanatically devoted to Napoleon.

_____ 3. A ? studies the similarities and the differences among languages.

_____ 4. Learning the basic rules of ? will help you pronounce unfamiliar words correctly.

_____ 5. Some say English ? is the most difficult to learn because so many of its rules have exceptions.

_____ 6. According to English ?, we place the owner's name before his or her possession, as in "Marie's paper."

_____ 7. The ? "break a leg" actually means "good luck" and is an expression used in the theater.

_____ 8. The engineer's ? was so technical that none of us could understand her.

_____ 9. Instead of describing me as clumsy, my coach used this ?: "He needs to improve his motor control."

_____ 10. A single word can have so many meanings that a knowledge of ? can aid communication.

_____ 11. When I talk to my friends, I usually use ? language rather than formal language.

_____ 12. The professor of ? specialized in the Sino-Tibetan languages, which consist of one-syllable words.

_____ 13. *Groovy, right on,* and *far out* were part of the ? of the 1960's.

_____ 14. Many different English ? are spoken in the United States.

_____ 15. The name of their group is GASP, an ? that stands for "Group Against Smoking in Public."

Number correct _____ (total 15)

FOCUS ON: *The Sounds of Language*

How often have you listened to a radio ad or song lyrics that made you react emotionally, perhaps with joy or sorrow? This effect was not a coincidence; it was planned by a writer who knew about the sounds of words and how to use them to create certain effects. The following devices can help you use the sounds of words to create certain effects in your writing.

Alliteration

Alliteration is the repetition of consonant sounds at the beginnings of words. Writers of both prose and poetry use alliteration to emphasize certain words, to reinforce meaning, and to impart a musical quality to poems. Study the following examples:

the *s*ilver *s*weep of the *s*ea   *p*olicy and *p*olitics
a *h*elping *h*and   hot *r*od's *r*oar and *r*umble

Alliteration can also be used to emphasize an idea in a passage or it can reinforce a certain mood or feeling. In this line from Edgar Allan Poe's "The Raven," notice how the *d* sound helps to convey a feeling of heaviness and foreboding.

"*D*oubting, *d*reaming *d*reams no mortal ever *d*ared to *d*ream before"

Consonance

Like alliteration, consonance is the repetition of similar or identical consonant sounds. However, consonance refers to sounds found *within* or *at the ends of words* that are close together. Such sounds can produce a type of sound effect that unifies a work or enhances a mood. Note the repetition of sounds in the following examples:

whi*rr* of the propell*er*   conso*l*ed by the co*l*d go*l*d
di*s*turbing whi*s*pers in the darkne*ss*   the pain*t* hi*t* the pavemen*t* with a spla*t*

Assonance

Assonance is often called "vowel rhyme." It is the repetition of vowel sounds within words that are close to each other. The repeated vowel sounds can give a musical quality to the words. Read aloud the examples below.

al*o*ne at h*o*me   br*a*ve and v*ai*n
l*i*ke the t*i*de   a r*o*se in a b*o*wl

The emphasis of a vowel sound can also help reinforce meaning in a piece of writing. For example, the long *i* sound can heighten or excite emotion, as in these lines from a William Blake poem.

"T*y*ger! T*y*ger! burning br*i*ght
In the forest of the n*i*ght. . . ."

Onomatopoeia

Onomatopoeia occurs when the sound of a word mimics its meaning. Consider the examples below.

snap   pop   murmur   flop   fizz   crackle

These words not only name a sound but also echo the sounds they name. Onomatopoetic words allow readers to hear and feel sounds.

Identifying Sound Devices Identify the occurrences of alliteration, assonance, consonance, and onomatopoeia in the following sentences. Write the name of the device in the blank. Each sentence has only one main sound device.

_____ 1. Ted tore past the tackle to score the touchdown.

_____ 2. The dry corn stalks snapped and crackled as fire moved through the field.

_____ 3. He who laughs last laughs best.

_____ 4. Oh, how cold I felt, hearing the groan of that closing door.

_____ 5. Pam came home with her gleaming diamond.

_____ 6. The river water gurgled and splashed at my feet.

_____ 7. She spilled the soup and slipped on the stair.

_____ 8. Bats fluttered in the darkly lit basement.

_____ 9. Cruising through the town, Conrad made a smooth mo͟ ͟ .

_____ 10. Suddenly, from the hum of the jungle emerged the his͟ of a python.

Number correct _____ (total

Number correct in Vocab Lab _____ (tota

Tongue Twisters A tongue twister is a phrase or sentence that contains series of similar sounds. Although usually quite difficult, the object of tongue twister is to repeat it as many times as possible, as quickly as possib without mispronouncing it. Study the examples of tongue twisters below, then try to create five of your own.

knapsack strap
mixed biscuits
a proper copper coffee pot
Some shun sunshine.
a dozen double damask dinner
    napkins
six slim slender saplings

lemon liniment
preshrunk shirts
The sinking steamer sank.
Whistle for the thistle sifter.
There's no need to light a night
    light on a night like tonight.

Special Unit   Taking Standardized Vocabulary Tests

During the next few years, you will be taking many standardized tests that contain vocabulary questions. Employment tests, placement tests, and college entrance examinations include such questions in order to measure your basic language skills. It is to your advantage to prepare yourself for these tests so that you will do as well as you possibly can.

One way to prepare for these tests is to work hard in your English classes to improve your language skills. Another effective method of preparation is to study the different types of test questions you are likely to encounter in standardized tests. In the area of vocabulary, these types of questions include **antonyms, analogies,** and **sentence completion.**

The exercises in this book have provided practice with these types of vocabulary questions. The following pages of this special unit offer additional practice in and specific strategies for taking standardized tests.

Part A   Antonyms

As you know, **antonyms** are words that are opposite in meaning. Standardized test questions covering antonyms are answered by selecting the word choice most opposite in meaning to the given word. A typical question looks like this:

> _____ CAREFUL: (A) easy   (B) acute   (C) careless   (D) unprepared
> (E) cautious

To answer an antonym question, use the following strategies:

1. Remember that you must find a word that is *opposite* in meaning. Do not be thrown off by *synonyms*—words that are similar in meaning. In the example above, choice *E*, *cautious*, is a synonym for the given word, *careful*.
2. Decide whether the given word is positive or negative, and then eliminate all possible choices that are in the same category as the given word. *Careful* has a positive connotation. Therefore choice *A*, *easy*, and choice *E*, *cautious*, can be eliminated.
3. Remember that many words have more than one meaning. If no word seems to fit your sense of the opposite meaning, think about other meanings for the given word. For example, *acute* means both "sharp" and "serious." However, since neither of these meanings is opposite that of *careful*, choice *B* also can be eliminated.
4. If you do not know the meaning of a given word, try to analyze the word's parts—the prefix, suffix, base word, or root—in order to define the word. *Careful* and *careless* share the same base word. Their suffixes, *-ful* and *-less*, have opposite meanings, however. Therefore, the words themselves have opposite meanings, and choice *C* is the correct answer.

Exercise Write the letter of the word whose meaning is most nearly *opposite* that of the capitalized word.

_____ 1. ABRUPTLY: (A) quickly   (B) noisily   (C) gradually   (D) carefully   (E) unexpectedly

_____ 2. NEVER :   (A) later   (B) seldom   (C) soon   (D) always   (E) frequently

_____ 3. EXTERIOR :   (A) outside   (B) superficial   (C) visible   (D) integral   (E) interior

_____ 4. REMEMBER :   (A) recollect   (B) know   (C) memorize   (D) forfeit   (E) forget

_____ 5. HINDER :   (A) disguise   (B) block   (C) help   (D) end   (E) forget

_____ 6. DISCARD :   (A) regard   (B) lose   (C) win   (D) throw away   (E) save

_____ 7. ODD :   (A) unusual   (B) rare   (C) favorite   (D) special   (E) normal

_____ 8. PORTABLE :   (A) handy   (B) flexible   (C) legible   (D) immovable   (E) mobile

_____ 9. EXCLUDE :   (A) forget   (B) include   (C) exit   (D) omit   (E) infect

_____ 10. CLEVER :   (A) happy   (B) smart   (C) sad   (D) cutting   (E) stupid

Number correct _____ (total 10)

Part B   *Analogies*

Analogies, as you will recall, are pairs of words that are related in some way to each other. In most analogy problems on standardized tests, you are given two words that are related to each other in some way. Your job is to determine this relationship and to find another pair of words that are related in the same way. A typical analogy question looks like this:

_____ BUTTON : SNAP: (A) zipper : jacket   (B) pencil : pen
(C) fork : utensil   (D) crayon : draw   (E) book : read

To answer analogy questions, use the following strategies:

1. First, be aware of the types of relationships that may be expressed in analogies. Refer to the chart on page 50 for a list of the most common of these relationships.
2. Then determine the relationship of the given pair of words. Do this by creating a sentence that contains both words and that shows the relationship between them. In the above example, the relationship can be expressed this way:

A *button* and a *snap* have the same function.

3. Third, find the pair of words among the answers that could logically replace the given pair in your sentence. In the example, answer *B* does this.

A *pencil* and a *pen* have the same function.

Exercise Write the letter of the word pair that best expresses a relationship similar to that expressed in the original pair.

_____ 1. SHOE : FOOT :: (A) head : hat (B) glove : hand (C) glasses : frame (D) toothbrush : teeth (E) ear : earplug

_____ 2. MICROSCOPE : GERMS :: (A) doctor : illness (B) shot : serum (C) patient : nurse (D) vision : glasses (E) telescope : stars

_____ 3. JUICE : ORANGE :: (A) beef : steer (B) apple : core (C) pie : crust (D) milk : cheese (E) clouds : rain

_____ 4. WIND : SAILBOAT :: (A) astronaut : space shuttle (B) music : dance (C) fan : air conditioner (D) bike : pedal (E) gas : car

_____ 5. COLD : HOT :: (A) arctic : tropical (B) warm : tepid (C) alien : foreign (D) upset : violent (E) majestic : regal

_____ 6. ANNOY : PESTER :: (A) laugh : cry (B) laugh : tickle (C) talk : listen (D) entertain : amuse (E) create : exterminate

_____ 7. INFANT : CHILD :: (A) adolescent : adult (B) dog : puppy (C) plant : seed (D) root : plant (E) sister : brother

_____ 8. GIRAFFE : MAMMAL :: (A) human : man (B) grasshopper : insect (C) web : spider (D) feline : cat (E) daisy : rose

_____ 9. HAMMER : NAIL :: (A) screw : screwdriver (B) stapler : staple (C) ax : blade (D) pen : ink (E) thread : needle

_____ 10. TAILOR : THREAD :: (A) baker : oven (B) bricklayer : brick (C) architect : building (D) brush : painting (E) clay : sculptor

Number correct _____ (total 10)

Part C *Sentence Completion*

Sentence Completion questions test your ability to use words and to recognize relationships among parts of a sentence. You are given a sentence in which one or two words are missing. You must then choose the word or words that best complete the sentence. A typical sentence completion question looks like this:

_____ Our team has a great ⸻?⸻ to win, but a lack of practice will ⸻?⸻ us from attaining first place.
(A) knowledge . . . understand (B) amount . . . inspire
(C) desire . . . prevent (D) spirit . . . sadden
(E) game . . . disappoint

To answer sentence completion questions, use the following strategies:

1. Read the entire sentence carefully. Pay particular attention to words that indicate contrast or similarity. For example, the word *but* in the question above gives you a clue that the correct word pair will contain words that are opposite in meaning. Therefore, the correct answer is *C*, desire . . . prevent.
2. Try each of the choices. Eliminate choices that make no sense, that are grammatically incorrect, or that contradict some other part of the statement.
3. Look for grammatical clues within the sentence. Does the structure of the sentence call for a verb, an adjective, a noun? If the answer is a verb, in what tense must the verb be written to correspond with the rest of the sentence? Asking such questions may help you eliminate some incorrect answers.

Exercise Write the letter of the word or words that best complete the sentence.

_____ 1. The ? rules of the coach demand that each player be in bed by 9 P.M.
(A) loose (B) rigid (C) legal (D) medical (E) flexible

_____ 2. Julio was impressed with the ? of the merchandise.
(A) technique (B) absence (C) quality (D) selling (E) mediocrity

_____ 3. The lack of ? value in Janet's lunches was alarming.
(A) monetary (B) nutritional (C) educational (D) lethal (E) liquid

_____ 4. Sherry was ? to see the movie but ? to pay the high admission price.
(A) eager . . . reluctant (B) quick . . . eager (C) told . . . not
(D) eager . . . anxious (E) reluctant . . . unhappy

_____ 5. The ? speech bored the audience and ? them to sleep.
(A) exciting . . . enticed (B) dull . . . relieved (C) brief . . . sang
(D) technical . . . taught (E) monotonous . . . lulled

_____ 6. The teacher ? the students ? at 3 P.M.
(A) isolated . . . randomly (B) dismissed . . . promptly (C) diverted . . .
rigidly (D) acknowledged . . . remotely (E) resembled . . . distinctly

_____ 7. The candidate was ? as she ? victory.
(A) tired . . . chose (B) hostile . . . declined (C) elusive . . . relished
(D) astonished . . . dismissed (E) jubilant . . . proclaimed

_____ 8. Tom's ? situation was so good that he was able to ? in a new home.
(A) health . . . live (B) debt . . . survive (C) financial . . . invest (D)
domestic . . . admire (E) poverty . . . assemble

_____ 9. ? behavior is not ? in the classroom.
(A) Superlative . . . memorable (B) Obvious . . . typical (C) Mediocre
. . . toxic (D) Hostile . . . contemptuous (E) Immature . . . appropriate

_____ 10. The ? businesswoman was honored by her ?.
(A) passive . . . parents (B) abrupt . . . bankers (C) liberal . . .
trends (D) prominent . . . colleagues (E) elite . . . clothes

Number correct _____ (total 10)

Number correct in unit _____ (total 30)

Part D   General Strategies

No matter what type of question you are solving, certain strategies can be applied to any part of a standardized test. Keep the following guidelines in mind. They can help you increase your chance of success. Remember, too, that a good mental attitude, plenty of rest the night before a test, and the ability to relax will further enhance your test performance.

Basic Strategies for Taking Standardized Tests

1. **Read and listen to directions carefully.** This may seem obvious, but many students do poorly on tests because they misunderstand the directions. For each question, read all of the choices before choosing an answer.

2. **Budget your time carefully.** Most standardized tests are timed, so it is important that you not spend too much time on any single item.

3. **Complete the test items you know first.** Mark the difficult ones and return to them later. More difficult questions are often at the end of each section.

4. **Mark the answer sheet carefully and correctly.** Most standardized tests make use of computerized answer sheets. You are required to fill in a circle corresponding to the correct answer in the test booklet, as follows:

When using such computerized answer sheets, follow these guidelines.

   a. Always completely fill in the circle for the correct answer.
   b. Periodically check your numbering on the answer sheet, particularly if you skip an item. Make sure that the number you are marking corresponds to the number of the test question.
   c. Never make notes or stray marks on the answer sheet. These could be misread as wrong answers by the scoring machine. Instead, write on the test booklet itself or on scratch paper, as indicated in the directions.

5. **Be aware of distractors.** Distractors are answer choices that may seem correct at first glance but are actually wrong. For example:

   _____   HOT : COLD   (A) cool : frozen   (B) good : bad   (C) first : second
           (D) warm : lukewarm

   Two choices, *A, cool : frozen* and *D, warm : lukewarm*, are distractors. Both relate to temperature, as does *hot : cold*. You may be tempted to choose one of these as the correct answer. However, neither of these choices presents the same relationship as *hot : cold*. The correct answer, *B, good : bad*, shows the relationship of opposites shown by *hot : cold*.

6. **Do not make random guesses.** Guessing is unlikely to improve your score. In fact, on some standardized tests, points are deducted for incorrect answers. On such a test, you should guess only if you are almost certain of the answer. If no points are deducted for a wrong answer, however, it is to your benefit to guess if you can eliminate one or more of the choices.

UNIT 9

Target Words and Their Meanings

1. affluent (af′ loo wənt, sometimes af loo′-) adj.
2. array (ə rā′) n., v.
3. azure (azh′ ər) adj.
4. bazaar (bə zär′) n.
5. comparable (käm′ pər ə b'l) adj.
6. convey (kən vā′) v.
7. cubicle (kyoo bi k'l) n.
8. elusive (i loo siv) adj.
9. essence (es′ 'ns) n.
10. existence (ig zist′ əns) n.
11. flare (fler) n., v.
12. incense (in′ sens) n.
13. incrustation (in′ krus tā′ shən, in krus′-) n.
14. intensity (in ten′ sə tē) n.
15. intermingle (in′ tər min′ g'l) v.
16. iridescent (ir′ ə des′ n't) adj.
17. seep (sēp) v.
18. spacious (spā′ shəs) adj.
19. subtle (sut′ 'l) adj.
20. symbolic (sim bäl′ ik) adj.

Inferring Meaning from Context

For each sentence write the letter of the word or phrase that is closest to the meaning of the italicized word or words. Use context clues to help you.

B 1. Scott comes from *an affluent* family, one of the wealthiest in the country.
   a. a happy b. a rich c. a large d. a treacherous

B 2. The museum's new exhibit featured a fascinating *array* of ancient Egyptian jewelry.
   a. book b. display c. history d. image

C 3. The gem in Juanita's ring was *azure* in color, like the sky on a clear day.
   a. gray b. dark c. blue d. yellow

A 4. Our neighbors purchased beautiful Turkish rugs at one of the many colorful stalls in a *bazaar* near Istanbul.
   a. market b. home c. embassy d. church

D 5. Although North Carolina and South Carolina are two different states, they are *comparable*, having many features in common.
   a. beautiful b. difficult to compare c. magnificent d. similar

C 6. Large ferryboats *convey* passengers, cars, trucks, and even buses across the beautiful waters between Seattle and Victoria.
   a. overtake b. assemble c. carry d. circulate

C 7. Behind the mirror was a *cubicle*, which held the family documents.
   a. mechanism b. corridor c. small compartment d. reflection

97

A 8. The boys tried to catch the Siamese cat, but the animal proved *elusive* as she darted under furniture and behind curtains.
   a. hard to catch   b. un-catlike   c. affectionate   d. picturesque

D 9. The *essence* of a happy marriage is love.
   a. opposite   b. psychology   c. beginning   d. most important quality

D 10. Automobiles have been *in existence* for over a century; in 1885, Karl Benz used the first internal-combustion engine in a vehicle.
   a. voluminous   b. treacherous   c. extinct   d. present

B 11. The dying campfire *flared up* again, and another log caught fire.
   a. matured   b. blazed   c. went out   d. dissolved

A 12. A beautiful-smelling *incense* pervaded the temple.
   a. substance with a pleasant odor   b. noxious gas   c. glamor
   d. mystery

B 13. The *incrustation* of shellfish and algae on the ship's hull told the divers that it had been on the ocean floor for about two hundred years.
   a. deficiency   b. covering   c. color   d. aperture

B 14. In her training, track athlete Jackie Joyner can be easygoing, but in competition, she shows *an intensity* of concentration.
   a. a lack of   b. an extreme degree   c. a moderation
   d. an avoidance

D 15. In a petting zoo, children are free to wander about and *intermingle* with goats, calves, deer, and ducks.
   a. reside   b. get lost   c. eat lunch   d. mix together

A 16. The fortuneteller stared into her magic ball, which was *iridescent*, a rainbow of colors glowing mysteriously.
   a. showing shifting changes in color   b. hazardous   c. clear, colorless
   d. psychological

B 17. One concern about storing hazardous chemicals in the ground is that they might *seep from* the containers and enter the soil or water supply.
   a. be retrieved from   b. leak from   c. remain in   d. gush from

C 18. With its hundreds of rooms, the *spacious* palace at Versailles was one of the most magnificent sights on our trip to France.
   a. sufficient   b. ominous   c. large   d. crowded

C 19. Wishing to leave the party but not wishing to offend the hostess, Jason gave Julie *a subtle* nod that only she would notice.
   a. a blunt   b. a spectacular   c. an undetected   d. a meaningless

A 20. The dove on the flag *is symbolic of* that nation's peaceful history.
   a. stands for   b. derides   c. illuminates   d. negates

Number correct _____ (total 20)

You should now have a general idea of the meaning of each target word. Refine your understanding by examining the shades of meaning the words have in the following excerpt.

The Labyrinthine City of Fez

Anaïs Nin

Fez is a city in the North African country of Morocco. The many connecting passageways in this city make it labyrinthine, or mazelike. The busy marketplace of Fez is a feast for the senses. As you read this excerpt, note all the sensory details this observant writer uses to create a vivid picture.

Colors **seep** into your consciousness as never before: a sky-blue jellaba[1] with a black face-veil, a pearl-grey jellaba with a yellow veil, a black jellaba with a red veil, a shocking-pink jellaba with a purple veil. The clothes conceal the wearers' figures so that they remain **elusive**, with all the **intensity** and expression concentrated in the eyes. The eyes speak for the body, the self, for the age, **conveying** innumerable messages from their deep and rich **existence**.

After color and the graceful sway of robes, the **flares**, the stance, the swing of loose clothes, come the odors. One stand is devoted to sandalwood from Indonesia and the Philippines. It lies in huge round baskets and is sold by weight, for it is a precious luxury wood for burning as **incense**. The walls of the **cubicle** are lined with small bottles containing the **essence** of flowers—jasmine, rose, honeysuckle, and the rose water that is used to perfume guests. In the same baskets lie the henna leaves that the women distill and use on their hair and hands and feet. For the **affluent**, the henna comes in liquid form. And there is, too, the famous kohl, the dust from antimony[2] that gives the women such a soft, **iridescent**, smoky radiance around their eyes.

The smell of fruit, the smell of perfumes, and the smell of leather **intermingle** with the smell of wet wool hanging outside of the shops to dry—gold bedspreads hanging like flags in the breeze, sheep's-wool rugs, the favored

5

10

15

---

[1] jellaba: a long, loose outer garment
[2] antimony: a silver-white crystalline element

cherry-red wool blankets, and rose carpets, like fields of daisies, lilies, apple   20
blossoms. Blue is the **symbolic** color of Fez, a sky blue, a transparent blue, the
only blue that evokes the word long-forgotten and loved by the poets: **azure**.
Fez is azure. You rediscover the word *azure.*

The smell of cedar grows stronger. We are now in the carpenters' quarter. It
is **spacious**, high enough for the beams of wood, brought by the donkeys, to be   25
turned into tables, chairs, trunks. The smell is delicious, **comparable** only to
that of fresh-baked bread. The wood is blond, and the carpenters, work with
care and skill. The art of working mother-of-pearl **incrustations** is rare. Two
members of the distinguished family that alone knows the art are teaching it to
children. I watch them work in the aisle of the museum, with pieces as tiny as   30
one-eighth of an inch, shaping and fitting them to a sculptured rosewood box. It
is not an art found in tourist **bazaars**. To watch hands at such delicate work is to
understand the whole of the Moroccan character—patience, timelessness,
care, devotion.

And now we are in the street of spices. They look beautiful in their baskets,   35
like an **array** of painter's powders. There is the gold-red saffron, the silver
herbs, the scarlet-red peppers, the sepia[3] cinnamon, the ochre[4] ginger, and the
yellow curry. The smells surround you, enwrap you, drug you. You are tempted
to dip your whole hand in the powdery colors. Later these herbs and spices will
appear **subtly** in the local cooking.   40

---

[3] sepia: a dark reddish-brown color
[4] ochre: a dark yellow color

Refining Your Understanding

For each of the following questions, consider how the target word is used in the
passage. Write the letter of the word or phrase that best completes the sentence.

B   1. The people seem *elusive* (line 4) because of   a. the variety of colors
b. the clothes they wear   c. their eyes.

A   2. ". . . bottles containing the *essence* of flowers . . . " (lines 11-12). Used
in this way, *essence* refers to the   a. fragrance   b. color   c. leaves.

B   3. "For the *affluent,* the henna comes in liquid form (line 14)." From this
statement you should infer that   a. henna is used only by the lower
classes   b. henna in liquid form is expensive   c. the affluent people can
be tricked easily.

A   4. The various smells *intermingle* (line 17), meaning they   a. mix
b. explode   c. smell bad.

B   5. The fact that the various herbs and spices "will appear *subtly* in the local
cooking" (lines 39-40) means that   a. your mouth might burn from
these herbs and spices   b. you would notice these herbs and spices only
slightly   c. these herbs and spices have no taste at all.

Number correct _____ (total 5)

7/24

Part C   Ways to Make New Words Your Own

This section presents reinforcement activities that will help you make the target words part of your permanent vocabulary.

Using Language and Thinking Skills

Finding the Unrelated Word Write the letter of the word or phrase that is not related in meaning to the other words or phrases in the set.

D 1. a. wealthy b. affluent c. prosperous d. poor

B 2. a. open b. subtle c. direct d. obvious

D 3. a. seep b. ooze c. flood d. trickle

D 4. a. reality b. existence c. actuality d. nothingness

B 5. a. rainbow-like b. white c. iridescent d. many-colored

A 6. a. musical b. representative c. expressive d. symbolic

B 7. a. elusive b. eloquent c. evasive d. hard-to-catch

C 8. a. bazaar b. trade center c. excitement d. marketplace

A 9. a. wither b. flame c. flare d. glow

D 10. a. convey b. transport c. conduct d. confide

Number correct _____ (total 10)

Practicing for Standardized Tests

Synonyms Write the letter of the word that is closest in meaning to the target word.

A 1. AFFLUENT: (A) wealthy (B) poor (C) lawless (D) moderate (E) coarse

D 2. COMPARABLE: (A) critical (B) mature (C) unequaled (D) similar
(E) pervasive

E 3. CONVEY: (A) suffice (B) deplete (C) expose (D) recline (E) transport

B 4. CUBICLE: (A) door (B) small compartment (C) circle (D) expanse
(E) spectacle

C 5. ELUSIVE: (A) involved (B) responsive (C) baffling (D) wet (E) suitable

D 6. ESSENCE: (A) noxious gas (B) taciturnity (C) odorless gas
(D) fragrance (E) mechanism

A 7. IRIDESCENT: (A) colorful (B) cumbersome (C) hearty (D) tragic
(E) potent

B 8. SEEP: (A) urge (B) ooze (C) decline (D) incline (E) see into

7/24

E 9. SPACIOUS: (A) crowded   (B) empty   (C) majestic   (D) complex
(E) roomy

D 10. SUBTLE: (A) obvious   (B) sturdy   (C) typical   (D) understated
(E) adaptive

Number correct _____ (total 10)

Analogies Write the letter of the pair of words that best expresses a relationship similar to that of the original pair.

E 1. IRIDESCENT : COLORLESS ::   (A) wintry : cold   (B) bright : shiny
(C) noxious : poisonous   (D) noisy : smelly   (E) smooth : jagged

C 2. INTERMINGLE : MIX ::   (A) coincide : diverse   (B) advertise: buy
(C) worsen : decline   (D) develop : stunt   (E) adapt : adopt

C 3. BAZAAR : SHOPPING ::   (A) song : singing   (B) salesperson : selling
(C) restaurant : eating   (D) horse : riding   (E) education : reading

B 4. AZURE : BLUE ::   (A) stress : involvement   (B) melodrama : play
(C) technology: mechanism   (D) heraldry : herald   (E) destiny : mystery

B 5. SPACIOUS : CRAMPED ::   (A) hearty : warm   (B) mature : childish
(C) funny : comical   (D) romantic : glamorous   (E) exhausted : depleted

D 6. ARRAY : ARRANGEMENT ::   (A) steppe : mountain   (B) urgency :
moderation   (C) phenomenon : experiment   (D) image : picture
(E) glamor : plainness

D 7. SPY : ELUSIVE ::   (A) gymnast : agile   (B) farmer : agricultural
(C) navigator : lost   (D) detective : mysterious   (E) moon: lunar

B 8. EXISTENCE : EXIST ::   (A) transportation : travel   (B) domination :
dominate   (C) painting : create   (D) recreation : swim   (E) mob : riot

B 9. PERFUME : ESSENCE ::   (A) input : exhaust   (B) corridor : hallway
(C) fire : explosion   (D) song : opera   (E) psychology : psychiatry

B 10. INTENSITY : RELAXATION ::   (A) curiosity : fascination   (B) enclosure :
expanse   (C) hazard : stress   (D) table : chair   (E) snake : poison

Number correct _____ (total 10)

Word's Worth: *bazaar and bizarre*

Bazaar is sometimes confused with the word *bizarre*, but their meanings and origins are very different. The first term comes from the Persian word *bazar*, meaning "market." The second comes from the language of the Basque, a group of people living in Northern Spain. In Basque, *bizar* meant "beard." The word became associated with Spanish soldiers, who were bearded—and who also were considered bold and spirited. Over the centuries the meaning of *bizarre* evolved from "bold" to "strange."

7/24

Spelling and Wordplay

Crossword Puzzle Read the clues and print the correct answer to each in the proper squares. There are fifteen target words in this puzzle.

Across

1. Life
5. Abbr. advertisement
7. Alike
12. Headgear
14. Prefix meaning "two"
15. Shopping place
16. Abbr. United States
18. Conj. supposing that
19. High cards
21. To make an error
22. Understated
25. Told an untruth
26. Abbr. morning
27. To encourage
29. Abbr. For Your Information
30. Sky-blue
32. Frozen water
33. Pleasant burning odor
36. To embrace
37. Inside of
38. Prep. meaning "from"
40. At present
41. To blaze up
43. Modern
45. Roman numeral four
46. To view
47. __ __ and behold!
48. To ooze
49. To carry out an act
51. Abbr. tuberculosis
52. Representative

Down

1. Elaborate coatings
2. Tree's juice
3. Hearing organ
4. Small compartment
5. Abbr. atomic
6. To mix together
8. Myself
9. Wealthy
10. Abbr. American Boxing Association
11. Perfume
12. Garden tool
13. Display
17. Abbr. Syracuse University
18. That thing
20. Abbr. East Indies
23. Abbr. British Thermal Unit
24. Noun suffix
28. __ __ __ Whiz!
31. Circle
32. Third person singular of "to be"
34. To carry
35. Information
36. To restore to health
39. We walk on them
41. To touch
42. Fishing tool
44. Spider's net
50. Not off

Part D   *Related Words*

The words below are closely related to the target words you have studied. Use your knowledge of the target words and of word parts to determine the meaning of the related words. (For information about word parts analysis, see pages 6-12.) Learning these related words expands your vocabulary and helps you learn the target words more thoroughly.

1. affluence (af′ lōō wəns, sometimes
    af lōō′-) n.
2. compare (kəm per′) v.
3. conveyance (kən vā′ əns) n.
4. cube (kyōōb) n., v.
5. elude (i lōōd′) v.
6. exist (ig zist′) v.
7. incrust (in krust′) v.
8. intense (in tens′) adj.
9. intensify (in ten′ sə fī′) v.
10. iridescence (ir′ ə des′ ′ns) n.
11. seepage (sēp′ ij) n.
12. spaciousness (spā′ shəs nis) n.
13. subtlety (sut′ il tē) n.
14. symbol (sim′ b'l) n.
15. symbolize (sim′ b'l īz′) v.

Understanding Related Words

Finding Examples Write the letter of the situation that best demonstrates the meaning of each word.

A   1. **conveyance**
    a. a truck making a delivery
    b. a tree bending in the wind
    c. a comfortable chair

C   2. **elude**
    a. to take medicine
    b. to plan a vacation
    c. to avoid the tacklers in a football game

B   3. **subtlety**
    a. a bright red dress
    b. small difference between two meanings of a word
    c. a shout to a policeman for help

B   4. **intensify**
    a. to take a nap
    b. to practice harder to better an athletic record
    c. to make peace with an enemy

A   5. **symbol**
    a. the basketball team's mascot
    b. a history book
    c. an odor in the kitchen

Number correct _____ (total 5)

7/24

> Turn to **The Prefix ad-** on pages 189–190 of the **Spelling Handbook.**
> Read the rule and complete the exercises provided.

Sound-alikes The words *flare* and *flair* are homonyms, words that sound alike but have a different meaning and spelling. Study the definitions below and then complete the sentences by writing the correct word in the blank.

> **flair** (fler) n.
> a. a natural talent
> b. a sense of style
>
> **flare** (fler) v., n.
> a. to blaze up
> b. to burst out in anger
> c. to spread out like the bell of a trumpet
> d. a signal light (n.)

1. Lori has a _flair_ for the latest fashion.

2. We set a _flare_ by our stranded truck.

3. Don't put charcoal lighter on warm coals or a dangerous blaze can _flare_ up.

4. Allan has a _flair_ for athletics.

5. Sally's temper seems to _flare_ up at inopportune times.

Number correct _____ (total 5)

Analyzing Word Parts

The Latin Root ten *Intense* and *intensify* both come from the Latin word *tendere*, meaning "to stretch." When you stretch beyond your usual efforts, you become *intense*. When your nerves are stretched, you feel *tension*. Other words with this root are *extensive*, *attentive*, and *tendon*. Using sentence clues and your knowledge of the root *ten*, complete the following sentences with words from this list.

attentive   intense   tendon   extensive   intensify

1. While running, Lorraine strained a (an) _tendon_ in her knee.

2. The lamp has a switch that allows you to _intensify_ the light beam.

3. Because of the _intense_ heat, the football practice was shortened.

4. Dr. Stein has done _extensive_ research in the field of microbiology.

5. Having had only two hours of sleep, Elaine found it difficult to stay _attentive_ in class the next day.

Number correct _____ (total 5)

Number correct in unit _____ (total 70)

7/24

The Last Word

Writing

Choose one item from each of the three columns below. Then write a story based on these three items. Use your imagination.

Characters	Incidents	Conditions
• an *intense* runner	• *existing* as an animal; not human	• in a *cubicle*
• an *affluent* teacher	• *flaring* his nostrils	• in a *spacious* mansion
• a *bizarre* speaker	• *eluding* the principal	• the *essence* of a skunk
• a *subtle* salesperson	• *intermingling* with strangers	• *incrusted* with jewels
• an *iridescent* dresser	• *conveying* an idea	• evidence of *seepage*

Speaking

To compare means to find similarities and differences in things: "He compared California oranges with Florida oranges." Choose two items for comparison and prepare a speech that discusses their similarities and differences. Suggested items are listed below.

- an amateur and a professional
- a person's life and a story about a character
- wisdom and knowledge
- movie acting and TV acting

Group Discussion

What are some of the *symbols* of patriotism? How do people react to these symbols? Are they being used for positive or negative purposes? What are the differences between real patriotism and the symbols of patriotism? In groups, discuss these questions. For each question, answer with specific examples; make a list of these answers to share with the full class.

U N I T 10

Part A Target Words and Their Meanings

1. careen (kə rēn′) v.
2. catapult (kat′ ə pult′, -poolt′) v., n.
3. comprehension (käm′ prə hen′ shən) n.
4. curdle (kur′ d'l) v.
5. disfigure (dis fig′ yər) v.
6. exultant (ig zult′ 'nt) adj.
7. flank (flank) n., v.
8. grace (grās) n., v.
9. hurtle (hurt′ 'l) v.
10. level (lev′ 'l) v., adj., n.
11. mottled (mät′ 'ld) adj.
12. pent-up (pent′-up′) adj.
13. plume (ploom) n.
14. pulverize (pul′ və rīz′) v.
15. pyrotechnic (pī′ rə tek′ nik) adj.
16. reel (rēl) v., n.
17. stratosphere (strat′ ə sfir′) n.
18. strewn (stroon) v.
19. summit (sum′ it) n., adj.
20. vista (vis′ tə) n.

Inferring Meaning from Context

For each sentence, write the letter of the word or phrase that is closest to the meaning of the italicized word.

_____ 1. Caught in a fierce storm, the ship *careened* from side to side.
   a. signaled   b. tilted   c. sailed   d. aligned

_____ 2. Stan the Human Cannonball was *catapulted* from a cannon through the air and into a huge net.
   a. pulled   b. shot   c. retrieved   d. exhausted

_____ 3. Previewing the assignment and asking some questions before reading the textbook increases one's *comprehension*.
   a. moderation   b. appraisal   c. understanding   d. intensity

_____ 4. Milk will *curdle* if you mix it with vinegar.
   a. deplete   b. thicken   c. turn white   d. accumulate

_____ 5. Vandals *disfigured* the statue, breaking off its left arm.
   a. marred   b. glamorized   c. assembled   d. thrust

_____ 6. When World War II ended in 1945, *exultant* people danced in the streets.
   a. defeated   b. talented   c. elusive   d. joyful

_____ 7. One colt had a star-shaped white patch on his right *flank*.
   a. underbelly   b. side   c. tail   d. face

_____ 8. Praising the ballerina's performance, critics said that "Swan Lake" had never been performed with such *grace* before.
a. moderation   b. odd style   c. derision   d. beauty of movement

_____ 9. It is the high velocity with which a meteorite *hurtles* through space that makes the bright streaks you may see on a clear, starry night.
a. seeps   b. speeds   c. drifts   d. circulates

_____ 10. Construction workers *leveled* the old building, creating a parking lot where there was once a beautiful hotel.
a. built   b. depleted   c. identified   d. flattened

_____ 11. Sara developed a rash that gave her face a *mottled* appearance.
a. coarse   b. marked with blotches   c. surprised   d. azure

_____ 12. After being in the house all day, the dog enjoyed running in the park and releasing its *pent-up* energy.
a. held in   b. wonderful   c. free   d. physical

_____ 13. We need three hats with ostrich *plumes* for the actors who play the Three Musketeers.
a. veils   b. flowers   c. feathers   d. symbols

_____ 14. Chunks of salt need to be *pulverized* before use in a saltshaker.
a. picked   b. boxed   c. crushed   d. shaken

_____ 15. On the Fourth of July, an entire skyrocket program went off in two thunderous minutes—apparently because of a *pyrotechnic* error.
a. military   b. shrewd   c. fire-fighting   d. fireworks-related

_____ 16. Suffering from a high fever, Steve climbed out of bed, *reeled* unsteadily across the room, and sank into a chair beside the phone.
a. staggered   b. hopped   c. walked as if on a tightrope   d. strolled

_____ 17. Aircraft flying above 35,000 feet are in the *stratosphere*, which extends from about six to fifteen miles above the earth.
a. azure   b. upper part of the earth's atmosphere
c. circumference   d. interior

_____ 18. After the hurricane debris was *strewn* across the village.
a. moved   b. scattered   c. assembled   d. missing

_____ 19. Some say that the first place in the United States to receive the sun's rays each morning is the *summit* of Mt. Katahdin, in Maine.
a. enactment   b. mystery   c. lowest point   d. highest point

_____ 20. The picturesque *vista* in front of the ranch included a prairie expanse in the foreground and a quaint old ghost town in the distance.
a. view   b. automobile   c. community   d. version

Number correct _____ (total 20)

Part B   Target Words in Reading and Literature

You should now have a general idea of the meaning of each target word. Refine your understanding by examining the shades of meaning the words have in the following excerpt.

Volcano

News staffs of The Daily News *and* The Journal-American

The time was 8:32 A.M., Sunday, May 18, 1980. The place—Mount St. Helens, 100 miles south of Seattle, Washington. Geologist David Johnston, as well as campers Bruce Nelson and his friends, looked forward to a beautiful day in the mountain forests. But an unnatural stillness pervaded the region. The greatest volcanic explosion of the twentieth century was about to happen.

Suddenly, the northern face of the mountain, swollen and **disfigured** for nearly two months by pressure from magma and gases below, began to collapse. Jarred loose by the earthquakes, it slipped down the mountain's **flanks**.

At almost the same instant, a **plume** of steam shot from the **summit**. Within   5
seconds, the cloud turned black, a horrifying, deathly, **mottled** black, and roared into the sky.

The rock and ice cap that had been holding back pressure from the **pent-up** gases and magma in the core of the mountain was open. The fury was free. It was as if someone had shaken a bottle of champagne, tipped it on its side, and   10
popped the cork.

Hot gas and ash and huge chunks of rock and ice **catapulted** from the weakened north face of the volcano. Shooting out of the side of the mountain, [the explosion] was completely unexpected, something that had happened only once in the recorded history of volcanoes.   15

The blast was almost beyond **comprehension**, 500 times greater than the 20-kiloton atomic bomb that fell on Hiroshima, and it washed over the foothills and valleys beneath the mountain in the shape of a fan. In moments, it covered 150 square miles, **leveling** all that stood in its way.

Millions of 200-year-old fir trees that had **graced** St. Helens' northern **vista**   20
were flattened, **strewn** like matchsticks, their bark scarred, branches stripped, entire forests lying like so many strands of an enormous windswept hairdo. Howling at nearly 200 miles an hour, the explosion tore some of the old giants out by their roots, throwing them up and over nearby ridges 1,500 feet high.

The top of the mountain went too, throwing 1,300 feet of the once-graceful 25
and snow-covered cone, now **pulverized**, into the **stratosphere**. The growling
black plume, laced with pink and purple sheets of lightning, shot 63,000 feet into
the air in a **pyrotechnic** display that was to last all day.

Many of the people watching as the mountain exploded never knew what hit
them. The mountain would never let some of them be found. 30

Moments after his **exultant** cry that Mount St. Helens was erupting, David
Johnston vanished in a storm of hurricane winds and hot ash.

A geologist friend who landed there several days later told Johnston's parents
the ridge, five miles north of the peak, had been wiped clean.

"The trees are gone," he said. "David's trailer, the jeep, everything was 35
blown away." Johnston had been in the direct line of the blast.

[At the time of the eruption, thirteen miles northwest of the peak, camper]
Bruce Nelson saw the yellow and black cloud **hurtling** toward him.

He grabbed his girlfriend and they stood in each other's arms while trees
crashed around them and ash nearly buried them. They were finally able to 40
crawl to safety, but two of their friends died just a few feet away, their tent
crushed in the wreckage.

On the fringes of the blast, some people had time, but little more than a few
precious seconds to run for their cars as the cloud came at them.

Some of them survived. **Careening** madly down logging roads at 80 miles an 45
hour, they drove, pursued by the spitting, **curdling** cloud of death. But many of
them didn't make it. One man, standing atop his car, was taking pictures when
the cloud enveloped him. Others, speeding from the scene, were simply
overtaken at the wheel.

Mount St. Helens was **reeling**. 50

Refining Your Understanding

For each of the following questions, consider how the target word is used in the
passage. Write the letter of the word or phrase that best completes the sentence.

_____ 1. One could see that the mountain was *disfigured* (line 1), because it
a. had changed shape   b. was leveled   c. was torn open.

_____ 2. The word *plume* (line 5) suggests that the jet of steam was   a. barely
noticeable   b. feather-shaped   c. cloud-shaped.

_____ 3. Gas, ash, rock, and ice *catapulted* (line 12) from the mountain, meaning
these materials   a. were flung   b. were pent-up   c. seeped downward.

_____ 4. Fir trees *graced* (line 20) the slopes of Mount St. Helens; in other words,
the trees   a. made the region more susceptible to fire   b. made the
scene religious   c. made the slopes beautiful.

_____ 5. By referring to lightning as a *pyrotechnic* display (line 28) the writers
imply it was   a. hot   b. dangerous   c. visually spectacular.

Number correct _____ (total 5)

Part C Ways to Make New Words Your Own

By now you are familiar with the target words and their meanings. This section presents a variety of reinforcement activities that will help you make the words a part of your permanent vocabulary.

Using Language and Thinking Skills

Finding Examples Write the letter of the situation or subject that best demonstrates the meaning of each word.

_____ 1. **summit**
   a. Pike's Peak
   b. Death Valley
   c. Waikiki Beach

_____ 2. **pyrotechnic**
   a. a tidal wave
   b. a hurricane
   c. a skyrocket

_____ 3. **grace**
   a. a person slips on a banana peel
   b. a skater glides across a frozen pond
   c. a fire roars through a building

_____ 4. **reel**
   a. a boxer staggers back and forth after being punched
   b. the front of a house
   c. anything that can be proved true

_____ 5. **comprehension**
   a. a classmate misinterprets an assignment
   b. someone understands what another person is saying in Spanish
   c. a student attends a dance at your school

_____ 6. **pulverize**
   a. a steamroller rolls over a rock, crushing it totally
   b. an ape swings in a tree
   c. a basketball team wins a game by one point

_____ 7. **exultant**
   a. the winner of a million-dollar lottery
   b. the smallest building in town
   c. the losers in the first round of a tournament

_____ 8. **careen**
   a. the guard changes in front of a palace
   b. a car slides from side to side on a wet road
   c. a train moves slowly down a track

_____ 9. **vista**

    a. the view from the top of the Empire State Building

    b. a large television screen

    c. a doll's house

_____ 10. **plume**

    a. a pancake with syrup

    b. a glassy lake

    c. a peacock's feather

Number correct _____ (total 10)

Practicing for Standardized Tests

Sentence Completion Write the letter of the word that best completes the meaning of the sentence.

_____ 1. The windstorm left branches and fallen leaves ? over yards and streets.

    (A) hurtled (B) careening (C) mottled (D) strewn

_____ 2. The vaulter's pole acts as a ? to launch the vaulter over the bar.

    (A) plume (B) flank (C) summit (D) catapult

_____ 3. Dan suspected he was not following the recipe correctly when the milk started to ?.

    (A) level (B) catapult (C) curdle (D) disfigure

_____ 4. Shortly after takeoff, the space vehicle was soon shooting up through the ?, en route to the planet Mars.

    (A) stratosphere (B) plume (C) vista (D) summit

_____ 5. In 1925, the worst tornado in history ? buildings and even entire communities as it roared through Missouri, Illinois, and Indiana.

    (A) leveled (B) flanked (C) graced (D) hurtled

_____ 6. Many people were ashamed of the graffiti that ? the school walls.

    (A) graced (B) pulverized (C) leveled (D) disfigured

_____ 7. Meteors make bright streaks in the night sky as they ? through space.

    (A) hurtle (B) wobble (C) pulverize (D) curdle

_____ 8. The army jeep was ? with various shades of green and brown to blend in with the surroundings.

    (A) strewn (B) pent-up (C) graced (D) mottled

_____ 9. Psychologists tell us that we should express our feelings rather than keep them ? inside of us.

    (A) exultant (B) pent-up (C) level (D) mottled

_____ 10. Despite a wound in its left ?, the deer leaped to safety.

    (A) plume (B) summit (C) flank (D) vista

Number correct _____ (total 10)

Spelling and Wordplay

Antonym Fill-ins Use the antonyms on the left to determine the letters of the target words that will fit into the blanks to the right.

1. beautify: __ __ __ __ __ __ __ __

2. raise: __ __ __ __ __

3. released: __ __ __ __ __ - __ __

4. bottom: __ __ __ __ __ __

5. gathered: __ __ __ __ __ __

6. move straight: __ __ __ __ __

7. go slowly: __ __ __ __ __ __

8. clumsiness: __ __ __ __ __ __

9. sad: __ __ __ __ __ __ __ __

10. misunderstanding: __ __ __ __ __ __ __ __ __ __ __ __ __ __ __

Number correct _____ (total 10)

Part D   Related Words

Use your knowledge of the target words to determine the meaning of the related words.

1. comprehend (käm′ prə hend′) v.
2. comprehensible (käm′ prə hen′ sə b'l) adj.
3. comprehensive (käm′ prə hen′ siv) adj.
4. configuration (kən fig′ yə rā′ shən) n.
5. curd (kʉrd) n.
6. disgrace (dis grās′) n., v.
7. exult (ig zult′) v.
8. exultation (eg zəl tā′ shən) n.
9. graceful (grās′ f'l) adj.
10. graceless (grās′ lis) adj.
11. gracious (grā′ shəs) adj.
12. plumage (ploo′ mij) n.

Understanding Related Words

Sentence Completion Write the related word that best completes each of the sentences. Do not use a related word more than once.

_____ 1. The dairy worker poured the _?_ (s) of soured milk into a large vat to begin the cheese-making process.

_____ 2. After being caught repeatedly misusing the public's funds, the governor finally resigned in _?_ .

_____ 3. Our dog Lulu is the most _?_ animal I've ever seen. She constantly runs into doors and knocks things over.

113

_____ 4. During the half-time show, the band members formed a spectacular _?_ that looked like an eagle in flight.

_____ 5. We _?_(ed) in the news that our band would march in the Rose Bowl Parade.

_____ 6. The _?_ of the peacock is perhaps the most beautiful of that of all birds.

_____ 7. In the early days of radio, speakers often were barely _?_ because of the static.

_____ 8. When performed by a group of _?_ ballet dancers, Tchaikovsky's *Sleeping Beauty* is an unforgettable experience.

_____ 9. If you want to _?_ your science lesson well, skim the chapter before you read it, note the main headings, and then read the chapter carefully.

_____ 10. The _?_ hosts welcomed me warmly, gave me a wonderful meal, and encouraged me to stay as long as I wanted.

Number correct _____ (total 10)

Turn to **The Letter c** and **The Letter g** on pages 205-206 of the **Spelling Handbook**. Read the rules and complete the exercises provided.

Analyzing Word Parts

The Suffix *-ation* The suffix *-ation* forms nouns and means "the act or result of." Accordingly, *exultation* means "the act of exulting." Change each of the following words by adding *-ation*. Write the newly formed word and then write the meaning of the new word, using your dictionary to check your work.

1. expect: _____

2. alter: _____

3. compute: _____

4. imagine: _____

5. visit: _____

Number correct _____ (total 5)

Number correct in unit _____ (total 70)

The Last Word

Writing

The following passage contains a number of colorless words and expressions, some in italics. Replace these italicized words and phrases with one of the following target words: *flank, grace, hurtle, plume, strewn, summit, vista.*

Pyrotechnic Extravaganza

It was a warm July evening, with the rosy glow of the sunset slowly turning to night blue. Hundreds of townspeople had gathered on the western *side* of Sutter's Hill near the river. From there they waited expectantly and admired the *view* before them. The fireworks show was about to begin.

Darkness had just set in when the watchers heard a loud "thunk!" A sparkling flare began to *go* skyward. The spark hovered just beneath the blue, then blasted open with a flash and an earth-pounding roar, launching showers of gold sparkles in several directions simultaneously. A giant gold sunflower blazed in the sky.

Another blast came from below, and a bright arc soared high over the *top* of the hill. The skyrocket exploded, shooting sparks still higher. In the sudden darkness that followed, some watchers dodged bits of cardboard, ash, and even a few live sparks that were *scattered* over the site below.

Then came the "Geyser," a ground display with hundreds of white lights rising in the shape of a *feather*. For a moment the vertical array hovered in mid-air, glowing and bubbling upward with *elegance and easy movement* before it faded out.

For over an hour people stood there in the dark; intermittently their faces would illuminate, the whole scene flashing bright as day, then fade back into the dark.

Speaking

The Mount St. Helens eruption is one of the most dramatic natural phenomena of our time. Find out more about this giant volcanic event. What caused the eruption? What effect has it had on the weather, the climate, and the quality of life in the Northwest? Or you might prefer to read about other famous volcanic eruptions. To find information, make use of books, encyclopedias, and periodicals. Then, individually or in groups, report your findings to the class.

UNIT 11

Part A   Target Words and Their Meanings

1. alternative (ôl tur′ nə tiv, al-) n., adj.
2. barter (bär′ tər) v., n.
3. commerce (käm′ ərs) n.
4. confine (kən fīn′) v. (kän′ fīn) n.
5. evolve (i välv′) v.
6. expand (ik spand′) v.
7. expire (ik spīr′) v.
8. exploit (ik sploit′) v. (eks′ ploit) n.
9. formal (fôr′ məl) adj., n.
10. inheritable (in her′ it ə b'l) adj.
11. integral (in′ tə grəl) adj.
12. mobility (mō bil′ ə tē) n.
13. precede (pri sēd′) v.
14. restriction (ri strik′ shən) n.
15. servitude (sur′ və tōōd, -tyōōd′) n.
16. sordid (sôr′ did) adj.
17. status (stāt′ əs, stat′-) n.
18. statute (stach′ ōōt) n.
19. system (sis′ təm) n.
20. textile (teks′ tīl, -t'l, til) n., adj.

Inferring Meaning from Context

For each sentence write the letter of the word or phrase that is closest to the meaning of the italicized word or words. Use context clues to help you determine the correct answer. (For information about how context helps you understand vocabulary, see pages 1–5.)

_____ 1. If Rick did not drive to the city, the *alternative* was to take the train.
a. development   b. hazard   c. compulsion   d. choice

_____ 2. The fisherman stopped at the general store, where he would *barter* his fish for groceries.
a. clean   b. catch   c. trade   d. enjoy

_____ 3. There is a great deal of *commerce* taking place between Japan and America; various manufactured goods, food, and raw materials are exchanged between the two countries.
a. business   b. formality   c. distance   d. similarity

_____ 4. His health has deteriorated so much that he is now *confined to* his bed.
a. restricted to   b. out of   c. contented in   d. reading in

_____ 5. The plan *evolved* gradually over a period of three years, and now it will be put into effect.
a. developed   b. encountered   c. closed   d. dissolved

_____ 6. My father's business *expanded* tremendously—from a small grocery store twenty-five years ago to a huge chain of supermarkets today.
a. migrated   b. expired   c. grew   d. conveyed

116

_____ 7. We feared that in one year, when the contract *expired*, workers would again strike unless their demands were met.
a. was settled b. intermingled c. ended d. evolved

_____ 8. Nineteenth century labor union leaders charged some businesses with *exploiting* employees by working them hard and paying them little.
a. rewarding b. hurtling c. increasing the security of
d. taking advantage of

_____ 9. The dance was *formal*, with women in long dresses and men in tuxedos.
a. inferior b. stately c. undignified d. systematic

_____ 10. Are personality traits *inheritable*? For example, can you inherit shyness from a parent?
a. comparable b. curbed by parents c. obvious
d. acquired genetically from parents

_____ 11. We searched carefully for the missing part because it was an *integral* part of the ignition system.
a. unessential b. necessary c. hazardous d. inferior

_____ 12. Having a bicycle provides a great deal of *mobility*.
a. movability b. stability c. recognition d. restriction

_____ 13. The table of contents usually *precedes* the first chapter of a book.
a. stresses b. comes after c. includes d. comes before

_____ 14. There are *restrictions* on the maximum height of buildings in our town; no building can be higher than fifty stories.
a. theories b. estimates c. limitations d. no limitations

_____ 15. In a beehive, the drones lead lives of *servitude*, working constantly and enjoying little freedom.
a. slavery b. derision c. treachery d. exultation

_____ 16. The pile of rusted automobiles in the junkyard was a *sordid* mess.
a. filthy b. forgettable c. pretty d. potent

_____ 17. Many nineteenth-century British prisoners and debtors were allowed to help settle Australia, where they enjoyed the *status* of free citizens.
a. punishment b. position c. stress d. exertion

_____ 18. Congress enacted a *statute* to change some immigration quotas.
a. course b. development c. law d. condition

_____ 19. Fred's *system* for cleaning his garage works very well.
a. mechanism b. book c. procedure d. excellence

_____ 20. One of the chief uses of cotton is for *textile* products, especially clothing.
a. advertising b. glamorous c. little-known d. fabric

Number correct _____ (total 20)

Part B Target Words in Reading and Literature

You should now have a general idea of the meaning of each target word. Refine your understanding by examining the shades of meaning the words have in the following excerpt.

The Slave Trade

Richard B. Morris

The corrupt business of slavery began long before the first blacks arrived in colonial Virginia. In this selection, historian Richard Morris explains how the slave trade came to America.

Potentially America was a land of Eden. Labor was in demand to build homes, cultivate the earth, **exploit** the natural resources of the North Atlantic coast and the interior of the continent, sail the ships, and fish the seas. The colonists quickly discovered that the Indians, the native Americans who had settled the continent centuries before the Europeans, would not make compliant workers **confined** to settled abodes. The **alternatives** for labor power were to be found in the British Isles, on the European Continent, and along the West Coast of Africa. . . .   5

For black Africans a very special **system** of bound labor **evolved**. Slavery, it must be remembered, was not invented in the English colonies. For nearly two centuries before the settlement of Virginia, a trade in slaves had been carried on along the West African Coast. As the English empire **expanded** to the New World, the slave trade grabbed at the chance to make huge profits from this **sordid** business. Slave traffic became an **integral** part of a pattern of **commerce**, known as the triangular trade,'' that operated between New England, Africa, and the West Indies or the Southern colonies. New England rum, guns, gunpowder, utensils, **textiles**, and food were **bartered** for slaves provided by West African chiefs. The human cargo was packed aboard ships, chained together by twos, with hardly any room to stand, lie, or sit down. During voyages that sometimes lasted as long as 14 weeks, epidemics took an alarming death toll.   10   15   20

When the first blacks came to Virginia in 1619, they were treated as bound servants and were freed when their terms **expired**. In all there were probably not more than a few hundred such cases. Sometime in the 1640's, the practice

began of selling imported blacks as servants for life. In short this form of de 25 facto[1] slavery **preceded** legalized slavery. In the 1660's and 1670's, **statutes** in Virginia and Maryland gave slavery its **formal** distinguishing feature, an **inheritable status** of **servitude** for life. Soon, **restrictions** on slave **mobility**, along with a harsh system of discipline, were written into the "Black Codes."

---

[1] de facto: in fact, actual

Refining Your Understanding

For each of the following questions, consider how the target word is used in the passage. Write the letter of the word or phrase that best completes the sentence.

_____ 1. The fact that "bound labor *evolved*" (line 9) for Africans suggests that a. the system never really began   b. the system grew over a period of years   c. the system came into being quite suddenly.

_____ 2. The author states that slavery "became an *integral* part of a pattern of *commerce*" (lines 14–15), which suggests that the slave trade   a. was a shameful aspect of business   b. was a key ingredient in the economy c. disrupted the business world.

_____ 3. In the early 1600's, when their terms of slavery *expired* (line 23), bound servants became   a. slaves for life   b. soldiers   c. free people.

_____ 4. Since slavery became "an *inheritable status*" (lines 27–28), the children of slaves   a. would also be slaves   b. would be free people   c. would be given a choice.

_____ 5. "*Restrictions* on slave *mobility*" (line 28) meant that   a. slaves moved about freely   b. slaves could not move about freely   c. slaves could own vehicles.

Number correct _____ (total 5)

Part C   Ways to Make New Words Your Own

By now you are familiar with the target words and their meanings. This section presents reinforcement activities that will help you make the words part of your permanent vocabulary.

Using Language and Thinking Skills

True–False Based on your knowledge of the target word, decide whether each statement is true or false. In the blank, write **T** for True or **F** for False.

_____ 1. If your magazine subscription *expires*, you will receive twelve more issues.

_____ 2. There is a *statute* requiring people to stop at a stop sign.

_____ 3. The color of a person's eyes, as well as hair color and height, are _inheritable_ traits.

_____ 4. The amount of _commerce_ taking place depends on phases of the moon.

_____ 5. Curfews are _restrictions_.

_____ 6. The Revolutionary War, one of the major events in American history, _preceded_ the War of 1812.

_____ 7. When you trade a favorite shirt for a record album, you engage in a form of _barter_.

_____ 8. A football team tries to _exploit_ the weaknesses of its opponent.

_____ 9. Most picnics are _formal_ occasions.

_____ 10. Although important as a community service, a garbage dump is a _sordid_ place.

Number correct _____ (total 10)

Practicing for Standardized Tests

Antonyms Match each word on the left with its antonym on the right. Write the letter of the antonym in the blank at the left.

_____ 1. EVOLVE : (A) create (B) involve (C) assemble (D) deteriorate (E) develop

_____ 2. EXPAND : (A) recline (B) contract (C) broaden (D) enact (E) explain

_____ 3. EXPIRE : (A) begin (B) build (C) end (D) expel (E) perspire

_____ 4. FORMAL : (A) fancy (B) busy (C) casual (D) occasional (E) ominous

_____ 5. INTEGRAL : (A) essential (B) innate (C) subtle (D) numerical (E) unimportant

_____ 6. MOBILITY : (A) inability (B) looseness (C) status (D) recognition (E) immovability

_____ 7. PRECEDE : (A) approach (B) stop (C) tell the truth (D) come before (E) succeed

_____ 8. RESTRICTION : (A) declaration (B) limitation (C) holiday (D) freedom (E) reformation

_____ 9. SORDID : (A) foul (B) grave (C) sad (D) interesting (E) pristine

_____ 10. SYSTEM : (A) chaos (B) phenomenon (C) freedom (D) horde (E) mechanism

Number correct _____ (total 10)

Spelling and Wordplay

Crossword Puzzle Read each clue to determine what word will fit in the corresponding squares. There are several target words in the puzzle.

Across
1. Position
6. Long ___ ___ ___
9. To command
10. To conform
11. To get free from
12. To choose
13. Last course of a meal
15. Abbr. South
16. Contraction of "I would"
17. Abbr. Electrical Engineer
19. To end
25. To bring in goods
26. Large-scale buying and selling
28. Female reproductive cells
29. Noun suffix
30. Abbr. Veteran
31. Firm; stable
33. Prefix meaning twice; symbol for didymium
34. That thing
35. Capable of being inherited

Down
1. Filthy
2. Attempted
3. Increases
4. Symbol for tellurium
5. To coax
6. To love greatly
7. Breach
8. Makes a choice
10. Advertisement [Colloq.]
12. There
14. Male or female
18. To develop
20. To go before
21. Reduced to a rice-like consistency
22. Material used for filing fingernails
23. A law
24. Abbr. Governor
26. Center of an apple
27. Bricklayer
32. Atmosphere
34. Abbr. Illinois

Turn to **Words with the "Seed" Sound** on pages 204–205 of the **Spelling Handbook.** Read the rule and complete the exercises provided.

Word's Worth: textile

What do *text*, *texture* and *textile* have in common? Each has something to do with weaving. All three come from the same source—the Latin verb *texere*, meaning "to weave." A *textile*, of course, is something that is woven. In a *text*, the words could be described as "woven together." *Texture* also suggests *how* something is woven together, specifically, how a material feels.

Part D   Related Words

A number of words are closely related to the target words you have studied. Use your knowledge of the target words and of word parts to determine the meaning of the related words. (For information about word parts analysis, see pages 6-12.) Learning these related words expands your vocabulary and helps you learn the target words more thoroughly.

1. alternate (ôl′ tər nit) n., (-nāt′) v., adj.
2. commercial (kə mur′ shəl) adj., n.
3. constrict (kən strikt′) v.
4. expansion (ik span′ shən) n.
5. expansive (ik span′ siv) adj.
6. expiration (ek′ spə rā′ shən) n.
7. exploitation (eks′ ploy tā′ shun) n.
8. formality (fôr mal′ ə tē) n.
9. heritage (her′ ət ij) n.
10. immobilize (i mō′ bə līz) v.
11. inherit (in her′ it) v.
12. integrate (in′ tə grāt′) v.
13. integrity (in teg′ rə tē) n.
14. mobile (mō′ b'l) adj.
15. mobilize (mō′ bə liz′) v.
16. precedence (pres′ ə dəns, pri sēd′ 'ns) n.
17. restrict (ri strikt′) v.
18. strict (strikt) adj.
19. stricture (strik′ chər) n.
20. systematic (sis′ tə mat′ ik) adj.

Understanding Related Words

Finding Examples Write the letter of the situation or subject that best demonstrates the meaning of each word.

_____ 1. **commercial**
   a. cleaning your room
   b. your sister bakes cookies for the whole family
   c. a record company sells copies of a rock star's autograph

_____ 2. **constrict**
   a. the guest speaker loosens his tie
   b. a balloon gradually inflates
   c. muscles shrink and cramp together

_____ 3. **expansion**
   a. a store owner who decides to open a second store
   b. a singer who decides to sing two songs instead of twelve
   c. a successful dieter

_____ 4. **expiration**
   a. the explanation of a mechanical process
   b. the date a subscription ends
   c. the date a President takes office

_____ 5. **immobilize**
   a. to have a body cast
   b. to ride a bicycle
   c. to go to a dance

_____ 6. **integrate**
   a. to separate a class into smaller groups
   b. to call various groups together into one classroom
   c. to check out books from a library

_____ 7. **integrity**
   a. a coach bends the rules for the top athlete on the team
   b. someone shoplifts
   c. you do not allow someone else to take the blame for your mistakes

_____ 8. **precedence**
   a. a great-aunt always sits at the head of the table
   b. moving a paragraph to the end of a composition
   c. a randomly arranged family portrait

_____ 9. **strict**
   a. a "dieter" who eats anything and everything
   b. a coach who tells his team to be in bed by 9:00 P.M.
   c. a flexible curfew

_____ 10. **systematic**
    a. a student uses the card catalog to locate a library book
    b. a mob riots in the streets
    c. you clean your room by picking up whatever you happen to stumble over

Number correct _____ (total 10)

Analyzing Word Parts

The Latin Root *strict* The target word *restriction* comes from the Latin word *strictus*, meaning "drawn tight" or "compressed." The following related words also come from this Latin word: *constrict, restrict, restrictive, strict, stricture.* Look up these words in a dictionary and use them to complete the sentences below.

_____ 1. When my grandmother attended school, teachers required ? compliance with classroom rules.

_____ 2. Jan's collar was tight enough to ? her breathing.

_____ 3. A law was passed to ? the use of pesticides on crops.

_____ 4. The town's leaders placed a ? upon the construction of high-rise buildings.

_____ 5. The village allowed no restaurants along the lake, and this policy was criticized as being too ? .

Number correct _____ (total 5)

The Latin Root *pan* The target word *expand* derives from the Latin word *pandere*, meaning "to spread." The related words *expansion* and *expansive* belong to the same word family. Each of these three words functions as a different part of speech. Determine which word, *expand*, *expansion*, or *expansive*, best completes the following sentences. Write the word in the blank.

_____ 1. The ? gymnasium has doors that can slide back to double the space available.

_____ 2. These doors ? the gym enough to accommodate two classes.

_____ 3. The ? of the gym makes it large enough to seat two thousand spectators.

_____ 4. The ? spirits of the crowd inspire our team.

_____ 5. It is a shame that the parking lot cannot ? the way the gymnasium can.

Number correct _____ (total 5)

Number correct in unit _____ (total 65)

The Last Word

Writing

Rewrite each sentence, using one of the words from the list.

alternate	exploitation	heritage	integral	precede
evolved	expires	inheritable	mobility	system

Example:
Original: The robins flew for hundreds of miles to the south for the winter.
Revision: The robins *migrated* south for the winter.

1. The workers complained of being taken advantage of by their boss.

   _____

2. Property is something that is passed on from generation to generation.

   _____

3. Oil is something that the American economy cannot get along without.

   _____

4. A quick tire check should be done before you take your long car trip.

   _____

5. Because people move so much, neighbors often don't get to know each other.

   _____

6. The date on which Buzz's subscription runs out is December 31.

   _____

7. The clever detective used a set of procedures for gathering clues.

   _____

8. We should treasure that which our ancestors have handed down to us.

   _____

9. If one answer doesn't work, try the other one.

   _____

10. The use of computers has developed and changed to a point never imagined by the original inventors.

    _____

    _____

Group Discussion

Most people learn more, and remember more, when there is a *system* to their studying. Compare the various systems of studying used by you and your fellow students. Discuss how they might be improved.

UNIT 12: Review of Units 9–11

Part A   Review Word List

Unit 9 Target Words

1. affluent
2. array
3. azure
4. bazaar
5. comparable
6. convey
7. cubicle
8. elusive
9. essence
10. existence
11. flare
12. incense
13. incrustation
14. intensity
15. intermingle
16. iridescent
17. seep
18. spacious
19. subtle
20. symbolic

Unit 9 Related Words

1. affluence
2. compare
3. conveyance
4. cube
5. elude
6. exist
7. incrust
8. intense
9. intensify
10. iridescence
11. seepage
12. spaciousness
13. subtlety
14. symbol
15. symbolize

Unit 10 Target Words

1. careen
2. catapult
3. comprehension
4. curdle
5. disfigure
6. exultant
7. flank
8. grace
9. hurtle
10. level
11. mottled
12. pent-up
13. plume
14. pulverize
15. pyrotechnic
16. reel
17. stratosphere
18. strewn
19. summit
20. vista

Unit 10 Related Words

1. comprehend
2. comprehensible
3. comprehensive
4. configuration
5. curd
6. disgrace
7. exult
8. exultation
9. graceful
10. graceless
11. gracious
12. plumage

Unit 11 Target Words

1. alternative
2. barter
3. commerce
4. confine
5. evolve
6. expand
7. expire
8. exploit
9. formal
10. inheritable
11. integral
12. mobility
13. precede
14. restriction
15. servitude
16. sordid
17. status
18. statute
19. system
20. textile

Unit 11 Related Words

1. alternate
2. commercial
3. constrict
4. expansion
5. expansive
6. expiration
7. exploitation
8. formality
9. heritage
10. immobilize
11. inherit
12. integrate
13. integrity
14. mobile
15. mobilize
16. precedence
17. restrict
18. strict
19. stricture
20. systematic

Inferring Meaning from Context

For each sentence write the letter of the word or phrase that is closest to the meaning of the italicized word.

_____ 1. The *array* of baked goods on the countertop made my mouth water.
   a. bazaar   b. existence   c. display   d. aroma

_____ 2. Jackie spent two days shopping in a Turkish *bazaar*.
   a. cubicle   b. marketplace   c. grocery store   d. system

_____ 3. Aircraft carriers use a special device to *catapult* planes into the sky.
   a. launch   b. drop   c. navigate   d. urge

_____ 4. *Commerce* between China and the United States is expanding; these countries sell each other more goods than they did twenty years ago.
   a. mobility   b. intensity   c. business   d. friendship

_____ 5. We were unable to finish because the puzzle's answer was so *elusive*.
   a. exposed   b. brilliant   c. evasive   d. easy

_____ 6. King Arthur's sword handle was *encrusted* with emeralds and diamonds.
   a. strewn   b. decorated   c. assembled   d. spawned

_____ 7. During the fall, their casual dating *evolved* into a serious relationship.
   a. expired   b. developed   c. careened   d. receded

_____ 8. A sudden *flare* from our bonfire lit up the entire camping area.
   a. blaze   b. exultation   c. stricture   d. intensity

_____ 9. The wood cabinets had an unusual, *mottled* grain, dark in some places and almost blonde in others.
   a. shiny   b. typical   c. brilliant   d. blotched

_____ 10. Do high winds and dark clouds usually *precede* a thunderstorm?
   a. come before   b. come after   c. come during   d. avoid

_____ 11. Sue knew her car needed repairs when oil began to *seep* from the engine.
   a. flow   b. intensify   c. curdle   d. ooze

_____ 12. Maria felt that doing the dishes six nights in a row was *servitude*.
   a. slavery   b. derision   c. stress   d. enactment

_____ 13. The building was a *sordid* mess. It was infested with rats and insects.
   a. leveled   b. mottled   c. filthy   d. potential

_____ 14. Pamela's promotion to lieutenant gave her higher *status* than before.
   a. maturity   b. subtlety   c. rank   d. mobility

_____ 15. A *statute* must be approved by Congress before it becomes a regulation.
   a. marble figure   b. stricture   c. law   d. iron sculpture

Number correct _____ (total 15)

Using Review Words in Context

Using context clues, determine which word from the list fits best in each blank in the story below. Each word from the list may be used only once.

alternating   conveys   existence   formal   integral
array   evolved   expanded   heritage   symbolized

The Stars and Stripes

Have you ever thought about the values the American flag _____ ?
Understanding the flag's design and the way it has _____ over the
years sheds light on our _____ and our ideals.

After the colonies declared their independence from Britain, representatives to
the Continental Congress soon realized their young country needed a new flag.
The number of stars and stripes, of course, represented the thirteen colonies
in _____ at that time. Although the Congress made no
_____ statement about the arrangement of the stars, the most
common design during this period was an arrangement of _____
rows of stars—3, 2, 3, 2, 3. As the young country _____ and more
states came into the Union, a star was added for each new state. Consequently,
the _____ of stars has changed many times.

No records from the Continental Congress indicate why the colors red, white,
and blue were chosen. However, when the Great Seal of the United States was
designed in 1782, the same three colors were used, and this time the meanings
were given. The red stood for courage and hardiness. The white
_____ purity and innocence; and the blue represented vigilance,
perseverance, and justice. These were the values thought to be _____
to the making of a strong and prosperous country.

Number correct _____ (total 10)

Part B   Review Word Reinforcement

Using Language and Thinking Skills

Understanding Multiple Meanings Write the letter of the correct definition in
the blank to the left of the sentence the definition fits.

---

exploit
a. to make use of productively (v.)
b. to make unethical use of for one's own advantage (v.)

_____ 1. Mr. Zilch was trying to *exploit* his workers by paying them low wages.

_____ 2. The city was able to *exploit* its location on the river by building a dam.

---

incense
a. a substance that produces a pleasant odor when burned (n.)
b. any pleasant odor (n.)
c. to make very angry (v.)

_____ 3. The crowd was *incensed* by the speaker's unfair and negative statements.

_____ 4. The burning sticks of *incense* filled the room with a sweet aroma.

_____ 5. As the chest's lid was opened, the *incense* of cedar filled the air.

Number correct _____ (total 5)

Practicing for Standardized Tests

Antonyms Write the letter of the word that is most nearly opposite in meaning to the review word.

_____ 1. AFFLUENT : (A) wealthy (B) pretty (C) moderate (D) poor (E) able

_____ 2. COMPREHENSION : (A) understanding (B) servitude (C) formality (D) restriction (E) confusion

_____ 3. CUBICLE : (A) compartment (B) ballroom (C) aperture (D) interior (E) angle

_____ 4. EXPIRE : (A) live (B) ascend (C) die (D) exhaust (E) enact

_____ 5. INTEGRAL : (A) unnecessary (B) vital (C) inheritable (D) numerous (E) involved

_____ 6. LEVELED : (A) excavated (B) inclined (C) destroyed (D) rebuilt (E) surveyed

_____ 7. SORDID : (A) pure (B) potent (C) exposed (D) noxious (E) wretched

_____ 8. SPACIOUS : (A) immoderate (B) depleted (C) interior (D) vast (E) cramped

_____ 9. SUBTLE : (A) exultant (B) mysterious (C) psychological (D) elusive (E) obvious

_____ 10. SUMMIT : (A) high point (B) middle point (C) meeting place (D) mechanism (E) low point

Number correct _____ (total 10)

Synonyms Write the letter of the word nearest in meaning to the review word.

_____ 1. BARTER : (A) trade (B) import (C) persuade (D) deplete (E) respond

_____ 2. EXPLOITATION: (A) applause (B) hatred (C) concern (D) abuse (E) organization

_____ 3. CONVEY : (A) involve (B) transport (C) pulverize (D) constrict (E) incense

_____ 4. DISFIGURE : (A) condition (B) mar (C) mystify (D) err (E) adapt

_____ 5. EXULTANT : (A) expired (B) compulsive (C) persuasive (D) responsive (E) jubilant

_____ 6. PENT-UP : (A) odd (B) confined (C) romantic (D) lawful (E) weak

_____ 7. SEEP : (A) flare (B) convey (C) intermingle (D) leak (E) reel

_____ 8. STATUS : (A) statehood (B) volume (C) wish (D) legality (E) standing

_____ 9. STATUTE : (A) art (B) response (C) law (D) system (E) sculpture

_____ 10. VISTA : (A) view (B) home (C) conversation (D) version (E) porch

Number correct _____ (total 10)

Analogies Write the letter of the pair of words that best expresses a relationship similar to that of the original pair.

_____ 1. MOBILIZE : IMMOBILIZE :: (A) limit : restrict (B) dive : dove (C) expand : restrict (D) travel : drive (E) study : learn

_____ 2. EVOLVE : DEVELOP :: (A) elude : catch (B) incline : decline (C) bewilder : confuse (D) have done : will do (E) add : subtract

_____ 3. PRECEDE : FOLLOW :: (A) explode : ignite (B) seep : expand (C) charge : retreat (D) supersede : succeed (E) disfigure : mar

_____ 4. AFFLUENT : MANSION :: (A) hospitable : host (B) interior : room (C) spacious : suite (D) message : urgent (E) poor : shack

_____ 5. BARTER : ECONOMY :: (A) immigraton : emigration (B) summit : top (C) cash : dollar (D) tradegy : comedy (E) politics : government

_____ 6. GRACE : BALLERINA :: (A) privacy : cubicle (B) subtlety : spy (C) clouds : sky (D) formality : dance (E) penmanship : typist

_____ 7. EYE : VISTA :: (A) stroll : feet (B) scene : photographer (C) ship : voyage (D) ear : symphony (E) sight : view

_____ 8. INCENSE : SMELL :: (A) ice : skate (B) editor : edit (C) food : taste (D) harvest : gather (E) involvment : involve

_____ 9. SERVITUDE : SLAVERY :: (A) king : rule (B) limitation : restriction (C) author : book (D) system : chaos (E) maelstrom : water

_____ 10. JUDGE : STATUTE :: (A) rule : game (B) sculpture : art (C) hazard : road (D) volume : sound (E) doctor : illness

Number correct _____ (total 10)

130

Spelling and Wordplay

Proofreading Find the misspelled words that appear in the following news report. Write the words correctly in the blanks provided.

Risky Business

Yesterday, in one of the more afluent sections of town, something bizarre happened in the bizare. The window of one of the shops featured a display of bottles containing chemicals. When viewed in the sunlight, the chemicals produced an aray of colors.

In addition to producing the lovely colors, the sunlight had another effect. The sun's rays intramingled with the chemicals, heating them. The glass, of course, increased the intencity of the heat. As a result, the gases in some of the bottles began to expand. Finally, these pent-up gases exploded with a thunderous roar.

Glass was hertled into the air. Flames flaired up and a white plum of smoke rose from the now-leaveled display case. The floor was strune with glass and cork. The store was a sorded scene.

This morning the local Chamber of Comerce issued a news release conveing the idea that yesterday's piroteknic display had been purposely set off. The blast was supposed to act as a "catepult to launch the new SPACE BLAST SALE into commercial orbit." The owner of the shop declined to comment.

1. _____   9. _____

2. _____   10. _____

3. _____   11. _____

4. _____   12. _____

5. _____   13. _____

6. _____   14. _____

7. _____   15. _____

8. _____

Number correct _____ (total 15)

Part C   Related Words Reinforcement

Using Related Words

Sentence Completion Write the word from the following list that best completes each of the sentences.

comprehensive	curds	plumage	strict	summitry
conveyance	integrity	precedence	subtlety	symbolize

_____ 1. _?_, or top-level meetings between world leaders, is relied upon to resolve matters of international diplomacy.

_____ 2. Professor Pound has invented a new form of motorized transportation, a _?_ that can carry passengers five hundred miles on one gallon of gas.

_____ 3. Our new principal, Ms. Astrup, implemented _?_ new rules about talking in the hallways.

_____ 4. Although Tricia understood the plot of the story, she missed the _?_ of the humor in it.

_____ 5. My father is a man of _?_; he always keeps his promises.

_____ 6. What does the eye on the top of the pyramid on a one dollar bill _?_?

_____ 7. Earth's invasion of Mars will take _?_ over all other news items tonight.

_____ 8. The small clots of cheese-like material that are in soured milk are called _?_.

_____ 9. I can tell by that bird's _?_ that it is a peacock.

_____ 10. At the end of the history class, we took a _?_ examination that covered our entire system of government.

Number correct _____ (total 10)

Reviewing Word Structures

The Latin Roots *ten*, *strict*, **and** *pan* Complete each of the following sentences with a word from the Review List (page 126). Follow the directions in parentheses, using a word with a *pan*, *ten*, or *strict* root.

_____ 1. The rapid _?_ of that suburb's population has contributed to traffic jams and overcrowded schools. (Use a word with the root *pan*.)

_____ 2. Dexter refused to wear a tie, saying it would _?_ his breathing. (Use a word with the root *strict*.)

_____ 3. The airlines announced a _?_ against smoking on board their planes. (Use a word with the root *strict*.)

_____ 4. With only one job opening and over a thousand applicants, the competition was _?_. (Use a word with the root *ten*.)

_____ 5. The midday sun beat down on the weary band of explorers with an _?_ that nearly overwhelmed them. (Use a word with the root *ten*.)

Number correct _____ (total 5)

Number correct in unit _____ (total 90)

Vocab Lab 3

FOCUS ON: *The Physical World*

The following words are related to the study of our physical world and its components—air, earth, and water.

Air Words

aerodynamics (er′ ō dī nam′ iks) n. the branch of physics dealing with the forces exerted by air or other gases in motion. • Wind tunnels are used to determine the *aerodynamics* involved in airplane wing designs.

barometer (bə räm′ ə tər) n. an instrument for measuring atmospheric pressure. • Many people have a *barometer* at home to help them predict rain.

ionosphere (ī än′ əs fir′) n. the outer part of the earth's atmosphere, consisting of changing layers of heavily ionized molecules. • The *ionosphere* begins at an altitude of twenty-five miles.

meteorology (mēt′ ē ə räl′ ə jē) n. the science of the atmosphere and its phenomena, including weather. • Norma studied *meteorology* in college before becoming a weather forecaster.

ozone (ō′ zōn) n. a blue gas, a type of oxygen, with a strong odor; it is formed by electrical discharge or exposure to ultraviolet radiation. • The sun's ultraviolet rays create a layer of *ozone* in the upper atmosphere of the earth.

Earth Words

agronomy (ə grän′ ə mē) n. the management of farm land. • Future farmers sometimes study *agronomy* in college.

bench mark (bench märk) n. a surveyor's mark made on a permanent landmark for use as a reference point in determining other altitudes. • When making accurate measurements, surveyors depend on *bench marks*.

geology (jē äl′ ə jē) n. the science dealing with the structure of the earth's crust and the development of its various layers. • Knowing where to drill for oil requires a knowledge of *geology*.

seismology (sīz mäl′ ə jē) n. the science dealing with earthquakes. • An expert in *seismology* spoke to our class about the increasing number of earth tremors in our region.

topography (tə päg′ rə fē) n. the science of representing, as on maps and charts, the surface features of a region, such as hills, rivers, roads, and cities. • The map showed the *topography* of the region.

Water Words

artesian well (är tē′ zhən wel) n. a deep well in which water is forced up by underground pressure. ● The water from the *artesian well* came to the surface without being pumped.

ebb tide (eb tīd) n. the outgoing tide. ● The boats went out with the *ebb tide* and came back in with the flood tide.

hydrology (hī dräl′ ə jē) n. the science dealing with the waters of the earth, especially surface and underground sources of water and the cycle of evaporation and rainfall. ● When the wells in their village dried up, the people sought the help of experts in *hydrology* to locate new sources of water.

riparian (ri per′ ē ən, rī-) adj. of, adjacent to, or living on the bank of a river or lake. ● The attorneys argued about which client had the rights to the *riparian* property.

undertow (un′ dər tō′) n. a current of water beneath the water surface that flows in a different direction from that of the surface water. ● The waters off our beach have a dangerous *undertow* that can pull you out to sea.

Matching Focus Words to Examples Write the *air*, *earth*, or *water* focus word that best applies to each situation below.

_____ 1. a good time to look for seashells

_____ 2. lakeshore property

_____ 3. designing a jet to travel through extremely high wind currents

_____ 4. created by a bolt of lightning

_____ 5. scientists learning new ways to prevent drought

_____ 6. a surveying crew looking for a starting point to begin its measurements of a piece of land

_____ 7. an earthquake measuring 6.5 on the Richter scale.

_____ 8. a naturally flowing fountain of water

_____ 9. a military commander asking for maps of a region

_____ 10. a meteor burning up as it passes through heavily ionized gases in the atmosphere

_____ 11. predicting weather for the upcoming weekend

_____ 12. high air pressure indicating good weather

_____ 13. a warning to swimmers at an ocean beach about dangerous currents

_____ 14. a soils specialist talking about the best way to prepare a field for cultivation

_____ 15. an exhibit set up to show layers in the earth's crust

Number correct _____ (total 15)

FOCUS ON: *The Best Word*

If you were writing a newspaper article, which word would you use in the following sentence to suggest that a person was evasive and did not quite tell the truth?

When the curious reporters confronted him, Mr. Sanderson _____.
(lied, fibbed, hedged, tergiversated, pussy-footed, beat around the bush).

The words and phrases in the parentheses above have nearly the same meaning, but only *one* of them is the best to use in this particular sentence. How do you determine which word is the best word when several seem to fit? To answer this question, follow three general guidelines.

1. **Use the word your audience will understand.** If you use words that are too unusual, you not only fail to communicate meaning, but you also suggest that you are trying to impress someone with your knowledge. In the above example, well-educated readers will probably know the meaning of all the choices given except for *tergiversated*. That word should be ruled out.

2. **Use the word that conveys the right shade of meaning.** All the words in the example have the same general meaning of "made a statement not completely true," but they all have different shades of meaning. Shades of meaning are reflected in the word's **connotation**—the emotional weight of a word. *Lie* has the negative connotation of stating a flat-out untruth. *Fib* suggests an inconsequential or trivial falsehood, of the sort a child would tell about taking a cookie. Neither word quite fits the meaning you want in the example sentence. *Lie* is too strong, *fib* is too weak, and neither one suggests the idea of "being evasive."

3. **Use the word that best fits the occasion or the situation.** Like the clothing you wear, your language has different degrees of formality. You can use slang and very informal language in talking with your friends. However, you should use more formal language when you write for audiences you cannot see. On the basis of this guideline, you would probably rule out such informal phrases as *pussy-footed* and *beat around the bush*.

These three tests suggest, then, that a careful writer would use the word *hedged*, meaning "to avoid giving direct answers." *Hedged* communicates with intelligent readers, it suggests the right shade of meaning, and it has the proper degree of formality. Use these guidelines to choose the best word in your own writing.

Choosing the Best Word In each of the following sentences, write the word that *best* fits the situation. Apply the three guidelines discussed above. The type of writing in which the sentence appears is indicated after each sentence.

_____ 1. King Henry VIII was so (*chubby, obese, porky*) that he had to be lifted onto his horse with a crane. (a high school social studies report)

_____ 2. From what I've seen, distrust seems to be (*pervasive, everywhere, endemic*). (a chatty column in a newsletter)

_____ 3. Senior citizens often choose to retire to Florida because the climate is so (*invigorating, healthful, salubrious*). (a guide to the Southeastern states)

_____ 4. After fasting for twenty-five days, the protester was weak and (*skinny, lean as a rake, emaciated*). (a newspaper article)

_____ 5. After their miraculous win in the championship game, the players were (*delighted, ecstatic, glad*). (a newspaper article)

_____ 6. This gentle, bearded (*isolationist, hermit, weirdo*) had lived by himself in a lonely wooded area for several years. (a narrative composition for English class)

_____ 7. When the judges gave Evansville's star gymnast a low 8.0 score, the crowd became (*unruly, fractious, obstreperous*). (high school newspaper article)

_____ 8. Now, set the (*aperture, hole, opening*) of the camera as wide as it will go. (the instruction manual for a camera)

_____ 9. The seemingly minor border dispute resulted in a major (*brouhaha, controversy, fuss*) that eventually led to war. (an article in a history textbook)

_____ 10. The protagonist in Dickens's *A Christmas Carol*, Ebenezer Scrooge, is the epitome of a (*stingy, penny-pinching, parsimonious*) man. (an article for English scholars)

_____ 11. I don't like being around Marie because she (*is pugnacious, is bellicose, has a chip on her shoulder*). (a letter to a friend)

_____ 12. Spectacular spectacles! We know you'll agree that our carnival shows are truly (*good, splendiferous, pleasant*). (an ad for a carnival)

_____ 13. To finish off our perfect day, we decided that a banana split was absolutely (*necessary, requisite, fundamental*). (a letter to a friend)

_____ 14. Late Monday night, the police detectives (*collared, apprehended, busted*) the murder suspect. (a newspaper article)

_____ 15. His suspenders were no longer (*elastic, extensile, stretchy*). (a descriptive composition for English class)

Number correct _____ (total 15)

UNIT 13

Part A   Target Words and Their Meanings

1. acknowledge (ək näl′ ij) v.
2. advocate (ad′ və kāt′) v. (-kit) n.
3. confrontation (kän′ frən tā′ shən) n.
4. equality (i kwäl′ ə tē, -kwôl′-) n.
5. foster (fôs′ tər, fäs′-)v., adj.
6. indictment (in dīt′ mənt) n.
7. intend (in tend′) v.
8. mentality (men tal′ ə tē) n.
9. militant (mil′ i tənt) adj., n.
10. naive (nä ēv′) adj.
11. pessimistic (pes′ ə mis′ tik) adj.
12. pious (pī′ əs) adj.
13. prominence (präm′ ə nens) n.
14. propel (prə pel′) v.
15. prophet (präf′ it) n.
16. puritanical (pyoor′ ə tan′ i k'l) adj.
17. rigid (rij′ id) adj.
18. shrewd (shrood) adj.
19. sophisticated (sə fis′ tə kāt′ id) adj.
20. strategist (strat′ ə jist) n.

Inferring Meaning from Context

For each sentence write the letter of the word or phrase that is closest to the meaning of the italicized word. Use context clues to help you determine the correct answer. (For information about how context helps you understand vocabulary, see pages 1–5.)

_____ 1. At first, John did not want to *acknowledge* that he had witnessed a crime.

a. admit   b. know   c. learn   d. resist

_____ 2. In his speeches, Dr. Cooper *advocates* physical fitness as the prime ingredient of good health.

a. accuses   b. opposes   c. admits   d. promotes

_____ 3. Although Terri hated *confrontations*, she knew she had to admit to her brother that she had broken his tennis racket.

a. agreements   b. conflicts   c. applause   d. avoiding people

_____ 4. Getting the same grades in the same classes gave Bill and Betty a certain *equality*.

a. dependence   b. difference   c. moderation   d. sameness

_____ 5. Julia's parents tried to *foster* good study habits by providing her with a quiet, well-lighted study area.

a. acknowledge   b. force   c. encourage   d. ignore

_____ 6. Cora cried bitterly as she listened to the judge read the *indictment* against her.

a. restriction   b. release   c. exultation   d. charge

137

_____ 7. Rita told everyone that she really did *intend* to be on time next week.
a. plan b. precede c. rush d. proclaim

_____ 8. Inventing a new product requires a creative *mentality* that allows a person to approach a situation or problem with a new perspective.
a. heritage b. college education c. equality d. way of thinking

_____ 9. Growing up on the streets had made him *a militant* defender of homeless people.
a. a disciplined b. a formal c. an aggressive d. an integral

_____ 10. He was more than innocent; he was *naive*. Trusting everyone, he was often disappointed and tricked.
a. knowledgeable b. integrated c. childishly simple d. comically wise

_____ 11. Angelica had *a pessimistic* outlook that prevented her from feeling good about her future.
a. a possessive b. a glamorous c. a negative d. an exultant

_____ 12. People adopted *a pious* attitude as they entered the great cathedral.
a. a religious b. an unholy c. a distinguished d. a militant

_____ 13. The singer gained *prominence* with her award-winning record album.
a. complexity b. mobility c. wisdom d. fame

_____ 14. The burning of liquid hydrogen is what *propels* most rockets into space.
a. thrusts b. careens c. precedes d. pulls

_____ 15. Our coach told us we would win the game, 100 to 90. When we did win by that exact score, we started to consider him a *prophet*.
a. comical character b. predictor of the future c. professor
d. militant

_____ 16. Colin was a troublemaker; in contrast, Ian had a *puritanical* nature.
a. clumsy b. morally strict c. disorganized d. restorative

_____ 17. The doctor told my aunt to lose thirty pounds; now she is on a *rigid* diet.
a. easy b. strict c. creative d. mature

_____ 18. Attorneys learn to be very *shrewd* in the way they word contracts.
a. clever b. voluntary c. pessimistic d. coarse

_____ 19. Her extensive travels and her reading made Tanya more *sophisticated* than many of her friends.
a. worldly wise b. unfortunate c. affluent d. comical

_____ 20. General Patton was an excellent *strategist*, capable of winning difficult battles under unfavorable conditions.
a. speaker b. planner c. follower d. advocate

Number correct _____ (total 20)

You should now have a general idea of the meaning of each target word. Refine your understanding by examining the shades of meaning the words have in the following excerpt.

The Days of Martin Luther King, Jr.

Jim Bishop

Martin Luther King, Jr., (1929–68) was one of America's most important social reformers. King strove for racial equality, believing that racial justice could be achieved through nonviolent means. In the following article writer Jim Bishop describes this complex man.

He was short and chubby, a man with a boy's grin, the **mentality** of a **sophisticated prophet,** and the voice of a hollow log drum booming in the Congo. Dr. Martin Luther King, Jr., was, on the surface, a typical black preacher who called down fire and brimstone on sinners but thought it would happen in the next world rather than this one. A black woman who refused to move to the back of a bus **propelled** Dr. King into world **prominence.** Fearful and **pessimistic,** he fought her cause and was stunned when he won. In time he was to lead the Southern black man to fresh freedoms after hundreds of years of servitude. In a span of thirteen years, the preacher saw himself as a black Mohandas Gandhi,[1] perhaps a Jesus, because he won victory after victory by **advocating** nonviolence and the unselfish love for the hating whites.

Nonviolence was not only his credo,[2] but his rationale.[3] He reminded the

[1] Mohandas Gandhi: leader and social reformer of India
[2] credo: approximately the same meaning as *creed*—"religious belief"
[3] rationale: reasoned principle

militants that twenty-two million blacks had neither the weapons nor the possibility of winning a fight against a white government of one hundred eighty million people. He was **shrewd;** he was **naive.** He was courageous; he was 15 cowardly. He was a leader, but not a **strategist.** Almost always, he was willing to settle for less than he asked for his people. However, he got more for them than they had been able to achieve in three centuries of servitude.

At times his attitude was almost saintly. His life became a series of violent **confrontations,** each different from the others. To the historian the joke was on 20 the white man because King was asking for **equality** in what was considered a classless society. It was demeaning[4] to both sides to **acknowledge** the fact that America, the **puritanical** democracy, **fostered** a caste system, every bit as **rigid** as India's, of at least four main classes—white, "poor white trash," Spanish-speaking people, and blacks. 25

The black leadership was aware of this [caste system] but refused to admit it. The men on Capitol Hill and in the White House were born into it and contented themselves with **pious** promises. This broad-blessed land of sparkling streams and tall forests had sparrows living on one branch and swallows on another, but men pretended not to be aware of it. 30

Dr. King was given a short time to accomplish a brotherhood of many kinds of birds, and his **indictments** of his enemies left ruffled feathers and bloody beaks. He asked equal pay for equal skills, voting rights for blacks, the extermination of ghettos, an anti-distinctive status called equality; but his true goal was social acceptability of all blacks by all whites. When he spoke of "brotherhood," the 35 reverend **intended** more than the integration of schools and buses.

---

[4] demeaning: humbling; shameful

Refining Your Understanding

For each of the following questions, consider how the target word is used in the passage. Write the letter of the word or phrase that best completes the sentence.

_____ 1. Bishop tells us that at first King was *pessimistic* (line 7), which means he
a. expected to succeed   b. didn't expect to succeed   c. didn't succeed.

_____ 2. By *advocating* (line 10) nonviolence, King   a. mistrusted it
b. supported it   c. opposed it.

_____ 3. *Militants* (line 13) would probably have favored action involving
a. nonviolence   b. marching   c. fighting.

_____ 4. The term *rigid* (line 23) suggests that the caste system in India and in the United States   a. allowed for little movement between social classes
b. did exist but was not harmful   c. was tailored to each country.

_____ 5. *"Indictments* (line 32) of his enemies" suggests that King's relationship to his opponents was sometimes   a. forgiving   b. questioning
c. accusing.

Number correct _____ (total 5)

Part C Ways to Make New Words Your Own

This section presents a variety of reinforcement activities that will help you make the words part of your permanent vocabulary.

Using Language and Thinking Skills

Matching Ideas In the blank write the word from the list that is most clearly related to the situation conveyed in the sentence.

equality   indictment   militant   pious   rigid

_____ 1. The mob grew to several hundred. The people were angry, and one could sense the hatred growing. Soon words would not be enough to satisfy them.

_____ 2. As the spiritual leader entered, there was a hush in the room—a hush that was a devout moment for all.

_____ 3. The grand jury had been investigating the case for eight months. Finally the jurors felt they had enough evidence to bring charges against the people involved in the crime.

_____ 4. The law requires that all individuals be given the same rights

_____ 5. Some people insist on following strict rules. They refuse to alter their views or allow room for others to interpret the rules differently.

Number correct _____ (total 5)

Understanding Multiple Meanings Study the definitions of the target word and then read the sentences that use the word. Write the letter of the definition that fits each sentence.

---

acknowledge
a. to admit to be true; to confess (v.)
b. to recognize the authority or claims of (v.)
c. to express thanks for (v.)
d. to state that one has received something (such as a letter, gift, favor, or payment) (v.)

_____ 1. In the introduction, the author *acknowledged* the assistance of her editor.

_____ 2. Lincoln is *acknowledged* as being a key figure in the abolition of slavery.

_____ 3. Frank *acknowledged* that he received help while preparing to take the test.

_____ 4. The Bureau of Indian Affairs *acknowledged* my letter requesting more information on the Sioux Indians.

> **advocate**
> a. a person who pleads another's cause; a lawyer (n.)
> b. a person who speaks or writes in support of someone or something (n.)
> c. to speak or write in support of; to be in favor of (v.)

_____ 5. In her role as an adviser to the senator, she became an *advocate* of lower utility bills for consumers.

_____ 6. Although the defendant's case seemed hopeless, the *advocate* worked hard in hopes of obtaining an acquittal.

_____ 7. The politician *advocated* the lowering of taxes to revive the economy.

_____ 8. Because Cal is a good speaker, he acted as Tom's *advocate* during the trial.

> **pious**
> a. having or showing religious devotion (adj.)
> b. pretending to be virtuous without really being so (adj.)

_____ 9. The religious leader was a *pious* individual who had great respect for the teachings of his church.

_____ 10. The defendant looked *pious* as the lawyers presented their final arguments to the jury.

Number correct _____ (total 10)

Finding the Unrelated Word Write the letter of the word that is not related in meaning to the other words in the group.

_____ 1. a. settlement b. agreement c. confrontation d. resolution

_____ 2. a. advocate b. defender c. counselor d. opponent

_____ 3. a. propel b. catapult c. push d. hesitate

_____ 4. a. strategist b. destroyer c. planner d. organizer

_____ 5. a. pessimistic b. optimistic c. positive d. upbeat

_____ 6. a. puritanical b. liberal c. strict d. prim and proper

_____ 7. a. overtrusting b. crafty c. clever d. shrewd

_____ 8. a. simple b. naive c. innocent d. worldly

_____ 9. a. encourage b. foster c. hinder d. assist

_____ 10. a. mature b. experienced c. gullible d. sophisticated

Number correct _____ (total 10)

Practicing for Standardized Tests

Analogies Write the letter of the pair of words that best expresses a relationship similar to that of the original pair.

_____ 1. ADVOCATE : COURTROOM :: (A) commerce : business (B) opponent : enemy (C) peacock : plume (D) cook : kitchen (E) servitude : plantation

_____ 2. PROPHET : PROFIT :: (A) emigration : immigration (B) moral : morale (C) flair : flare (D) fortune : seer (E) verse : curse

_____ 3. MILITANT : SOLDIER :: (A) sordid : building (B) persuasive : salesperson (C) modern : artist (D) illiterate : librarian (E) grave : clown

_____ 4. FUEL : PROPEL :: (A) push : pull (B) textile : weave (C) flag : wave (D) tragedy : laugh (E) magnet : attract

_____ 5. CONFRONTATION : SHOWDOWN :: (A) intensity : youthfulness (B) persuasion : barter (C) depletion : derision (D) moderation : excess (E) hazard : danger

_____ 6. STRATEGIST : PLAN :: (A) advocate : courtoom (B) horde : crowd (C) doctor : professional (D) mystery : romance (E) prophet : vision

_____ 7. NAIVE : CHILD :: (A) young : politician (B) affluent : millionaire (C) sophisticated : infant (D) sordid : cleanliness (E) formal : dance

_____ 8. JURY : INDICTS :: (A) legislature : votes (B) system : confuses (C) hazard : exposes (D) bazaar : buys (E) mechanism : stresses

_____ 9. ACKNOWLEDGE : ADMIT :: (A) send : receive (B) comprehend : understand (C) increase : deplete (D) swim : dive (E) suffer : heal

_____ 10. PURITANICAL : PURITAN :: (A) scientific : psychologist (B) prophetic: prophet (C) pyrotechnic : celebration (D) hopeful : pessimist (E) religious : Pilgrim

Number correct _____ (total 10)

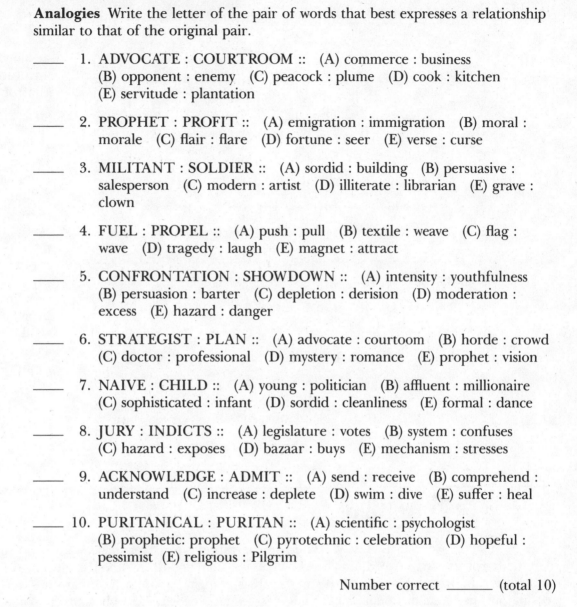

Word's Worth: prophet

Prophet is a word that has a long history. It is a combination of two Greek word parts, the prefix *pro-*, meaning "for," and the root *phemi*, meaning "to speak." The word was first used in ancient Greek times to describe special people who would speak for and deliver the messages of Zeus and other Greek gods and goddesses. The term was later applied to Jewish prophets of the Old Testament who were especially known for their concern for social justice. Today, the word *prophet* is often used to refer to a leader or individual who predicts future events.

Spelling and Wordplay

Word Maze Find and circle the target words in this maze.

```
A  C  O  V  M  P  L  I  H  S  A  G  D  A
D  C  D  I  G  I  R  P  R  O  P  E  L  E
V  E  K  P  L  O  F  O  S  T  E  R  H  S
O  V  T  N  R  U  X  Z  A  Q  P  M  Q  T
C  I  W  A  O  S  E  T  U  U  R  E  H  I
A  A  D  S  C  W  U  A  R  T  O  N  E  C
T  N  T  K  P  I  L  I  J  Y  P  T  D  I
E  C  N  Q  V  I  T  E  M  G  H  A  U  T
F  W  E  O  T  A  F  S  D  M  E  L  T  S
O  M  M  Y  N  I  L  V  I  G  T  I  I  I
S  B  T  I  N  T  E  N  D  H  E  T  C  M
K  E  C  N  E  N  I  M  O  R  P  Y  R  I
C  A  I  M  I  L  I  T  A  N  T  O  E  S
L  M  D  R  N  U  N  D  W  E  R  H  S  S
C  O  N  F  R  O  N  T  A  T  I  O  N  E
T  S  I  G  E  T  A  R  T  S  J  E  B  P
```

acknowledge
advocate
confrontation
equality
foster
indictment
intend
mentality
militant
naive
pessimistic
pious
prominence
propel
prophet
puritanical
rigid
shrewd
sophisticated
strategist

Part D   Related Words

A number of words are closely related to the target words you have studied. Use your knowledge of the target words and of word parts to help you determine the meaning of these words. (For information about word parts analysis, see pages 6–12.) If you are unsure of any definitions, use your dictionary. Learning these related words expands your vocabulary and helps you learn the target words more thoroughly.

1. acknowledgment (ək näl′ ij mənt, ak-) n.
2. confront (kən frunt′) v.
3. equalize (ē′ kwə līz′) v.
4. equation (i kwā′ zhən) n.
5. equilibrium (ē′ kwə lib′ rē əm) n.
6. indict (in dīt′) v.
7. intention (in ten′ shən) n.
8. naiveté (nä ēv tā′, ēv′ tā) n.
9. pessimism (pes′ ə miz′m) n.
10. piety (pī′ ə tē) n.
11. prominent (präm′ ə nənt) adj.
12. prophecy (präf′ ə sē) n.
13. prophetic (prə fet′ ik) adj.
14. propulsion (prə pul′ shən) n.
15. rigidity (ri jid′ ə tē) n.
16. shrewdness (shrood′ nes) n.
17. sophistication (sə fis′ tə kā′ shən) n.
18. strategy (strat′ ə jē) n.

Understanding Related Words

Finding Examples Match each noun with the appropriate example. Write the correct letter in the blank.

a. pessimism   f. propulsion
b. acknowledgement   g. piety
c. equation   h. shrewdness
d. equilibrium   i. sophistication
e. intention   j. strategy

_____ 1. a rocket sending a satellite into orbit

_____ 2. two children balanced on a seesaw

_____ 3. a friend's plan to attend your party

_____ 4. $2 \div 3y = 36$

_____ 5. knowing what to wear and how to act at a formal party

_____ 6. a characteristic of a keen-witted detective who collects important clues

_____ 7. the best plan to beat the opposing team

_____ 8. a letter that says someone has received what you sent

_____ 9. going to church daily to pray

_____ 10. always leaning toward the negative side of every issue

Number correct _____ (total 10)

Synonyms–Antonyms Decide if the following pairs of words are synonyms or antonyms. In the blank write **S** for Synonym or **A** for Antonym.

_____ 1. equalize – balance

_____ 2. shrewdness – stupidity

_____ 3. equilibrium – poise

_____ 4. pessimism – optimism

_____ 5. sophistication – worldliness

_____ 6. prophecy – prediction

_____ 7. indict – charge

_____ 8. prominent – well-known

_____ 9. confront – avoid

_____ 10. rigidity – flexibility

Number correct _____ (total 10)

Homonyms The words *prophet* and *profit* are homonyms—words that sound alike but have different meanings. Each of these words has several definitions, as listed below.

> **prophct**
> a. one who claims to speak for God (n.)
> b. a spokesperson for some cause, group, etc. (n.)
> c. one who predicts the future (n.)

profit
a. advantage; benefit (n.)
b. financial gain (n.)
c. to make a financial profit; to benefit; to gain (v.)

Complete each of the following sentences with *prophet* or *profit*. To determine which word to use, note the context of the sentence and refer to the definitions above. Write the words in the blanks on the left.

_____ 1. The _?_ claimed to speak for a god.

_____ 2. We expect to _?_ from our education.

_____ 3. I wish I were a _?_ so that I would know who will win the game tomorrow.

_____ 4. Every business hopes to make a _?_.

_____ 5. Isaiah is a _?_ in the Bible.

_____ 6. My _?_ last year was less than sixty dollars.

_____ 7. Most people believe that there is little _?_ in war.

_____ 8. The weather forecaster was correct so often that he seemed to be a _?_.

_____ 9. Many cults have their own _?_.

_____ 10. We _?_ from each book we read.

Number correct _____ (total 10)

Analyzing Word Parts

The Latin root *equ* The target word *equality* and the related words *equalize*, *equation*, and *equilibrium* come from the Latin word *aequus*, meaning "equal." Other words in the family of *equ* roots include *equanimity* and *equinox*. Use a dictionary to familiarize yourself with the meanings of these words. Then write the word from this list that completes the meaning in the following sentences.

equalize   equation   equinox
equanimity   equilibrium

_____ 1. Einstein's most famous _?_, $E = mc^2$, means "energy = mass x the speed of light^2."

_____ 2. During the _?_, day and night are of equal length.

_____ 3. After getting off the spinning "Rotor" at the amusement park, it took me several minutes to regain my _?_.

_____ 4. Players were traded in order to _?_ the strengths of the two teams.

_____ 5. The man was known for his calmness and _?_ during difficult times.

Number correct _____ (total 5)

Number correct in unit _____ (total 95)

Turn to **Doubling the Final Consonant** on pages 199–201 of the **Spelling Handbook.** Read the rules and complete the exercises provided.

The Last Word

Writing

According to an old saying, "The road to failure is paved with good *intentions*." What does this quotation say about good intentions? Write a short explanation.

Speaking

Prepare a speech on one of the following topics.

1. The *shrewdest* person I know
2. Justifiable reasons to be *militant*
3. A *prominent* person I admire

Group Discussion

Divide the class into groups of four. Choose one of the topics below to discuss. For three minutes, two group members should *advocate* one side of the issue. Then the other two group members should *advocate* the opposing side of the issue for three minutes.

- Students in schools should wear uniforms.
- The lyrics of record albums should be given a rating the way movies are.
- Some of our school rules are too lax—they should be made stricter.
- The penny should be abolished.

UNIT 14

Part A Target Words and Their Meanings

1. accessible (ak ses′ ə b'l) adj.
2. acute (ə kyo͞ot′) adj.
3. appreciate (ə prē′ shē āt′) v.
4. arid (ar′ id, er′-) adj.
5. biosphere (bī′ ə sfir′) n.
6. compose (kəm pōz′) v.
7. compression (kəm presh′ ən) n.
8. distill (dis til′) v.
9. document (däk′ yə mənt) n. (-ment′) v.
10. expeditious (ek′ spə dish′ əs) adj.
11. innovative (in′ ə vāt′ iv) adj.
12. obstacle (äb′ sti k'l) n.
13. quantity (kwän′ tə tē) n.
14. tabular (tab′ yə lər) adj.
15. technological (tek′ nə läj′ i k'l) adj.
16. tedious (tē′ dē əs) adj.
17. trace (trās) n., v.
18. utilize (yo͞ot′ 'l īz′) v.
19. visionary (vizh′ ən er′ ē) n., adj.
20. yield (yēld) v., n.

Inferring Meaning from Context

For each sentence write the letter of the word or phrase that is closest to the meaning of the italicized word or words. Use context clues to help you.

_____ 1. Halifax became a great port because it was *accessible to* ships.

a. easy to reach by   b. expensive for   c. uncharted by
d. dangerous for

_____ 2. The water shortage in that county has become *acute*; wells have gone dry, and the good soil is turning to dust.

a. beautiful   b. inconvenient   c. severe   d. interesting

_____ 3. We did not *appreciate* Jefferson's genius until we visited Monticello and realized what a brilliant architect and inventor he was.

a. value   b. advocate   c. predict   d. criticize

_____ 4. The desert is *arid* because it receives very little rainfall.

a. flat   b. azure   c. dry   d. beautiful

_____ 5. The *biosphere* of the desert supports varied life forms such as the saguaro cactus, the roadrunner, the coyote, and the rattlesnake.

a. bird life   b. number of animals   c. type of environment
d. list of extinct creatures

_____ 6. Canada *is composed of* ten provinces, which stretch from the Atlantic to the Pacific.

a. is made up of   b. is endangered by   c. is about to be divided into
d. is bordered by

_____ 7. A diesel engine is started by *the compression of* air rather than by the use of a spark plug; the motion of the tightly packed air molecules generates heat and ignites the gasoline in the cylinder.
a. the phenomenon of   b. the loss of   c. pollution of the
d. applying heavy pressure to

_____ 8. To prevent mineral deposits in your steam iron, use *distilled* water.
a. mineral   b. river   c. purified   d. colored

_____ 9. Many *documents*, such as wills and marriage certificates, must be witnessed.
a. works of art   b. legal records   c. ceremonies   d. important decisions

_____ 10. Copy machines allow us to be much more *expeditious* with our paperwork; a century ago important documents were copied by hand.
a. shrewd   b. rigid   c. honest   d. efficient

_____ 11. A top surgeon uses *innovative* techniques rather than conventional ones.
a. strict   b. new   c. regular   d. outdated

_____ 12. Worker absenteeism was the main *obstacle to* achieving production goals.
a. thing that led the way to   b. reason for   c. thing that encouraged
d. thing that got in the way of

_____ 13. The *quantity* of water in the barrel was barely adequate, but it was enough to keep the miner alive until the first-aid team reached him.
a. amount   b. temperature   c. cost   d. expansion

_____ 14. A butte is similar to other kinds of hills, except for its *tabular* surface; instead of tapering toward a peak, its top is flat.
a. table-like   b. triangular   c. forested   d. circular

_____ 15. *Technological* advances help the space program attain many goals.
a. scientific   b. pictorial   c. superstitious   d. immoderate

_____ 16. Doing the same job day after day was so *tedious* that Tara was yawning.
a. difficult   b. uncomfortable   c. frequent   d. boring

_____ 17. Even a *trace* of that poisonous gas can be dangerous to your health.
a. container   b. symbol   c. very small amount   d. large amount

_____ 18. The coach said Mary was not *utilizing* all her natural ability as a runner.
a. using   b. proclaiming   c. wasting   d. depleting

_____ 19. Bismarck was considered a *visionary*; he foresaw a time when many republics in central Europe would become one country—Germany.
a. professional   b. person who sees into the future   c. pessimistic
person   d. person who acts independently

_____ 20. At sea, captains should *yield to* ships coming from the starboard side.
a. attack   b. proceed before   c. ignore   d. give way to

Number correct _____ (total 20)

Part B   Target Words in Reading and Literature

You should now have a general idea of the meaning of each target word. Refine your understanding by examining the shades of meaning the words have in the following excerpt.

Is There an Iceberg in Your Future?

Kendrick Frazier

Penguins aren't the only creatures interested in icebergs. As the concern about droughts, climate changes, and water shortages increases, scientists are studying new sources of water. Icebergs, towed by boats to distant dry lands, present an interesting possibility.

Eight days before sailing for the first time into waters south of the Antarctic Circle, Captain James Cook found his ship the *Resolution* among loose pieces of ice. Cook had his crew hoist out three boats, and the sailors broke the ice with axes into pieces small enough to be loaded onto the boats and brought aboard ship. They "took up as much as **yielded** about 15 tons of fresh water," 5 Cook wrote in his journal. "The melting of the ice is a little **tedious,** otherwise this is the most **expeditious** way of watering I ever met with." That was in 1773.

Now, more than two centuries since this first **documented** use of Antarctic icebergs for fresh water, the concept of **utilizing** icebergs has reached a stage so bold and imaginative as to challenge the skills and knowledge of the most 10 **innovative** engineers, scientists, and seamen. As the First International Conference on Iceberg Utilization at Iowa State University showed, the idea of towing large **tabular** icebergs from Antarctic waters to the coasts of **arid** lands in both the Southern and Northern Hemispheres is alive and very well, despite enormous scientific and **technological obstacles** to be overcome. 15

The little-**appreciated** fact is that on a planet with widespread arid lands and

steadily increasing population, the need for additional fresh water in many regions is **acute.** However, the majority of all the world's fresh water (77.1 percent) is locked up in ice caps and glaciers. Nearly all the remaining water (22.3 percent) is underground and not always easily **accessible.** (Only a tiny 0.5   20 percent is in the lakes and rivers of the world, and the remaining **traces** are in the atmosphere and **biosphere.**) And of the three-quarters of the world's fresh water locked up in ice, 90 percent is in the Antarctic ice cap.

Icebergs, unlike sea ice, are **composed** of fresh water, not sea water. The ice in the Antarctic bergs was created by the buildup of snow and its **compression**   25 into ice during millions of years over the Antarctic continent. The ice flows toward the continent's edge. At the coast it forms floating ice shelves about 240 meters thick that are continually breaking off and forming icebergs.

The **quantities** are almost unimaginable. It has been estimated that the Antarctic ice shelves produce a trillion cubic meters (1,000 cubic kilometers) of   30 icebergs a year. One 90- by 35-kilometer iceberg at the end of the Antarctic peninsula contains enough water to serve a city the size of Washington, D.C., for thousands of years. The water in this ice is extremely pure, having the purity of **distilled** water. This frozen fresh water merely drifts northward and eventually melts uselessly into the sea. It is no wonder that **visionaries** in the   35 waterproof areas of the world are eyeing icebergs as a future freshwater resource.

Refining Your Understanding

For each of the following questions, consider how the target word is used in the passage. Write the letter of the word or phrase that best completes the sentence.

_____ 1. "The melting of the ice is a little *tedious*" (line 6) suggests that Cook's sailors experienced much   a. danger   b. excitement   c. boredom.

_____ 2. The first *documented* (line 8) use of icebergs for water was over two centuries ago. That is, this was   a. the first scientific use of icebergs   b. the first recorded use of icebergs   c. the first failed use of icebergs.

_____ 3. When the author refers to "*arid* lands in both the Southern and Northern Hemispheres" (lines 13-14), he is referring to countries with   a. steppes   b. deserts   c. resources.

_____ 4. The use of the word *expeditious* (line 7) indicates that melting ice   a. is expensive   b. is a good source of water   c. is found only south of the Antarctic Circle.

_____ 5. Which of the following would be considered a *visionary* (line 35)?   a. an official who will not consider a new plan to improve the country's food production   b. a scientist who is interested in trying new ways of raising crops   c. a citizen who sees no reason to change the way crops are grown.

Number correct _____ (total 5)

Part C *Ways to Make New Words Your Own*

This section presents a variety of reinforcement activities that will help you make the words part of your permanent vocabulary.

Using Language and Thinking Skills

Understanding Multiple Meanings Read the definitions that follow each target word. Then determine which of the four words best completes each sentence. In the blank write the word and also the letter of the definition that is conveyed.

---

acute
a. sharp, as in pain (adj.)
b. serious (adj.)

---

appreciate
a. to value or enjoy (v.)
b. to be sensitively aware of (v.)
c. to rise in value (v.)

---

document
a. a written record (n.)
b. to provide support for something said or written (v.)

---

trace
a. visible evidence; sign (n.)
b. to draw in lines (v.)
c. to find or "track down" (v.)

_____ 1. A responsible news reporter should keep good records and be able to _?_ any statements he or she reports.

_____ 2. Jane _?_ the compliment Mark gave her.

_____ 3. Jon will _?_ the design on paper and fill in the details later.

_____ 4. After a long investigation, he _?_ the rumor to its source.

_____ 5. A(n) _?_ pain on the right side of your midsection is a symptom of appendicitis.

_____ 6. After working in the factory last summer, I can _?_ the demands made now by the union.

_____ 7. A(n) _?_ shortage of electricity can black out an entire city.

_____ 8. By ten o'clock not even a (an) _?_ of fog could be seen.

_____ 9. The influx of new residents to our town caused the value of our land to _?_ considerably.

_____ 10. The old _?_, with signatures of the original inhabitants of the community, may be viewed at the courthouse.

Number correct _____ (total 10)

Practice for Standardized Tests

Analogies Write the letter indicating the pair of words that best expresses a relationship similar to that of the original pair.

_____ 1. DRY : ARID ::   (A) mathematical : algebraic   (B) moist : damp   (C) elusive : intrusive   (D) iridescent : red   (E) rigid : flexible

_____ 2. TABULAR : DESK ::   (A) triangular : circle   (B) talkative : friend   (C) spherical : basketball   (D) highlighted : feature   (E) hidden : secret

_____ 3. REPETITION : TEDIOUS ::   (A) innovation : refreshing   (B) surrender : victorious   (C) conclusion : initial   (D) summit : beautiful   (E) restriction : liberated

_____ 4. EXPANSION : COMPRESSION ::   (A) mass : volume   (B) taciturnity : trait   (C) growth : shrinkage   (D) conveyance : travel   (E) encrustation : buildup

_____ 5. DISTILL : WATER ::   (A) pulverize : wood   (B) refine : oil   (C) deride : enemy   (D) exhaust : fume   (E) spawn : fish

_____ 6. ABUNDANCE : TRACE ::   (A) flare : light   (B) biosphere : world   (C) display : array   (D) friend : enemy   (E) essence : odor

_____ 7. DREAMER : VISIONARY ::   (A) curd : milk   (B) textile : clothes   (C) constriction : expansion   (D) mind : body   (E) actuality : reality

_____ 8. ACUTE : PAIN ::   (A) graceful : clumsiness   (B) symbolic : symbol   (C) unrestrictive : boundary   (D) round : square   (E) severe : injury

_____ 9. OBSTACLE: PASSAGEWAY ::   (A) hurdle : track   (B) tunnel : mountain   (C) aperture : opening   (D) symbol : flare   (E) dam : electricity

_____ 10. INVENTION : INNOVATIVE ::   (A) eyesore : scenic   (B) parachute : essential   (C) comprehension : comparable   (D) sculpture : creative   (E) solitude : sociable

Number correct _____ (total 10)

Spelling and Wordplay

Crossword Puzzle Read each clue to determine what word will fit in the corresponding squares. There are several target words in the puzzle.

Across

1. Sharp
5. A mental image
9. Popular flower, usually red
10. Abbr. Associate of Arts
11. To bend the head forward
13. Contraction of "I am"
14. To go on
18. Abbr. Double Play
19. Past tense of "to have"
20. Small, poisonous snake
21. Abbr. District of Columbia
23. Third person singular of "to be"
24. Obstruction
29. — — — — Armstrong, moonwalker
31. Abbr. *id est* (Latin for "that is")
32. Not good
33. Act of being compressed
35. Not off
36. Toward
37. To give way
40. Not down
41. Advertisement
42. Evidence
46. Abbr. Alternating Current
47. Word of choice
48. Morning
49. Wicked
50. More than half

Down

1. Dry
2. To make up
3. You and me
4. Of technology
5. A large tank
6. Wrongs
7. A single thing
8. Negative
10. Conjunction
12. An official paper
15. Abbr. On Account
16. Abbr. Iowa
17. Not down
22. Tiresome
23. To introduce a new thing
25. To drink a little at a time
26. Abbr. Terrace
27. Major TV network
28. Opposite of first
30. Adjective suffix meaning "pertaining to"
34. Edward's nickname
38. Abbr. Lieutenant
39. Abbr. Doctor
43. A dove's sound
44. To fall into error
45. Girl's name
48. There

Turn to **Words with ie and ei** on pages 203–204 of the **Spelling Handbook.** Read the rule and complete the exercises provided.

Part D Related Words

A number of words are closely related to the target words you have studied. Use your knowledge of the target words and of word parts to help you determine the meaning of these words. (For information about word parts analysis, see pages 6–12.)

1. access (ak′ ses) n.
2. appreciation (ə prē′ shē ā′ shən) n.
3. aridity (ə rid′ ə tē) n.
4. composer (kəm pō′ zər) n.
5. composition (käm′ pə zish′ ən) n.
6. compress (käm′ pres) n. (kəm pres′) v.
7. dispose (dis pōz′) v.
8. documentary (däk′ yə men′ tə rē) adj., n.
9. expedite (ek′ spə dīt′) v.
10. expose (ik spōz′) v.
11. impose (im pōz′) v.
12. innovation (in′ ə vā′ shən) n.
13. sphere (sfir) n.
14. technical (tek′ ni k'l) adj.
15. technology (tek näl′ ə jē) n.
16. utility (yo͞o til′ ə tē) n.
17. utilization (yo͞o′ ti li zā′ shən) n.
18. visualize (vizh′ o͞o wə līz′, o͞o līz′) v.

Understanding Related Words

Definitions from Context Carefully consider the context of each italicized word below and write its definition in the blank. Check your answers with a dictionary.

1. Frequent *utilization* of the copy machine will cause it to wear out faster.

_____

2. *Access* to a telephone allowed Sandra to call in the story to her editor as soon as she left the crash site.

_____

3. The day before the performance, the *composer* sat in the concert hall listening to the orchestra rehearse her latest symphony.

_____

4. The *compress* applied to Peggy's cut finger was tight enough to stop the bleeding.

_____

5. Arnie called his grandparents to express his *appreciation* for the birthday gift.

_____

6. Although the travel book provided a detailed description, we found it difficult to *visualize* the actual size of the mountain range.

_____

7. Benjamin Franklin amazed the people of his time with his many *innovations*, such as bifocal eyeglasses.

   _____

8. Few plants other than the cactus thrive in the *aridity* of the desert climate.

   _____

9. It takes years to acquire the *technical* knowledge necessary to be a good electrical engineer.

   _____

10. The *documentary* film on World War II revealed what really occurred during the invasion of Poland.

   _____

Number correct _____ (total 10)

Analyzing Word Parts

The Latin Root *pos* The target word *compose* comes from the Latin word *positus*, meaning "to place." Related words with this root include *composer*, *composition*, *dispose*, *impose*, and *expose*. Use your knowledge of word parts to match each word with its correct definition. (For lists of word parts and their meanings, see pages 6–12.) Write the letter of the matching word in the blank.

a. compose   e. deposit   h. impose
b. composer   f. dispose   i. position
c. composition g. expose   j. propose
d. depose

_____ 1. To place a burden on or upon; to force on another

_____ 2. a person who creates something; a person who puts something together

_____ 3. to throw away

_____ 4. a unified placement of parts, as in writing or painting

_____ 5. to leave unprotected; to reveal

_____ 6. to remove from a position of power

_____ 7. to put forth for consideration or acceptance

_____ 8. to place for safekeeping, as in putting money in a bank

_____ 9. the visual or proper place

_____ 10. to create a literary work

Number correct _____ (total 10)

Number correct in unit _____ (total 65)

The Last Word

Writing

Visionary is a term used to describe someone with ideas that often do not seem practical at the time. However, sometimes the ideas of such imaginative thinkers prove to be quite practical. Visionaries include explorers such as Columbus and inventors such as the Wright brothers. Use an encyclopedia or some other reference work to gather information about a person who has been considered a visionary—past or present. Write a short biographical sketch about the person.

Speaking

How does *technology* affect the way we live? What *technological* changes have occurred during your lifetime? Ask your parents these same questions. Share your findings with the class.

Group Discussion

Spend ten minutes listing as many uses as you can think of for fresh water. After making the list, try to determine the amount of water (in gallons) you use each day. The class should then determine the total number of gallons of water used by the entire class each day. Discussion might center on ways to conserve the use of fresh water. Attempt to calculate how much water could be saved by the class in a day.

UNIT 15

1. anticipate (an tis′ ə pāt′) v.
2. approximate (ə präk′ sə mit) adj.
   (-māt′) v.
3. ascertain (as′ ər tān′) v.
4. contemplation (kän təm plā′ shən) n.
5. contemporary (kən tem′ pə rer′ ē) n.,
   adj.
6. continuous (kən tin′ yoo wəs) adj.
7. effect (ə fekt′, i-) n.
8. emotion (i mō′ shən) n.
9. extinct (ik stinkt′) adj.
10. indefinite (in def′ ə nit) adj.
11. mere (mir) adj.
12. perpendicular (pur pən dik yə lər) adj.
13. perpetual (pər pech′ oo wəl) adj.
14. philosopher (fi läs′ ə fər) n.
15. plunge (plunj) n., v.
16. reflection (ri flek shən) n.
17. species (spē′ shēz, -sēz) n.
18. surplus (sur′ plus, -pləs) adj., n.
19. testify (tes′ tə fī′) v.
20. vast (vast, väst) adj.

Inferring Meaning from Context

For each sentence write the letter of the word or phrase that is closest to the meaning of the italicized word. Use context clues to help you determine the correct answer. (For information about how context helps you understand vocabulary, see pages 1–5.)

_____ 1. We were over forty-five minutes late for our appointment with Mr. Rivera because we did not *anticipate* a traffic jam on the expressway.
a. encounter b. follow c. intermingle with d. expect

_____ 2. Because of the delays caused by the snowstorm, only *approximate* times for the arrival of the planes were given.
a. exact b. optimistic c. rigid d. estimated

_____ 3. "Spies" from other companies tried to *ascertain* our new formula.
a. find out b. abandon c. dismiss d. ignore

_____ 4. For hours, Sherlock Holmes sat in deep *contemplation* analyzing clues.
a. thought b. mystery c. convalescence d. relaxation

_____ 5. Because my cousin Elizabeth is *my contemporary*, we are taking several of the same classes.
a. my relative b. a person about the same age c. my neighbor
d. an intruder

_____ 6. Day and night, a *continuous* stream of fans arrived at the star's home.
a. sophisticated b. constant c. mournful d. sufficient

_____ 7. Our daily watering had a healthy *effect* on the willow tree.
  a. result   b. appraisal   c. intent   d. hindrance

_____ 8. Displaying great *emotion*, Robert broke into tears in the middle of his speech.
  a. prominence   b. moderation   c. theory   d. feeling

_____ 9. Many people believe that unless the hunting of whales stops, these creatures will soon become *extinct*.
  a. dangerously overpopulated   b. militant   c. hazardous
  d. no longer in existence

_____ 10. Raphael's plans for the weekend were *indefinite* because he had not found out yet whether he had to work at the pizzeria.
  a. sensible   b. unimportant   c. mysterious   d. uncertain

_____ 11. Joan of Arc was *a mere* child when she led French troops to victory.
  a. an ignorant   b. a pessimistic   c. a spoiled   d. nothing more than a

_____ 12. The two lines in the letter *T* are *perpendicular*.
  a. zig-zagged   b. at a 45-degree angle   c. exactly parallel
  d. at a right angle

_____ 13. A *perpetual* flame burns day and night at the grave of John F. Kennedy.
  a. formal   b. temporary   c. permanent   d. periodical

_____ 14. The main activity of a *philosopher* is contemplating the meaning of life.
  a. person who studies ideas   b. person who studies birds   c. gift-giver
  d. wise administrator

_____ 15. All the members of the gym class *plunged*, one by one, into the icy swimming pool.
  a. seeped   b. evolved   c. dived   d. expired

_____ 16. Jane studied her *reflection* in the mirror.
  a. determination   b. reputation   c. image   d. deficiencies

_____ 17. Many *species* of plants, including palms, ferns, and fruit trees, grow on the island.
  a. stems   b. features   c. kinds   d. correlations

_____ 18. Because of *a surplus* of peanut butter, the grocer lowered the price.
  a. an abundance   b. an avoidance   c. a depletion in the supply
  d. a new brand

_____ 19. George had to be sworn in before he could *testify* in court.
  a. make innovations   b. state falsehoods   c. observe procedures
  d. give evidence

_____ 20. The forest was so *vast* that we could not begin to estimate its size.
  a. sparse   b. enormous   c. typical   d. mottled

Number correct _____ (total 20)

159

Part B   Target Words in Reading and Literature

You should now have a general idea of the meaning of each target word. Refine your understanding by examining the shades of meaning the words have in the following excerpt.

Niagara Falls

Abraham Lincoln

Although Abraham Lincoln did not leave a great deal of his writing for us to read, the writing that does exist shows that he was a person of great insight. What follows is a thoughtful description of Niagara Falls, written in 1848.

Niagara Falls! By what mysterious power is it that millions and millions are drawn from all parts of the world to gaze upon Niagara Falls? There is no mystery about the thing itself. Every **effect** is just what any intelligent person, knowing the causes, would **anticipate**, without seeing it. If the water moving onward in a great river reaches a point where there is a **perpendicular** jog, of a hundred feet in descent, in the bottom of the river—it is plain that the water will have a violent and **continuous plunge** at that point. It is also plain that the water, thus plunging, will foam, and roar, and send up a mist, continuously, in which, during sunshine, there will be **perpetual** rainbows. The **mere** physical characteristic of Niagara Falls is only this. Yet this is really a very small part of that world's wonder. Its power to excite **reflection** and **emotion** is its great charm. The geologist will demonstrate that the plunge, or fall, was once at Lake Ontario, and has worn its way back to its present position; he will **ascertain** how fast it is wearing now, and so get a basis of determining how long it has been wearing back from Lake Ontario, and finally demonstrate by it that this world is at least fourteen thousand years old. A **philosopher** of a slightly different turn will say Niagara Falls is only the lip of the basin out of which pours all the **surplus** water which rains down on two or three hundred thousand square miles of the earth's

5

10

15

surface. He will estimate with **approximate** accuracy that five hundred
thousand tons of water falls with its full weight a distance of a hundred feet each   20
minute—thus exerting a force equal to the lifting of the same weight, through
the same space, in the same time. And then the further reflection comes that
this **vast** amount of water, constantly pouring down, is supplied by an equal
amount constantly lifted up, by the sun; and still he says, if this much is lifted up,
for this one space of two or three hundred thousand square miles, an equal   25
amount must be lifted for every other equal space; and he is overwhelmed in the
contemplation of the vast power the sun is constantly exerting in the quiet,
noiseless operation of lifting water up to be rained down again.

But still there is more. It calls up the **indefinite** past. When Columbus first
sought this continent—when Christ suffered on the cross—when Moses led   30
Israel through the Red Sea—nay, even, when Adam first came from the hand of
his Maker—then as now, Niagara was roaring here. The eyes of that **species** of
extinct giants, whose bones fill the mounds of America, have gazed on Niagara,
as ours do now. **Contemporary** with the whole race of people, and older than
the first, Niagara is strong, and fresh today as ten thousand years ago. The
mammoth and mastodon—now so long dead that fragments of their monstrous
bones alone **testify** that they ever lived, have gazed on Niagara. In that
long—long time, never still for a single moment. Never dried, never froze, never
slept, never rested.

Refining Your Understanding

For each of the following questions, consider how the target word is used in the
passage. Write the letter of the word or phrase that best completes the sentence.

_____ 1. Since Lincoln tells us that rainbows around Niagara Falls are *perpetual*
(line 9) when the sun is shining, we can assume that   a. we would have
a fifty-fifty chance of seeing a rainbow at Niagara   b. we will always see
a rainbow on a sunny day   c. rainbows seldom appear at Niagara.

_____ 2. When Lincoln mentions Niagara's power to "excite *reflection*" (line 11),
he means that, while watching Niagara, people   a. start cheering
b. meet other people   c. think more deeply.

_____ 3. Lincoln uses an older meaning of the word *philosopher* (line 16). He uses
philosopher to mean   a. a tourist   b. a scientist   c. a novelist.

_____ 4. Lincoln suggests that the scientifically minded person is caught up in
contemplation (line 27), meaning the person is   a. frozen by fear
b. wrapped in thought   c. prevented by the railings from looking
closer.

_____ 5. When Lincoln writes that Niagara Falls is "*contemporary* (line 34) with
the whole race of people," he means that   a. Niagara Falls, like a
human, races to its destination   b. Niagara Falls fits in well with the
modern spirit   c. these Falls have existed in every age of humankind.

Number correct _____ (total 5)

Part C Ways to Make New Words Your Own

This section presents a variety of reinforcement activities that will help you make the words part of your permanent vocabulary.

Using Language and Thinking Skills

True-False Decide whether each statement is true (**T**) or false (**F**).

_____ 1. A *philosopher* is likely to spend much time reflecting.

_____ 2. "Maybe" is an *indefinite* answer.

_____ 3. The population of a small town is usually *vast*.

_____ 4. If you buy a *surplus* of something, you buy only what you need.

_____ 5. An *approximate* answer to the math problem 10 x 17 is 170.

_____ 6. An *extinct* animal lives in the present.

_____ 7. A *perpetual* flame sometimes gets extinguished.

_____ 8. Abraham Lincoln was a *contemporary* of Julius Caesar.

_____ 9. If you *anticipate* an event, you can usually prepare for it.

_____ 10. During a blackout, electrical power is supplied in a *continuous* manner.

Number correct _____ (total 10)

Classifying Target Words Some words are frequently used in discussing certain subjects. For instance, *orbit* is a word you would expect to find in a book about space. Match each target word with the book in which you would expect to find that word. Write the letter of the matching target word in the blank.

Book Titles	**Target Words**
_____ 1. *Romance Forever*	a. contemporary
_____ 2. *Exploring Space Through a Telescope*	b. emotion
_____ 3. *The Witness Speaks*	c. extinct
_____ 4. *Luscious Meals from Leftovers*	d. perpendicular
_____ 5. *Geometry for Everyone*	e. philosopher
_____ 6. *Daring Divers of the Deep*	f. plunge
_____ 7. *What Does Life Mean?*	g. species
_____ 8. *Who Can Save the Whales?*	h. surplus
_____ 9. *Animals of the Desert*	i. testify
_____ 10. *Today's Fashion Fads*	j. vast

Number correct _____ (total 10)

Practicing for Standardized Tests

Synonyms Write the letter of the word that is closest in meaning to the capitalized target word.

_____ 1. PERPETUAL: (A) acute (B) continuous (C) brief (D) extinct (E) rigid

_____ 2. TESTIFY: (A) declare (B) unify (C) urge (D) astonish (E) align

_____ 3. ANTICIPATE: (A) prefer (B) prevent (C) await (D) foster (E) surprise

_____ 4. SURPLUS: (A) surrender (B) shortage (C) surprise (D) arc (E) oversupply

_____ 5. EMOTION: (A) contemplation (B) reflection (C) compression (D) passion (E) obstacle

_____ 6. INDEFINITE: (A) rigid (B) distinct (C) acute (D) unclear (E) tedious

_____ 7. SPECIES: (A) system (B) type (C) brain (D) slave (E) extinction

_____ 8. ASCERTAIN: (A) do (B) assemble (C) affect (D) utilize (E) determine

_____ 9. EFFECT: (A) result (B) essence (C) reflection (D) compress (E) effort

_____ 10. MERE: (A) pious (B) integral (C) only (D) naive (E) vast

Number correct _____ (total 10)

Spelling and Wordplay

Word Maze Find and circle each target word in this maze.

S	A	S	C	E	R	T	A	I	N	D	K	P	E	A
U	N	E	F	F	E	C	T	E	S	T	I	F	Y	R
O	T	J	P	H	I	L	O	S	O	P	H	E	R	C
U	I	N	D	E	F	I	N	I	T	E	S	A	A	O
N	C	R	W	T	D	Q	O	C	L	E	L	Q	R	N
I	I	T	C	A	K	S	N	T	I	U	X	M	O	T
T	P	M	P	M	Z	I	U	C	C	I	E	Y	P	E
N	A	E	H	I	T	A	E	I	B	R	M	S	M	M
O	T	R	V	X	E	P	D	J	V	Y	O	S	E	P
C	E	E	E	O	S	N	F	V	A	S	T	U	T	L
Z	R	E	F	R	E	O	T	A	O	N	I	L	N	A
Y	N	Q	B	P	G	H	D	W	N	H	O	P	O	T
W	A	G	R	P	L	U	N	G	E	Z	N	R	C	I
V	L	E	L	A	U	T	E	P	R	E	P	U	E	O
Z	P	R	E	F	L	E	C	T	I	O	N	S	O	N

anticipate
approximate
ascertain
contemplation
contemporary
continuous
effect
emotion
extinct
indefinite
mere
perpendicular
perpetual
philosopher
plunge
reflection
species
surplus
testify
vast

Part D Related Words

A number of words are closely related to the target words you have studied. Use your knowledge of the target words and of word parts to help you determine the meaning of these words. (For information about word parts analysis, see pages 6–12.) Learning related words not only expands your vocabulary; it helps you learn the target word more thoroughly.

1. anticipation (an tis′ ə pā′ shən) n.
2. approximation (ə präk′ sə mā′ shən) n.
3. contemplate (kän′ təm plāt′) v.
4. continuity (kän′ tə noo′ ə tē, -nyoo-) n.
5. emotional (i mō′ shən 'l) adj.
6. extinction (ik stink′ shən) n.
7. perpetuate (pər pech′ oo wāt′) v.
8. perpetuity (pʉr′ pə too′ ə tē) n.
9. philosophical (fil′ ə säf′ i k'l) adj.
10. philosophy (fi läs′ ə fē) n.
11. reflect (ri flekt′) v.
12. reflective (ri flek′ tiv) adj.
13. testimony (tes′ tə mō′ nē) n.
14. vastness (vast′ nes, väst′-) n.

Understanding Related Words

Finding Examples In the blank write the letter of the related word that best fits the situation expressed in the sentence.

a. anticipation
b. approximation
c. perpetuate
d. emotional
e. extinction
f. continuity
g. philosophy
h. reflect
i. testimony
j. vastness

_____ 1. The sad movie brought tears to the eyes of the people in the audience.

_____ 2. Kathy could hardly wait for the ski trip.

_____ 3. Randy has always believed that life must be lived to the fullest.

_____ 4. The farmer estimated that the next town was about twenty miles down the road, give or take a few miles.

_____ 5. The last saber-toothed tiger died many years ago.

_____ 6. The pond was so still that it acted as a giant mirror.

_____ 7. The feud was kept alive by the almost daily insults the two families shouted at each other.

_____ 8. On the stand, the witness gave her account of the accident.

_____ 9. Wheat fields in the Dakotas seem to reach to the ends of the earth.

_____ 10. On a film set, one assistant's job is to make sure the props are in the right places and that one scene flows evenly into the next.

Number correct _____ (total 10)

Turn to **The Prefix *ex-*** on pages 194–195 of the **Spelling Handbook**. Read the rules and complete the exercises provided.

Words Often Confused Although not related in structure, the word *affect* is often confused with the target word *effect*. Despite the similarity in spelling and pronunciation, there is a distinct difference in the use and meaning of these two words.

  affect: to influence or have an effect on someone or something (v.)
  effect: the result of something (n.)

By remembering the part of speech and the definition of each of these words, you can use them correctly. A memory aid may also help you: *affect* means "action"; *effect* means "end result."

Choose the correct word—*affect* or *effect*—for each of the following sentences. Write the word in the blank. You may have to add word endings.

_____ 1. The _?_ of the Gulf Stream are felt all the way across the Atlantic Ocean in England.

_____ 2. The horror movie did not _?_ Emily.

_____ 3. A scientist demonstrated that smoking _?_ the lungs.

_____ 4. Another possible _?_ of smoking is heart disease.

_____ 5. The new law _?_ all immigrants who have entered Canada since 1974.

_____ 6. Receiving an *A* on his test had a positive _?_ on Juan.

_____ 7. The _?_ spring has on people's moods is obvious.

_____ 8. We hope that studying will _?_ our grades.

_____ 9. The slightest amount of pollen in the air _?_ Ted.

_____ 10. Sympathy had no _?_ on Jim.

                    Number correct _____ (total 10)

Word's Worth: contemplate

Contemplate means "to gaze at" or "to consider seriously." This word derives from the religious practices of ancient Rome. The Latin *con* + *templum* meant "at temple." The word referred to what the priests did as they said their prayers and looked for sacred signs.

Analyzing Word Parts

The Latin Prefix *per-* This prefix comes from the Latin word *per*, meaning "through." Words with this prefix convey a sense of permanence or persistence—note that these two words themselves begin with *per-*. In what sense do *perpetual* and its related words *perpetuate* and *perpetuity* exhibit this meaning? In the following exercise, match the words on the right with their definitions on the left. Write the corresponding letter in the blank. Use a dictionary if necessary.

_____ 1. to spread through

_____ 2. a thorough alteration or change

_____ 3. a plant that lasts for more than one year

_____ 4. to poke holes through something

_____ 5. to follow a course of action in spite of opposition

_____ 6. to bring about or carry out (as a crime)

_____ 7. to become aware of through one of the senses

_____ 8. lying while under oath

_____ 9. to urge or convince

_____ 10. to cause to last indefinitely

a. perceive

b. perennial

c. perforate

d. perjury

e. permeate

f. permutation

g. perpetrate

h. perpetuate

i. persevere

j. persuade

Number correct _____ (total 10)

Number correct in unit _____ (total 85)

The Last Word

Writing

Make a list of the various types of *emotions* people can have. Then choose one that you have experienced. Write a short composition describing what caused you to feel the way you did.

Speaking

Use an encyclopedia to gather information about an unusual *species* of animal. Present this information to the class in a short speech.

Group Discussion

Sometimes an animal becomes *extinct* due to natural causes. In other cases, however, humans may have caused a particular species to become extinct. What species have disappeared? Why did it happen? Are there cases in which extinction could have been avoided? If so, what could have been done? Cite examples of animals today whose existence is threatened. What might be done to save them?

UNIT 16: Review of Units 13–15

Part A Review Word List

Unit 13 Target Words

1. acknowledge
2. advocate
3. confrontation
4. equality
5. foster
6. indictment
7. intend
8. mentality
9. militant
10. naive
11. pessimistic
12. pious
13. prominence
14. propel
15. prophet
16. puritanical
17. rigid
18. shrewd
19. sophisticated
20. strategist

Unit 13 Related Words

1. acknowledgment
2. confront
3. equalize
4. equation
5. equilibrium
6. indict
7. intention
8. naiveté
9. pessimism
10. piety
11. prominent
12. prophecy
13. prophetic
14. propulsion
15. rigidity
16. shrewdness
17. sophistication
18. strategy

Unit 14 Target Words

1. accessible
2. acute
3. appreciate
4. arid
5. biosphere
6. compose
7. compression
8. distill
9. document
10. expeditious
11. innovative
12. obstacle
13. quantity
14. tabular
15. technological
16. tedious
17. trace
18. utilize
19. visionary
20. yield

Unit 14 Related Words

1. access
2. appreciation
3. aridity
4. composer
5. composition
6. compress
7. dispose
8. documentary
9. expedite
10. expose
11. impose
12. innovation
13. sphere
14. technical
15. technology
16. utility
17. utilization
18. visualize

Unit 15 Target Words

1. anticipate
2. approximate
3. ascertain
4. contemplation
5. contemporary
6. continuous
7. effect
8. emotion
9. extinct
10. indefinite
11. mere
12. perpendicular
13. perpetual
14. philosopher
15. plunge
16. reflection
17. species
18. surplus
19. testify
20. vast

Unit 15 Related Words

1. anticipation
2. approximation
3. contemplate
4. continuity
5. emotional
6. extinction
7. perpetuate
8. perpetuity
9. philosophical
10. philosophy
11. reflect
12. reflective
13. testimony
14. vastness

Inferring Meaning from Context

For each sentence select the word or phrase that is closest to the meaning of the italicized word.

_____ 1. The *acute* pain in Mona's back needs prompt attention.
   a. bewildering   b. preceding   c. sharp   d. coarse

_____ 2. Sammy had difficulty showing his *appreciation* after being elected class president.
   a. theory   b. attribute   c. quality   d. thankfulness

_____ 3. By multiplying the number of rows by the number of seats in each row, we attempted to *ascertain* the size of the audience.
   a. formalize   b. determine   c. glamorize   d. compare

_____ 4. Mary *composed* her essay after analyzing the themes in the novel.
   a. put together   b. took apart   c. exposed   d. utilized

_____ 5. The quiet mornings on the lake were times of *contemplation* for Jack.
   a. emotion   b. fishing   c. convalescence   d. thinking

_____ 6. You and your classmates are *contemporaries*.
   a. friends   b. composers   c. people of about the same age   d. people who are together briefly

_____ 7. Amy could not *document* what happened after the accident, so we could only guess at the real truth.
   a. show proof of   b. comprehend   c. acknowledge   d. anticipate

_____ 8. Because he rarely showed any *emotion*, the coach's tears at the award ceremony surprised everyone.
   a. confidence   b. feeling   c. contemplation   d. anticipation

_____ 9. Most of the animals that lived before the Ice Age are now *extinct*.
   a. documented   b. restricted to certain areas   c. perpetual   d. no longer in existence

_____ 10. The ambassador tried to *foster* a better relationship between the two countries.
   a. encourage   b. incense   c. ascertain   d. restrict

_____ 11. The boy was too *naive* to recognize the danger in the streets.
   a. pious   b. sophisticated   c. shrewd   d. unsophisticated

_____ 12. After hearing the evidence, the grand jury handed down *an indictment*.
   a. a correlation   b. an inspection   c. an accusation   d. a contemplation

_____ 13. Anna, a *shrewd* debater, won first place in the competition.
   a. perpetual   b. pessimistic   c. clever   d. prophetic

_____ 14. We discovered a *species* of flowering shrub that had never been seen.
   a. type   b. surplus   c. multitude   d. trace

_____ 15. Inventors such as Thomas Edison are often characterized as *visionaries*.
a. likely suitors   b. foreseers of the future   c. militants   d. people with good eyesight.

Number correct _____ (total 15)

Using Review Words in Context

Using context clues, determine which word from the word list fits in each blank. Each word may be used once.

acknowledge	documented	intended	pessimistic	strategy
acute	emotional	mere	prominence	utilized
continuously	expeditiously	obstacles	shrewdly	vast

Race to the Pole

Who would be the first explorer to reach the South Pole? Would it be Robert F. Scott, an English explorer and naval captain who had gained _____ during an earlier exploration of Antarctica? Or would it be Roald Amundsen, a Norwegian explorer who had _____ to go to the North Pole until he learned that Robert Peary had reached there first? In October 1911, Scott's team and Amundsen's team set out for the South Pole.

The _____ of both men was to travel across the Ross Ice Shelf straight to the Pole. The _____ before them were brutal—the cold, the wind, the _____ , icy landscape. To haul the supplies, Scott _____ ponies and also sleds with motors. However, the motors and the ponies soon broke down, and Scott's men had to pull the sleds themselves.

_____ , Amundsen had chosen a somewhat shorter route, and he relied on hardy Eskimo dogs to pull the sleds. Amundsen's journey progressed _____ ; Scott's team struggled.

After an exhausting, eighty-one day trek, Scott's group reached the Pole. The Norwegian flag was already there. Scott and his men had to _____ defeat in an _____ , bitterly disappointing moment.

Amundsen and his men returned safely, but Scott's luck took another bad turn. The weather conditions deteriorated, the wind and cold becoming _____ . Running low on supplies, Scott and his other four men grew increasingly _____ about their chances of survival. They finally all perished during a blizzard that raged _____ for nine days. They had a _____ eleven miles to go to their destination. Later, Captain Scott's diary was found, which _____ this tragic expedition.

Number correct _____ (total 15)

Part B   Review Word Reinforcement

Using Language and Thinking Skills

Finding Examples Write the letter of the situation or subject that best demonstrates the meaning of each word.

_____ 1. **obstacle**
   a. A tree lies across the road following a storm.
   b. Pam gives free piano lessons to all the children in the neighborhood.
   c. A plane gets the message that all is clear for a landing.

_____ 2. **vast**
   a. Only fifty-two people watched the Tuesday basketball game.
   b. Africa's Sahara desert covers three million square miles.
   c. Donna observed the amoeba under the microscope.

_____ 3. **shrewd**
   a. Marcia convinces the store manager to reduce the price of a jacket.
   b. George cuts down the cherry tree and tells his father about it.
   c. Mary fails to study and thereby fails her driver's test.

_____ 4. **advocate**
   a. Billy tries to get public support for the new hockey rink.
   b. The country of Mexico is made up of twenty-nine states.
   c. Conrad thinks about giving his opinion, but says nothing.

_____ 5. **compose**
   a. Some students wore funny costumes to school on Halloween.
   b. Irving Berlin created some of America's best-loved songs.
   c. Bart spent the day taking apart an old shed.

_____ 6. **trace**
   a. Sherlock Holmes notices a bit of red clay on the suspect's shoes.
   b. Two football teams swarm onto the field to play the final game.
   c. Mr. Friedland's law office represents the Sugar Island group.

_____ 7. **confrontation**
   a. In just one hour Florence painted the entire front of the house.
   b. Jenny and Chris argued at the Bum Steer burger shop.
   c. Bill sat by the bend in the river.

_____ 8. **emotion**
   a. I have never seen Mr. Loeb arrive late for class.
   b. Jackie gets tears in her eyes when she thinks of sad times.
   c. I tend to get seasick very easily.

_____ 9. **extinct**
   a. The smell coming from the garbage dump was overwhelming.
   b. Mastodons did not survive the Ice Age.
   c. We watched the flock of geese fly over our heads.

_____ 10. **yield**

    a. Margaret wrote a best-selling novel about growing up on a farm.

    b. Ms. Astrup took her pupils to the museum's dinosaur exhibit.

    c. Rita Martinez finally gave in to her students' request to have class outside.

Number correct _____ (total 10)

Practicing for Standardized Tests

Antonyms Write the letter of the word that is most nearly the opposite in meaning to the review word.

_____ 1. ACCESSIBLE: (A) easy (B) affluent (C) unreachable (D) mottled (E) attainable

_____ 2. ACUTE: (A) dull (B) astonished (C) pretty (D) unified (E) sharp

_____ 3. COMPRESS: (A) expand (B) expend (C) expire (D) expose (E) extinct

_____ 4. CONFRONT: (A) bewilder (B) encounter (C) release (D) persuade (E) avoid

_____ 5. EQUALITY: (A) balance (B) difference (C) quality (D) freedom (E) integration

_____ 6. PERPETUAL: (A) peaceful (B) tedious (C) pessimistic (D) temporary (E) comparable

_____ 7. RIGID: (A) flexible (B) hard (C) arid (D) mere (E) pious

_____ 8. SURPLUS: (A) excess (B) enough (C) shortage (D) perpetuity (E) approximation

_____ 9. TEDIOUS: (A) temporary (B) grave (C) exciting (D) inferior (E) boring

_____ 10. VAST: (A) potent (B) naive (C) continuous (D) small (E) aligned

Number correct _____ (total 10)

Synonyms Write the letter of the word that is nearest in meaning to the review word.

_____ 1. APPRECIATE: (A) maintain (B) exhaust (C) despise (D) foster (E) value

_____ 2. EFFECT: (A) cause (B) result (C) destruction (D) persuasion (E) disclosure

_____ 3. EMOTION: (A) feeling (B) confrontation (C) psychology (D) reflection (E) derision

_____ 4. INDICT: (A) intrude (B) distinguish (C) charge (D) exclaim (E) expedite

_____ 5. MERE: (A) enough   (B) much   (C) luxuriant   (D) urgent   (E) only

_____ 6. OBSTACLE: (A) organism   (B) obstruction   (C) qualification
(D) deficiency   (E) dullness

_____ 7. REFLECTION: (A) image   (B) restriction   (C) vista   (D) iridescence
(E) estimation

_____ 8. VISIONARY: (A) symbol   (B) specialist   (C) prophet   (D) summit
(E) historian

_____ 9. FOSTER: (A) nurture   (B) propel   (C) kill   (D) visualize
(E) confront

_____ 10. INTENDED: (A) enclosed   (B) unplanned   (C) bored
(D) prophesied   (E) meant

Number correct _____ (total 10)

Analogies Write the letter of the pair of words that best completes each analogy.

_____ 1. CONTEMPORARY : PAST ::   (A) first : last   (B) fashionable : stylish
(C) current : former   (D) ancestral : future   (E) late : early

_____ 2. COMPOSER : SYMPHONY ::   (A) weaver : cloth   (B) indictment :
jury   (C) doctor : patient   (D) technology : factory   (E) intruder : theft

_____ 3. TEDIOUS : INTERESTING ::   (A) strict : puritanical   (B) arid : dry
(C) pessimistic : optimistic   (D) naive : innocent   (E) fierce : ferocious

_____ 4. APPRECIATION : GRATITUDE ::   (A) love : hatred   (B) business : profit
(C) success : failure   (D) advocate : supporter   (E) testimony : jury

_____ 5. PURITANICAL : RIGID ::   (A) careless : cautious   (B) diagonal :
perpendicular   (C) punctual : tidy   (D) militant : aggressive
(E) important : trivial

_____ 6. MILLION : QUANTITY ::   (A) conservation : wilderness   (B) teacher
: school   (C) course : student   (D) aridity : dryness   (E) anger: emotion

_____ 7. CONTEMPLATE : MIND ::   (A) sleep : dream   (B) exercise : body
(C) testify : lawyer   (D) talk : speech   (E) revolve : axis

_____ 8. PIOUS : CHURCH ::   (A) lawless : courtroom   (B) mental : stress
(C) studious : school   (D) brilliant : sun   (E) tall : athlete

_____ 9. REFLECTION : MIRROR ::   (A) anchor : ship   (B) catapult : force
(C) document : history   (D) prediction : prophet   (E) expedition :
adventure

_____ 10. MAP : STRATEGIST ::   (A) servitude : slave   (B) reflection :
contemplation   (C) prophet : future   (D) mechanism : propeller
(E) compass : navigator

Number correct _____ (total 10)

Spelling and Wordplay

Middle Message Fill in the blanks with the letters of target words in Units 13, 14, and 15. The letters appearing in the middle box will spell out a helpful message for spellers.

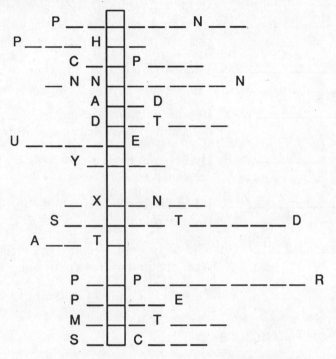

Number correct _____ (total 15)

Part C   Related Words Reinforcement

Using Related Words

Sentence Completion Write the related word from the list that best completes each sentence.

access	expedite	testimony
composer	naiveté	vastness
documentary	prominent	visualize
equilibrium		

_____ 1. Riding on the Flying Saucer at the carnival had affected Kari's _?_ ; afterward, she was so dizzy that she couldn't stand up.

_____ 2. Mrs. Myers decided to _?_ the registration procedure by passing out forms to everyone who was waiting in line.

173

_____ 3. Seeing the ? of the Pacific Ocean made me appreciate the courage of the early explorers.

_____ 4. The filmmakers were preparing a ? based on the life of Corazon Aquino and her rise to power in the Philippines.

_____ 5. ? citizens and others not as well-known expressed their concern over the mayor's housing plan.

_____ 6. Because of construction, there was only limited ? to the expressway.

_____ 7. Because of Karin's eyewitness ?, the police were able to determine which driver was at fault.

_____ 8. He believed every word anybody told him. Never have I seen such ?.

_____ 9. Johann Sebastian Bach was the ? of the Brandenberg Concertos.

_____ 10. The night before each track meet, Ellen would ? her race, imagining herself running perfectly.

Number correct _____ (total 10)

Reviewing Word Structure

The Word Parts _equ_, _pos_, and _per_ Complete each of the following sentences with a word from the Review List (page 167). Follow the directions in parentheses, using a word with an _equ_ or _pos_ root or a _per_ prefix.

_____ 1. That reporter's article did much to ? the corruption in our city government. (Use a word with the root _pos_.)

_____ 2. My grandfather has been trying to make a ? motion machine, a device that once set in motion, would continue forever. (Use a word with the prefix _per_.)

_____ 3. Carl Friedrich Gauss was the first mathematician to solve a geometric ? by using algebra. (Use a word with the root _equ_.)

_____ 4. The United States decided to ? trade restrictions on several Japanese products. (Use a word with the root _pos_.)

_____ 5. The mountain trail ended at a cliff, a ? drop of four hundred feet to the river below. (Use a word with the prefix _per_.)

Number correct _____ (total 5)

Number correct in unit _____ (total 100)

Vocab Lab 4

FOCUS ON: **History**

The following terms are frequently used in the field of history and in political news reports. Become familiar with these terms to enhance your reading comprehension.

apartheid (ə pärt′ hāt, -hīt) n.   an official policy of strict racial segregation and discrimination toward blacks and other non-white people. ● The government of South Africa is known for its policy of *apartheid*.

aristocracy (ar′ ə stäk′ rə sē) n.   those who are considered superior to others, such as a ruling class of nobility or an elite group within a profession. ● Many members of the French *aristocracy* were put to death during the Reign of Terror.

bourgeoisie (boor′ zhwä zē′) n.   the middle class of a society, neither aristocrats nor manual laborers. ● The leaders of the Russian revolution came from the *bourgeoisie*, not from the proletariat.

cartel (kär tel′) n.   a business or political group with a common cause. ● Representatives of a European banking *cartel* met to set interest rates.

fascism (fash′ iz′m) n.   a system of strict government control of industry and labor characterized by nationalism, racism, and militarism. ● Benito Mussolini, the founder of *fascism* in Italy, believed that everyone should work but that no one should work against the state.

humanism (hyo͞o mə niz′m) n.   the condition or quality of being human; the study of human beings, their art, and their culture. ● With its increased activity in art and classical learning, the Renaissance marked the revival of *humanism*.

imperialism (im pir′ ē əl iz′m) n.   the policy of extending the rule of one country over other countries and colonies. ● The British Empire's doctrine of *imperialism* included ruling America until 1776.

junta (ho͞on′ tə, jun′ tä) n.   a military or political group formed to hold power after a revolution. ● The *junta* now in power consists of three generals.

martyr (mär′ tər) n.   one who is tortured or killed because of his or her beliefs. ● Joan of Arc, who was burned at the stake, is considered a *martyr* in France.

nationalism (nash′ ə n′l iz′m) n.   a devotion to, and the promoting of, one's own nation.   ● A strong spirit of *nationalism* aided India in gaining independence.

Populist (päp′ yə list) n.   a member of a former American political party formed in 1891 and known as the Populist (or People's) party. The Populist party supported labor and agricultural interests. ● The Midwestern senator's ideas echoed the *Populists* of the 1800's.

proletariat (prō′ lə ter′ ē ət) n.   the social class with the lowest status, usually the working class.   ● During the Industrial Revolution, the *proletariat* often endured poor living conditions.

reparation (rep′ ə rā shən) n.   the repair or righting of a wrong. The plural word *reparations* refers to damages paid to another country by a defeated country.

• At the end of World War I, England demanded *reparations* from Germany.

socialist (sō′ shəl ist) n. one who believes in a type of government where the community owns and operates the means of production and distribution and where a private individual may only work for, but not own, any of these means. • Russia is an example of a *socialist* state.

totalitarian (tō tal′ ə ter′ ē ən) adj. a government controlled by one political party that allows no opposing political groups to exist. • *Animal Farm*, a novel by George Orwell, depicts the evils of a *totalitarian* state.

Sentence Completion In the blank write the word from the list that best completes the sentence.

_____ 1. Karl Marx used the word _?_ to refer to employers.

_____ 2. In order to rebuild after a war, the victorious country frequently demands _?_ from the defeated country.

_____ 3. Following the revolution, a _?_ made up of four popular leaders took control of the government.

_____ 4. American labor and agricultural interests joined together in the 1800's to form a group called the _?_.

_____ 5. The Afrikaner word _?_, meaning "apartness," aptly depicts the racial segregation policy in South Africa.

_____ 6. Of those who would die for a cause, Napoleon said, "It is the cause and not merely the death that makes a _?_."

_____ 7. In ancient Greece, the _?_, or assemblies of nobles, made governmental decisions and eventually replaced the kings.

_____ 8. The union leader, a hero of the _?_, asked his fellow workers to band together to challenge the management.

_____ 9. Great Britain's policy of _?_ led to extensive colonization and the saying "the sun never sets on the British Empire."

_____ 10. The international _?_ of oil producers agreed to regulate oil prices for the following year.

_____ 11. The dictator maintained _?_ rule by putting down all other political parties.

_____ 12. The philosophers of that period believed in _?_; they studied the classics and challenged religious doctrines.

_____ 13. Under Franco's dictatorship, Spain followed the nationalistic and militaristic practices of _?_.

_____ 14. Capitalism, where individuals can own and operate businesses for profit, stands in direct contrast to _?_.

_____ 15. Extreme patriotism is sometimes called _?_.

Number correct _____ (total 15)

FOCUS ON: *Pun Fun*

A pun is a play on words. The humor of a pun comes from the fact that words with the same sound or spelling may have different meanings. There are various kinds of puns. The three most common draw on words with multiple meanings, homonyms, and sayings. Study them—for the pun of it.

Multiple Meanings

The simplest pun works on the double meaning of a word. Consider the following examples:

Real estate agents know *a lot*.
My students have *class*.
A farmer *is outstanding in his field*.

If you just groaned, you are in good company. That is the way the ancient Greeks and Romans showed their appreciation for a good pun.

Creating Puns with Multiple Meanings Each of the following words has multiple meanings. Choose three of the words and, using their multiple meanings, create a pun for each. Then, choosing different words, write two original puns.

Example
court: In the annual Judges vs. Lawyers basketball game, Judge Lopez adjourned the *court* with his winning free throw in the final second.

face   foot   needle   pupil   run

1. _____

   _____

2. _____

   _____

3. _____

   _____

4. _____

   _____

5. _____

   _____

Homonyms

Homonyms, words that have the same pronunciation but different meanings, form the basis for many other puns. Study these examples:

Homonyms: need, knead   The bankrupt baker *kneaded* some dough.

Homonyms: pane, pain   The window maker's job is a real *pain*.

Creating Puns with Homonyms Each of the following items gives a pair of homonyms and an occupation. Incorporate the occupation and one of the homonyms to form a pun. Use the examples above as models.

6. scent, cent - florist: _____

7. deer, dear - hunter: _____

8. sale, sail - sailor: _____

9. profit, prophet - banker: _____

10. bough, bow - tree climber: _____

Pun Games

Puns can be the basis of inventive games. Sometimes the humor is based on sound-alike word relationships similar to homonyms or the slight alteration of one or two words. One game involves imaginary book titles and authors.

At the Eleventh Hour by Justin Time   *Crime Pays* by Robin Banks

Another game has you think of suitable verbs for the firing of workers in various jobs.

A writer is described. (de - *scribed*)   A musician is disconcerted. (dis - *concerted*)

Creating Puns Create five of your own puns for either of the games above.

11. _____

12. _____

13. _____

14. _____

15. _____

Number correct _____ (total 15)

Number correct in Vocab Lab _____ (total 30)

Units 1–8   *Standardized Vocabulary Test*

The following questions test your comprehension of words studied in the first half of the book. Test questions have been written in a way that will familiarize you with the typical standardized test format. As on most standardized vocabulary tests, questions are divided into the following categories: **antonyms, analogies,** and **sentence completion**.

Antonyms

Each question below consists of a word in capital letters followed by five words that are lettered. In the blank, write the letter of the word that is most nearly *opposite* in meaning to the word in capital letters. Since some of the questions require you to distinguish fine shades of meaning, consider all the choices before deciding which is best.

_____ 1. ABUNDANT: (A) wordy   (B) resigned   (C) misleading
(D) insufficient   (E) ample

_____ 2. DISCLOSE: (A) shut   (B) join   (C) conceal   (D) examine   (E) advance

_____ 3. UNCHARTED: (A) explored   (B) understood   (C) drawn
(D) blank   (E) incomplete

_____ 4. OMINOUS: (A) hopeful   (B) inflexible   (C) scarce   (D) lengthy
(E) threatening

_____ 5. SUPPLE: (A) inedible   (B) inflexible   (C) poisonous
(D) unmanageable   (E) agile

_____ 6. GRAVE: (A) carefree   (B) deep   (C) healthy   (D) serious   (E) contagious

_____ 7. CRITICAL: (A) superficial   (B) angry   (C) understandable
(D) eager   (E) insignificant

_____ 8. MATURE: (A) elderly   (B) feeble   (C) uncertain   (D) undeveloped
(E) strong

_____ 9. TACITURN: (A) intelligent   (B) talkative   (C) polished
(D) aggressive   (E) silent

_____ 10. POTENT: (A) tasty   (B) weak   (C) unsteady   (D) strong   (E) open

_____ 11. MYSTERIOUS: (A) sad   (B) fuzzy   (C) obvious   (D) feminine
(E) humorous

_____ 12. IMMODERATE: (A) outdated   (B) fashionable   (C) modern
(D) controlled   (E) cheerful

_____ 13. COARSE: (A) smooth   (B) evil   (C) hoarse   (D) course   (E) logical

_____ 14. DEPLETE: (A) dig   (B) restore   (C) float   (D) begin   (D) complete

_____ 15. UNERRINGLY: (A) anxiously (B) decoratively (C) mistakenly (D) intentionally (E) unconsciously

_____ 16. URGE: (A) discover (B) discourage (C) shout (D) request (E) punish

_____ 17. RESTORATIVE: (A) expensive (B) reestablished (C) careful (D) imaginary (E) destructive

_____ 18. DERIDE: (A) praise (B) dismount (C) encourage (D) complain (E) lie

_____ 19. EXPANSE: (A) enclosure (B) solidity (C) existence (D) development (E) prominence

_____ 20. TREACHEROUS: (A) dangerous (B) obtainable (C) harmless (D) disrespectful (E) careless

Number correct _____ (total 20)

Analogies

Each question consists of a pair of words followed by five pairs of words that are lettered. In the blank, write the letter of the pair that *best* expresses a relationship similar to that expressed in the original pair.

_____ 1. COMPLEX : SIMPLE :: (A) visible : clear (B) difficult : easy (C) popular : populous (D) approachable : friendly (E) supple : soft

_____ 2. APPRAISAL : JEWELRY :: (A) sparkle : diamond (B) market : value (C) progress : test (D) cost : estimate (E) evaluation : applicant

_____ 3. DRIZZLE : INTERMITTENTLY :: (A) hail : icily (B) sunshine : brightly (C) clouds: puffily (D) downpour: continuously (E) forecast: predictably

_____ 4. CONIFER : TREE :: (A) poem : literature (B) ocean : continent (C) mass : multitude (D) appraisal : praise (E) venture : adventure

_____ 5. EXPAND : DEPLETE :: (A) hide : mask (B) disclose : reveal (C) understand : undertake (D) inflate : expand (E) exhaust : invigorate

_____ 6. FEW : MULTITUDE :: (A) division : separation (B) gang : group (C) friend : acquaintance (D) horde : crowd (E) frenzy : calm

_____ 7. ILLNESS : CONVALESCENCE :: (A) quarantine : contagion (B) wedding : honeymoon (C) doctor : hospital (D) cure : treatment (E) injury : accident

_____ 8. ENACT : REPEAL :: (A) propose : marry (B) veto : approve (C) authorize : endorse (D) digest : eat (E) motivate : encourage

_____ 9. LAWLESS : LAWFUL :: (A) criminal : legitimate (B) judicial : judgmental (C) individual : solitary (D) useful : applicable (E) illegal : illegitimate

_____ 10. DEPLETE : RESOURCES ::   (A) erode : water   (B) waste : savings
(C) restore : energy   (D) cultivate : land   (E) complete : research

_____ 11. COMPASS : NAVIGATE ::   (A) pencil : educate   (B) ship : sink
(C) computer : travel   (D) calculator : compute   (E) thermometer:
convalesce

_____ 12. AMPLIFY : VOLUME ::   (A) magnify : size   (B) listen : video
(C) orchestrate : music   (D) add : addition   (E) shout : mumbling

_____ 13. GOSSIP : REPUTATION ::   (A) enemies : lies   (B) friendship :
secrets   (C) pollution : atmosphere   (D) hate : guilt   (E) glamour :
fame

_____ 14. SNEEZE : SPONTANEOUS ::   (A) anger : neutral   (B) habit :
unconscious   (C) stutter : deliberate   (D) break : effortless   (E) art :
typical

_____ 15. MAELSTROM : TREACHEROUS ::   (A) image : ominous
(B) automobile : tragic   (C) interior : external   (D) poison : noxious
(E) aperture : solid

Number correct _____ (total 15)

Sentence Completion

Each sentence below has one or two blanks. Each blank indicates that
something has been omitted. Beneath the sentence are five words or sets of words
that are lettered. In the blank at the left of each sentence, write the word or set
of words that *best* fits the meaning of the sentence.

_____ 1. The delivery boy _?_ as he carried the _?_ package along the trail.
(A) ventured . . . magnificent   (B) floundered . . . cumbersome
(C) proclaimed . . . ominous   (D) scuttled . . . grave
(E) adapted . . . potent

_____ 2. A robin is often said to _?_ the arrival of spring.
(A) enact   (B) mar   (C) venture   (D) herald   (E) overtake

_____ 3. In the show _?_ actors and actresses performed a funny _?_.
(A) compulsive . . . proclamation   (B) tragic . . . alignment
(C) multiple . . . enclosure   (D) pervasive . . . transition
(E) comic . . . spectacle

_____ 4. In recent years, many rural people have _?_ to the cities.
(A) navigated   (B) migrated   (C) envisioned   (D) scuttled
(E) conveyed

_____ 5. Through the _?_ at the mouth of the cave, Dr. Livingston caught a
glimpse of an _?_ resembling a prehistoric man.
(A) aperture . . . image   (B) corridor . . . illusion   (C) horde . . .
intruder   (D) organism . . . enclosure   (E) spectacle . . . assembly

_____ 6. The Presidential candidates were overwhelmed with questions from a _?_ of reporters.
(A) disclosure   (B) specialist   (C) migration   (D) horde   (E) transition

_____ 7. As an _?_ darkness replaced the noontime sun, a mood of tension _?_ the crowd of spectators.
(A) intruding . . . dissolved   (B) uncharted . . . heralded
(C) abundant . . . disclosed   (D) exhausting . . . involved
(E) ominous . . . pervaded

_____ 8. Unauthorized or _?_ use of certain common medications can be _?_ to one's health.
(A) compulsive . . . restorative   (B) urgent . . . indifferent   (C) lawless
. . . tragic   (D) immoderate . . . hazardous   (E) typical . . . treacherous

_____ 9. A weekend escape to the quaint, _?_ village was _?_ to the frazzled city dwellers.
(A) picturesque . . . restorative   (B) typical . . . advertised
(C) mysterious . . . suitable   (D) interior . . . comical
(E) glamorous . . . mystifying

_____ 10. Advertisements tend to _?_ even the most unexciting products and make them seem desirable.
(A) envision   (B) glamorize   (C) expose   (D) restore   (E) deride

Number correct _____ (total 10)

Number correct in Units 1–8 test _____ (total 45)

The following questions test your comprehension of words studied in the second half of the book. As on most standardized vocabulary tests, questions are divided into the following categories: **antonyms, analogies,** and **sentence completion**.

Antonyms

Each question below consists of a word in capital letters followed by five lettered words or phrases. Choose the word or phrase that is most nearly *opposite* in meaning to the word in capital letters. Since some of the questions require you to distinguish fine shades of meaning, consider all the choices before deciding which is best.

_____ 1. SUBTLE: (A) elusive   (B) superior   (C) extensive   (D) hard
(E) obvious

_____ 2. NAIVE: (A) sophisticated   (B) cooperative   (C) native   (D) innocent
(E) uninformed

_____ 3. EXPAND: (A) inject   (B) respond   (C) repeat   (D) disband
(E) contract

_____ 4. AFFLUENT: (A) simple   (B) unusual   (C) flowing   (D) poor
(E) prosperous

_____ 5. MILITANT: (A) peaceable   (B) defiant   (C) inadequate   (D) reliable
(E) combative

_____ 6. GRACEFUL: (A) clinging   (B) unnatural   (C) mature   (D) clumsy
(E) glamorous

_____ 7. STREWN: (A) stricken   (B) planted   (C) gathered   (D) antagonized
(E) lost

_____ 8. INTERMINGLE: (A) deliver   (B) separate   (C) mix   (D) depend
(E) relate

_____ 9. TRACE: (A) flank   (B) shortage   (C) surplus   (D) heritage
(E) alternate

_____ 10. EXULTANT: (A) spacious   (B) ecstatic   (C) tedious   (D) sad
(E) portable

_____ 11. EQUALITY: (A) formality   (B) impartiality   (C) unfairness
(D) inactivity (E) equilibrium

_____ 12. CONFINE: (A) release   (B) condemn   (C) distill   (D) restrict
(E) study

_____ 13. RIGID: (A) incorrect   (B) flexible   (C) angry   (D) forgiving
(E) cautious

_____ 14. SERVITUDE: (A) slavery   (B) impatience   (C) freedom   (D) hunger
(E) politeness

_____ 15. SHREWD: (A) loud   (B) vicious   (C) gentle   (D) naive   (E) insane

_____ 16. PESSIMISTIC: (A) hopeful   (B) neat   (C) timely   (D) tearful
(E) clever

_____ 17. ARID: (A) open   (B) remote   (C) damp   (D) breathless   (E) humorous

_____ 18. INNOVATIVE: (A) poetic   (B) affirmative   (C) extravagant
(D) explosive   (E) old-fashioned

_____ 19. PERPETUAL: (A) imperfect   (B) short-lived   (C) animalistic
(D) intense   (E) sharp-sighted

_____ 20. VAST: (A) broken   (B) limited   (C) unclear   (D) interior   (E) free

Number correct _____ (total 20)

Analogies

Each question consists of a pair of words followed by five pairs of words that are
lettered. In the blank, write the letter of the pair that *best* expresses a relationship
similar to that expressed in the original pair.

_____ 1. SIGNATURE : DOCUMENT ::   (A) write : paper   (B) person :
government   (C) trademark : product   (D) pen : scroll   (E) officer : law

_____ 2. CONFINE : FREE ::   (A) import : export   (B) confuse : confound
(C) curtail : limit   (D) barter : trade   (E) brace : strengthen

_____ 3. STRATOSPHERE : ROCKET ::   (A) history : art   (B) ocean :
submarine   (C) beliefs : proof   (D) myth : science   (E) racer : bicycle

_____ 4. AFFLUENT : MILLIONAIRE ::   (A) handy : finger   (B) interior :
shell   (C) landlocked : island   (D) earthly : comet   (E) poor : peasant

_____ 5. INTEGRAL : ESSENTIAL ::   (A) mysterious : misunderstood
(B) subordinate : secondary   (C) forgettable : memorable
(D) secure : temporary   (E) intentional : accidental

_____ 6. LIQUID : SEEP ::   (A) car : park   (B) snake : hiss   (C) river : flow
(D) restriction : prevent   (E) ice : solidify

_____ 7. OVERLOOK : ANTICIPATE ::   (A) govern : administer   (B) foretell :
foresee   (C) ignore : predict   (D) cancel : expire   (E) ascertain : discover

_____ 8. MILK : CURDLE ::   (A) affluence : save   (B) lamp : light   (C) iron :
rust   (D) egg : scramble   (E) cream : drink

_____ 9. PROMOTION : STATUS ::   (A) conformity : individuality   (B) new
clothes : appearance   (C) reformation : prisoner   (D) tiny room :
expansion   (E) deformity : movement

_____ 10. COTTON : TEXTILE ::   (A) pine : wood   (B) salad : lettuce
(C) horse : farm   (D) surplus : shortage   (E) desert : sand

_____ 11. NEGLECTED : SORDID ::   (A) maintained : tidy   (B) clean : dirty
(C) careful : overlooked   (D) sloppy : worse   (E) neat : spotless

_____ 12. PROPHET : FUTURE ::   (A) saint : religion   (B) expense : savings
(C) doctor : medication   (D) historian : past   (E) parent : child

_____ 13. STUBBORN : YIELD ::   (A) strong : bully   (B) withdrawn : socialize
(C) angry : fight   (D) eager : begin   (E) hungry : cook

_____ 14. QUANTITY : SEVERAL ::   (A) building : architecture   (B) freedom :
equality   (C) quality : excellence   (D) twins : two   (E) speech :
communication

_____ 15. MILITANT : AGGRESSIVE ::   (A) peaceful : nonviolent   (B) victimized
: victorious   (C) selfish : conceited   (D) dull : pyrotechnic   (E) neutral :
one-sided

Number correct _____ (total 15)

Sentence Completion

Each sentence below has one or two blanks. Each blank indicates that
something has been omitted. Beneath the sentence are five words or sets of words
that are lettered. In the blank, write the letter of the word or set of words that
best fits the meaning of the sentence.

_____ 1. Through the study of fossils, scientists can reconstruct models of _?_ that
have become _?_.
(A) documents . . . contemporary   (B) obstacles . . . technological
(C) prophets . . . legendary   (D) species . . . extinct
(E) systems . . . strewn

_____ 2. The witness was asked to _?_ about his involvement in the case.
(A) testify   (B) yield   (C) acknowledge   (D) comprehend   (E) visualize

_____ 3. Scientists studying the planet's _?_ have confirmed the _?_ of many
fascinating organisms.
(A) reflection . . . expansion   (B) equality . . . status
(C) biosphere . . . existence   (D) system . . . traces
(E) stratosphere . . . mobility

_____ 4. In order to make public places _?_ to handicapped persons, _?_ such as
steps and narrow doorways must be eliminated.
(A) effective . . . compressions   (B) accessible . . . obstacles
(C) sophisticated . . . confrontations   (D) specific . . . effects
(E) continuous . . . systems

_____ 5. Because the heat was so _?_, an air-conditioned arena was chosen for the
concert.
(A) mobile   (B) intense   (C) bizarre   (D) subtle   (E) intermingled

_____ 6. Scientists proved to be <u>?</u> when they predicted a <u>?</u> of food.
   (A) visionary . . . surplus   (B) contemporary . . . quantity
   (C) inheritable . . . restriction   (D) related . . . luxury
   (E) prominent . . . system

_____ 7. The cake recipe should <u>?</u> twelve servings.
   (A) intend   (B) curdle   (C) compose   (D) yield   (E) compress

_____ 8. Because it receives little rain, a desert is <u>?</u>.
   (A) tedious   (B) pessimistic   (C) level   (D) arid   (E) vast

_____ 9. The new voter registration <u>?</u> promises <u>?</u> to all citizens.
   (A) restriction . . . unpredictability   (B) system . . . equality
   (C) theory . . . quantity   (D) strategy . . . appreciation
   (E) document . . . servitude

_____ 10. Keeping taxes low while providing good services is a <u>?</u> problem in city
   management.
   (A) perpetual   (B) mysterious   (C) visionary   (D) formal
   (E) pessimistic

Number correct _____ (total 10)

Number correct in Units 9–16 test _____ (total 45)

SPELLING HANDBOOK

Knowing the meanings of words is essential to using language correctly. However, another important skill is knowing how to spell the words you use.

Almost everyone has at least some problems with spelling. If you have trouble spelling, you might be encouraged to know that many others like you have learned to avoid spelling errors by following these suggestions:

1. **Proofread everything you write.** Everyone occasionally makes errors through carelessness or haste. By carefully reading through what you have written, you will catch many of your errors.

2. **Look up difficult words in a dictionary.** If you are not sure about the spelling of a word, don't guess at it. Take the time to look up the word.

3. **Learn to look at the letters in a word.** Learn to spell a word by examining various letter combinations contained in the word. Note the prefix, suffix, or double letters. Close your eyes and visualize the word. Then write the word from memory. Look at the word again to check your spelling.

4. **Pronounce words carefully.** It may be that you misspell certain words because you do not pronounce them correctly. For example, if you write *probly* instead of *probably*, it is likely that you are mispronouncing the word. Learning how to pronounce words, and memorizing the letter combinations that create the sounds, will improve your spelling.

5. **Keep a list of your "spelling demons."** Although you may not think about it, you *do* correctly spell most of the words you use. It is usually a few specific words that give you the most trouble. Keep a list of the words you have trouble spelling, and concentrate on learning them. Also, look for patterns in the words you misspell and learn those patterns.

6. **Use memory helps, called mnemonic devices, for words that give you trouble.** *Stationery* has *er* as in *letter;* there is *a rat* in *separate; Wednesday* contains *wed*.

7. **Learn and apply the rules given in this section.** Make sure you understand these rules. Then practice using them until they become automatic.

Words with Prefixes

The Addition of Prefixes

A prefix is a group of letters added to the beginning of a word to change its meaning. When a prefix is added to a base word, the spelling of the base word remains the same. (For further information about word parts, see pages 6-12.)

con- + junction = conjunction   ex- + port = export
dis- + solve = dissolve   de- + hydrate = dehydrate
re- + cycle = recycle   in- + visible = invisible

A prefix can be added to a root as well as to a base word. A root is a word part that cannot stand alone; it must be joined to other parts to form a word. A root can be joined with many different prefixes to form words with different meanings. **However, the spelling of the prefix and the root remains the same.**

pro- + trude = protrude   per- + sist = persist
in- + trude = intrude   re- + sist = resist

Exercise A Add the prefixes as indicated and write the new word.

1. dis- + close   = _____

2. ad- + venture   = _____

3. pro- + claim   = _____

4. un- + consciousness   = _____

5. en- + counter   = _____

6. sub- + merge   = _____

7. de- + form   = _____

8. un- + desirable   = _____

9. in- + dependent   = _____

10. cor- + relation = _____

Number correct _____ (total 10)

Exercise B Complete each sentence with two words from the following list that have the same root.

composed	disclose	expend	import	involved
constrict	efficiency	export	inclined	reclined
deficiency	enclosed	exposed	inspect	respected
depend	evolved	exterior	interior	restriction

1. Although the _____ of the house looked old and weatherworn, its _____ was freshly painted and filled with modern furniture.

2. The guard _____ Dr. Khan's sense of privacy and did not _____ her briefcase.

3. Japan can _____ compact cars but must _____ oil from other countries.

4. Matthew _____ an essay that _____ the dangers of contact sports.

5. In first aid class, the health teacher placed a _____ on the use of tourniquets, which might _____ students' blood vessels unnecessarily.

6. You can _____ on Hal to _____ whatever effort is required to complete the task.

7. _____ with the job application form, Agnes found a statement asking her to _____ what she was paid at her last summer job.

8. The longer she _____ on the couch, the more Marion felt _____ to stay there.

9. The problem of litter in the parks _____ over a period of months until concerned citizens became _____ in finding a solution.

10. A lack of _____ in test-taking is often due to a _____ in organization.

Number correct _____ (total 20)

The Prefix ad-

When some prefixes are added to certain words, the spelling of the prefix changes. The prefix ad- changes in the following cases to create a double consonant:

ac- before c	ag- before g	an- before n	ar- before r	at- before t
af- before f	al- before l	ap- before p	as- before s	

Examples:

ad- + celerate = accelerate   ad- + pall = appall
ad- + fluent = affluent   ad- + rest = arrest
ad- + gressin = aggression   ad- + sure = assure
ad- + locate = allocate   ad- + sign = assign
ad- + nulment = annulment   ad- + tain = attain

Exercise Add the prefix *ad-* to each of the roots or base words below. Change the spelling of the prefix as appropriate, and write the word.

1. *ad-* + praisal   = _____

2. *ad-* + proach   = _____

3. *ad-* + complish   = _____

4. *ad-* + semble   = _____

5. *ad-* + nounce   = _____

6. *ad-* + cuse   = _____

7. *ad-* + proximate = _____

8. *ad-* + cessible   = _____

9. *ad-* + rive   = _____

10. *ad-* + firm   = _____

11. *ad-* + count   = _____

12. *ad-* + leviate   = _____

13. *ad-* + test   = _____

14. *ad-* + fix   = _____

15. *ad-* + ray   = _____

16. *ad-* + preciate   = _____

17. *ad-* + gravation = _____

18. *ad-* + cumulate   = _____

19. *ad-* + literation = _____

20. *ad-* + nex   = _____

21. *ad-* + lege   = _____

22. *ad-* + celerator = _____

23. *ad-* + fliction   = _____

24. *ad-* + tribute   = _____

25. *ad-* + fect   = _____   Number correct _____ (total 25)

The Prefix com-

The spelling of the prefix *com-* does not change when it is added to roots or to words that begin with the letters *m*, *p*, or *b*.

com- + mon = common   *com-* + ponent = component
com- + municate = communicate   *com-* + bat = combat

The prefix *com-* changes to *con-* when added to roots or words that begin with the letters *c*, *d*, *g*, *j*, *n*, *q*, *s*, *t*, or *v*.

com- + dition = condition   *com-* + vert = convert
com- + nect = connect   *com-* + cert = concert

The prefix *com-* changes to *col-* when added to roots or words that begin with the letter *l*, to create a double consonant.

com- + lect = collect   *com-* + lide = collide

The prefix *com-* changes to *cor-* when added to roots or words beginning with *r*, to create a double consonant.

com- + relation = correlation   *com-* + rupt = corrupt

Exercise A Add the prefix *com-* to each of the roots or base words below. Change the spelling of the prefix as appropriate, and write the word.

1. *com-* + laborate = _____

2. *com-* + strict = _____

3. *com-* + tact = _____

4. *com-* + bine = _____

5. *com-* + scious = _____

6. *com-* + gregation = _____

7. *com-* + jure = _____

8. *com-* + duct = _____

9. *com-* + respondent = _____

10. *com-* + valescence = _____

11. *com-* + merce = _____

12. *com-* + pression = _____

13. *com-* + cede = _____

14. *com-* + league = _____

15. *com-* + quer = _____

Number correct _____ (total 15)

Exercise B Find the misspelled word in each group. Write the word correctly.

_____ 1. conmence
continuous
conduct
concurrent

_____ 2. conrode
concentration
confound
congeal

_____ 3. corrugate
corroborate
corvey
corrosion

_____ 4. comlate
commotion
compass
combustion

_____ 5. compile
composure
contribute
conplain

_____ 6. consign
commission
comsider
commercial

_____ 7. concert
confide
conceal
conlision

_____ 8. conpose
companion
corrugate
confirm

_____ 9. corprehension
compact
conquest
collapse

_____ 10. commit
concise
comtemporary
conclude

Number correct _____ (total 10)

The Prefix *in-*

The spelling of the prefix *in-* does not change, except in the following cases:

(a) The prefix *in-* changes to *im-* when added to roots or words beginning with *m*, *p*, or *b*.

in- + moderate = immoderate   *in-* + position = imposition
in- + mature = immature   *in-* + becile = imbecile

(b) The prefix *in-* changes to *il-* when added to roots or words beginning with *l*, to create a double consonant.

in- + legal = illegal   *in-* + lusion = illusion

(c) The prefix *in-* changes to *ir-* when added to roots or words beginning with *r*, to create a double consonant.

in- + regular = irregular   *in-* + rational = irrational

Exercise A Add the prefix *in-* to each of the roots or base words below. Change the spelling of the prefix as appropriate, and write the word.

1. *in-* + mobilize   = _____

2. *in-* + legible   = _____

3. *in-* + relevant   = _____

4. *in-* + lustrate   = _____

5. *in-* + mortal = _____

6. *in-* + volve = _____

7. *in-* + herit = _____

8. *in-* + tend = _____

9. *in-* + luminate = _____

10. *in-* + definite = _____

11. *in-* + literate = _____

12. *in-* + port = _____

13. *in-* + reparable = _____

14. *in-* + genious = _____

15. *in-* + partial = _____

16. *in-* + logical = _____

17. *in-* + mobilize = _____

18. *in-* + resistible = _____

19. *in-* + patient = _____

20. *in-* + migration = _____ Number correct _____ (total 20)

Exercise B Find the misspelled word in each group. Write the word correctly.

_____ 1. incriminate
inmaterial
incur
inquire

_____ 2. immediate
imnovative
impossible
imbalance

_____ 3. inspection
intent
inrigation
incline

_____ 4. independent
inlicit
interior
inherit

_____ 5. inlegal
illusion
imprint
integrate

_____ 6. involuntary
indeed
indebted
inpulsive

_____ 7. irconceivable
irreverent
irresponsible
irradiate

_____ 8. implore
imlustration
impending
impair

_____ 9. immodest
imstruct
irrigate
incriminate

_____ 10. imsignificant
impeach
intrude
imposter

Number correct _____ (total 10)

The Prefix ex-

The spelling of the prefix *ex-* does not change when it is added to roots or to words beginning with vowels or with the consonants *p, t, h,* or *c*.

ex- + press = express   ex- + ception = exception
ex- + tinct = extinct   ex- + it = exit
ex- + hausted = exhausted ex- + ample = example

Exception: *Ex-* becomes *ec-* before *c* in the word *eccentric*.

The prefix *ex-* changes to *ef-* when added to roots or words beginning with *f*.

ex- + fort = effort   ex- + fect = effect

The prefix *ex-* changes to *e-* before most other consonants.

ex- + motion = emotion   ex- + vaporate = evaporate
ex- + rosion = erosion   ex- + lection = election

No common English words begin with the letters *exs*. When the prefix *ex-* is joined to roots that begin with the letter *s*, the *s* is dropped.

ex- + sert = exert   ex- + sist = exist

Exercise A Find the misspelled word in each group. Write the word correctly.

_____ 1. expect
                   expedition
                   elate
                   ellaborate

_____ 2. effective
                   extricate
                   exfusive
                   expound

_____ 3. extol
                   enormous
                   excursion
                   exvacuate

_____ 4. ehilarate
                   emergency
                   emit
                   exalt

_____ 5. excavate
                   exel
                   exchange
                   excite

_____ 6. exorbitant
                   examination
                   euberance
                   evaporate

_____ 7. expire
                   exsecute
                   extremely
                   exceed

_____ 8. exude
                   exrase
                   exasperate
                   extract

_____ 9. evasive
                   exhale
                   exhibit
                   exsistence

_____ 10. erupt
                    evolve
                    eplicate
                    exaggerate

Number correct _____ (total 10)

Exercise B Add the prefix *ex-* to each of the roots or base words below. Change the spelling of the prefix as appropriate, and write the word.

1. *ex-* + port = _____

2. *ex-* + volve = _____

3. *ex-* + ercise = _____

4. *ex-* + act = _____

5. *ex-* + pose = _____

6. *ex-* + merge = _____

7. *ex-* + longate = _____

8. *ex-* + radicate = _____

9. *ex-* + pend = _____

10. *ex-* + pansion = _____

11. *ex-* + spire = _____

12. *ex-* + terior = _____

13. *ex-* + lude = _____

14. *ex-* + ficiency = _____

15. *ex-* + ducate = _____

Number correct _____ (total 15)

Words with Suffixes

Words Ending in y

A suffix is a group of letters added to the end of a word that changes the word's meaning.

When a suffix is added to a word ending in *y* preceded by a consonant, the *y* is usually changed to *i*.

tragedy + *-es* = tragedies   mystery + *-ous* = mysterious
twenty + *-eth* = twentieth   merry + *-ly* = merrily
carry + *-er* = carrier

Exceptions:
(a) When *-ing* is added, the *y* does not change.

mystify + *-ing* = mystifying   unify + *ing* = unifying
carry + *-ing* = carrying   defy + *-ing* = defying

(b) In some one-syllable words the _y_ does not change.

dry + -_ness_ = dryness   shy + -_ness_ = shyness

When a suffix is added to a word ending in _y_ preceded by a vowel, the _y_ usually does not change.

array + -_ed_ = arrayed   destroy + -_er_ = destroyer
enjoy + -_able_ = enjoyable   joy + -_ful_ = joyful
Exceptions: day + -_ly_ = daily   gay + -_ly_ = gaily

Exercise A In these sentences, find each misspelled word and write the correct spelling on the line following the sentence. There may be more than one misspelled word in each sentence.

1. After attempting various strategyes, Laurie grabbed the magnifing glass out of the toddler's hand.

   _____

2. Todd did not feel qualified to comprehend the geometry theoryes.

   _____

3. True to the fortuneteller's prophecys, the man's future was marked by tragedis.

   _____

4. Why do television producers have a reputation for plaing "canned" laughter during comedies?

   _____

5. Feelings of inferiority and shiness typifyed my cousin's image of herself.

   _____

6. Deficiencyes in vitamins B and C lead to diseases such as beriberi and scurvy.

   _____

7. The heartyest laugh came from the woman wearing the luxurious mink stole.

   _____

Number correct _____ (total 10)

Exercise B Add the suffixes indicated, and write the word in the blank.

1. contemporary + -_es_ = _____

2. annoy + -_ed_   = _____

3. seventy + -_es_   = _____

4. majority + -_es_   = _____

5. joy + -_less_   = _____

6. involuntary + -_ly_ = _____

7. scary + -_est_   = _____

8. testify + -ed = _____

9. comply + -ing = _____

10. formality + -es = _____

11. multiplicity + -es = _____

12. qualify + -ing = _____

13. mystify + -er = _____

14. assembly + -es = _____

15. unify + -ing = _____

16. pray + -ed = _____

17. decay + -ing = _____

18. plenty + -ful = _____

19. clarify + -es = _____

20. magnify + -ed = _____

21. legendary + -ly = _____

22. rely + -able = _____

23. luxury + -ant = _____

24. classify + -ing = _____

25. testimony + -al = _____

Number correct _____ (total 25)

The Final Silent e

When a suffix beginning with a vowel is added to a word ending in a silent *e*, the *e* is usually dropped.

appraise + -al = appraisal　　retrieve + -er = retriever
circulate + -ion = circulation　　disclose + -ure = disclosure
retrieve + -al = retrieval　　dissolve + -ing = dissolving

When a suffix beginning with a consonant is added to a word ending in a silent *e*, the *e* is usually retained.

grave + -ness = graveness　　purpose + -less = purposeless
strange + -ly = strangely　　amaze + -ment = amazement
hope + -ful = hopeful　　whole + -ness = wholeness

Exceptions:

true + -ly = truly　　whole + -ly = wholly
argue + -ment = argument　　awe + -ful = awful

Exercise A In these sentences, find each misspelled word and write the correct spelling on the line following the sentence.

1. The expanseive Golden Gate Bridge is one of the most distinctive features of the San Francisco area.

   _____

2. The addition of spices can make bland-tasting food relatively desireable.

   _____

3. Each person in the assembly line has a specializeed job to perform.

   _____

4. The unitey of the workers should be important during the union negotiateions.

   _____

5. The jeweler made a determination as to the genuinness of the diamonds.

   _____

6. The literateure selections were made based on matureity and reading level.

   _____

7. Use your imagineation to write a truely creative story.

   _____

8. We have seen several groups of birds migrateing south in recent weeks.

   _____

9. We quietly peeked into the encloseure to see the newborn bear.

   _____

10. Ian's immoderate behavior was attributeable to his lack of sleep.

    _____

11. The clothes at the new store are moderatly priced.

    _____

12. Sam and Jason had an arguement concerning the estimatd profit they made.

    _____

13. The discontinueation of the professor's lectures was due to a lack of student responsivness.

    _____

14. Patti's involvment in the political campaign was time-consuming.

    _____

15. I'm afraid the expireation date for applying to colleges has passed.

    _____

Number correct _____ (total 20)

Exercise B Add the suffixes indicated, and write the new word in the blank.

1. expire + -ing = _____

2. image + -es = _____

3. relate + -ion = _____

4. discontinue + -ation = _____

5. convalesce + -ence = _____

6. attribute + -able = _____

7. symbolize + -ed = _____

8. coarse + -ly = _____

9. merge + -ing = _____

10. resemble + -ance = _____

11. coincide + -ence = _____

12. mature + -ation = _____

13. glamorize + -ation = _____

14. moderate + -ly = _____

15. advertise + -ment = _____

16. overtake + -en = _____

17. move + -ment = _____

18. horde + -ing = _____

19. evolve + -ing = _____

20. navigate + -ion = _____

21. grave + -ly = _____

22. accumulate + -ion = _____

23. adventure + -some = _____

24. restore + -ation = _____

25. intrude + -er = _____

Number correct _____ (total 25)

Doubling the Final Consonant

In one-syllable words that end with a single consonant preceded by a single vowel, double the final consonant before adding a suffix beginning with a vowel.

pin + -ing = pinning   beg + -ing = begging

Before adding a suffix beginning with a vowel to a word of two or more syllables, double the final consonant only if both of the following conditions exist:

1. The word ends with a single consonant preceded by a single vowel.
2. The word is accented on the second syllable.

pro pel′ + *-ed* = pro pelled′   re fer′ + *-al* = re fer′ ral

pro pel′ + *-er* = pro pel′ ler   per mit′ + *-ing* = per mit′ ting

com mit′ + *-ed* = com mit′ ted   de ter′ *-ence* = de ter′ rence

Note in the examples above that the syllable accented in the new word is the same syllable that was accented before adding the suffix.

If the newly formed word is accented on a different syllable, the final consonant is not doubled.

re fer′ *-ence* = ref′ er ence   pre fer′ + *-ence* = pref′ er ence

Exercise Each word below is divided into syllables. Determine which syllable in each word is accented, and insert the accent mark. Add the suffix indicated, noting whether or not the accent moves to a different syllable. Then write the new word. Repeat this procedure with the second suffix indicated.

Example: e mit′ + *-ed* = *emitted* + *-ing* = *emitting*

1. prof it + *-ed* = _____ + *-ing* = _____

2. a bet + *-ed* = _____ + *-ing* = _____

3. trans mit + *-ed* = _____ + *-ance* = _____

4. ad mit + *-ed* = _____ + *-ing* = _____

5. ab hor + *-ed* = _____ + *-ence* = _____

6. be gin + *-er* = _____ + *-ing* = _____

7. gov ern + *-ed* = _____ + *ing* = _____

8. con fer + *-ed* = _____ + *-ence* = _____

9. ex hib it + *-ed* = _____ + *-ing* = _____

10. com mit + *-ed* = _____ + *-ing* = _____

11. cor ral + *-ed* = _____ + *-ing* = _____

12. e quip + *-ed* = _____ + *-ing* = _____

13. in fer + *-ed* = _____ + *-ence* = _____

14. de liv er + *-ed* = _____ + *-ing* = _____

15. re mit + *-ed* = _____ + *-ance* = _____

Number correct _____ (total 30)

Exercise Add the suffixes indicated, and write the new word in the blank.

1. unravel + -ed = _____

2. put + -ing = _____

3. dispel + -ed = _____

4. control + -ing = _____

5. shrug + -ed = _____

6. abandon + -ing = _____

7. inherit + -ance = _____

8. transfer + -al = _____

9. tug + -ed = _____

10. defer + -ence = _____

Number correct _____ (total 10)

Words Ending in *ize* or *ise*

The suffix -*ize* is usually added to base words to form verbs meaning "to make or become."

neutral + -*ize* = neutralize (to make neutral)
memory + -*ize* = memorize (to make into a memory)

The -*ise* ending is less common. It is usually part of the base word itself rather than a suffix.

advertise   surprise   televise

Exercise Decide whether -*ize* or -*ise* should be added to each word or letter group. Then write the complete word in the blank.

1. special _____

2. adv _____

3. formal _____

4. exerc _____

5. commercial _____

6. critic _____

7. superv _____

8. modern _____

9. comprom _____

10. idol _____

11. magnet _____

12. organ _____

13. desp _____

14. dev _____

15. symbol _____

Number correct _____ (total 15)

The Suffix -ion

The -ion suffix changes verbs to nouns.

suggest + -ion = suggestion   separate + -ion = separation
discuss + -ion = discussion   migrate + -ion = migration
attract + -ion = attraction   immigrate + -ion = immigration

In the examples above, -ion is either added directly to the verb form, or the final *e* is dropped before -ion is added.

Some verbs when made into nouns have irregular spellings.

compose + -ion = composition   persuade + -ion = persuasion
assume + -ion = assumption   proclaim + -ion = proclamation

In the case of words that do not follow regular spelling patterns, you must memorize their spellings.

Exercise A Add -ion to each of the following words. Then write the new word.

1. inspect _____   9. compress _____

2. circulate _____   10. navigate _____

3. deplete _____   11. estimate _____

4. adopt _____   12. emigrate _____

5. sophisticate _____   13. transit _____

6. moderate _____   14. restrict _____

7. relate _____   15. profess _____

8. administrate _____

Number correct _____ (total 15)

Exercise B Each of the following nouns is formed by adding the -ion suffix to a verb. Write the verb from which the word was formed. Use a dictionary when needed.

1. intrusion _____   9. derision _____

2. descension _____   10. organization _____

3. imagination _____   11. composition _____

4. admission _____   12. expiration _____

5. expansion _____   13. propulsion _____

6. contraction _____   14. mobilization _____

7. qualification _____   15. proclamation _____

8. unification _____

Number correct _____ (total 15)

Other Spelling Problems

Words with *ie* and *ei*

When the sound is long *e* (*ē*), it is spelled *ie* except after *c*. If the vowel combination sounds like a long *a* (*ā*), spell it *ei*.

i **before** *e*

thief   grief   niece
chief   believe   relieve
yield   brief   fierce

except after *c*

ceiling   perceive   deceit
deceive   receive   receipt

or when sounded as *a*

neighbor   weigh   reign

Exceptions:

either   weird   seize   financier
neither   species   leisure

You can remember these words by combining them into the following sentence: *Neither financier seized either weird species of leisure.*

Exercise A In these sentences, find each misspelled word and write the correct spelling on the line following the sentence.

1. In his liesure time, Juan seized the opportunity to play ball.

   _____

2. There are many Christmas stories about Santa's sliegh being pulled by riendeer.

   _____

3. It was such a relief to retreive our cat from the animal shelter.

   _____

4. Neither the children nor the adults shreiked while the roller coaster was climbing the hill.

   _____

5. Ms. Parrish could not concieve of sewing a dress with so many different peices.

   _____

6. Abby's great acheivements in her field caused her to be concieted.

   _____

7. Janine was certain that she did not recieve a reciept for this piece of luggage.

   _____

8. Samuel shielded his identity by holding his handkercheif over his face.

   _____

9. The thief wieghed the worth of the necklace against his chances of being caught.

_____

10. The financeir was a wierd person who studied strange species.

_____

Number correct _____ (total 15)

Exercise B Fill in the blanks with *ie* or *ei*.

1. rec __ __ ve

2. br __ __ f

3. sl __ __ gh

4. y __ __ ld

5. f __ __ rce

6. p __ __ r

7. sh __ __ ld

8. n __ __ ce

9. bel __ __ f

10. __ __ ght

11. handkerch __ __ f

12. c __ __ ling

13. cash __ __ r

14. dec __ __ ve

15. r __ __ ndeer

Number correct _____ (total 15)

Words with the "Seed" Sound

One English word ends in *sede*:
supersede

Three words end in *ceed*:
exceed   proceed   succeed

All other words ending in the sound of *seed* are spelled *cede*:
accede   concede   precede   recede   secede

Exercise A In these sentences, find each misspelled word and write the correct spelling on the line following the sentence.

1. Before the Civil War, the Southern states proceded to secede from the Union.

_____

2. The referee had to intercede when the injured fighter refused to conceed.

_____

3. The procedes from the auction far exceeded our expectations.

_____

4. As the flood waters receeded, the rescue crews proceeded to look for stranded people.

_____

5. The professor announced that his present wishes will supercede all previous requests.

_____

6. According to the preseding announcement, management and the union are close to an agreement and will proceed to negotiate.

_____

7. Senator Lee acceded to be our candidate after Senator Turner's faction seceeded from our political party.

_____

8. My math teacher conceded that I could graduate even if I did not succede in his class.

_____

9. The teenagers receeded from the stage so that the concert could proceed.

_____

10. The apple picking, which preceeded making applesauce, went exceedingly well.

_____

Number correct _____ (total 10)

Exercise B Put a check by the five correctly spelled words below.

1. accede	_____	6. intercede	_____
2. excede	_____	7. prosede	_____
3. precede	_____	8. receed	_____
4. succede	_____	9. secede	_____
5. concede	_____	10. superseed	_____

Number correct _____ (total 10)

The Letter c

When the letter _c_ has a _k_ sound, it is usually followed by the vowels _a_, _o_, or _u_, or by any consonant except _y_.
_c_alendar   _c_ontinual   cir_c_ulate   predi_c_t

When the letter _c_ has an _s_ sound, it is usually followed by an _e_, an _i_, or a _y_.
des_c_end   differen_c_e   _c_irculate   _c_ycle

The Letter g

When the letter _g_ has a hard sound as in the word _go_, it is usually followed by the vowels _a_, _o_, or _u_, or by any consonant except _y_.
_g_arage   _g_ar_g_le   _g_oal   _g_uard

When the letter _g_ has a _j_ sound, it is usually followed by an _e_, an _i_, or a _y_.
_g_enuine   mer_g_e   ri_g_id   _g_ymnasium

Exceptions:
_g_iggle   _g_ill   _g_irl   _g_ive

Exercise A Decide if the *c* in each word below has a *k* sound or an *s* sound. Write *k* or *s* in the blank.

1. cumbersome _____
2. restriction _____
3. constantly _____
4. decimal _____
5. pictorial _____
6. caliber _____
7. recline _____
8. stricture _____

9. psychology _____
10. prophecy _____
11. ascend _____
12. faucet _____
13. precedent _____
14. encounter _____
15. suffice _____

Number correct _____ (total 15)

Exercise B Decide if the *g* in each word below has a soft *j* sound or a hard sound as in the word *go*. Write *j* or *go* in the blank.

1. glamorous _____
2. imagination _____
3. organism _____
4. signify _____
5. ingenuity _____
6. immigration _____
7. tragedy _____
8. plunge _____

9. legend _____
10. urge _____
11. plague _____
12. magnificent _____
13. integrate _____
14. guy _____
15. giraffe _____

Number correct _____ (total 15)

Exercise C Write the missing letter in each word.

1. imag __
2. trag __ c
3. mig __ ate
4. navig __ tion
5. asc __ rtain
6. g __ ave
7. ac __ nowledge
8. prec __ de

9. psycholog __
10. urg __ ncy
11. enc __ unter
12. c __ rcumstance
13. c __ ntinue
14. mag __ ify
15. g __ amor

Number correct _____ (total 15)

Spelling Review

Exercise A Add the prefix or suffix indicated, and write the new word.

1. *in-* + mobilize   = _____
2. *ad-* + tributable   = _____
3. *com-* + stitution   = _____
4. relate + *-ion*   = _____
5. *ad-* + proach   = _____
6. repute + *-able*   = _____
7. *un-* + consciousness   = _____
8. symbol + *-ize*   = _____
9. *dis-* + close   = _____
10. *ad-* + semble   = _____
11. *ex-* + volve   = _____
12. *in-* + port   = _____
13. mystify + *-ing*   = _____
14. exhaust + *-ion*   = _____
15. mere + *-ly*   = _____
16. *re-* + trieve   = _____
17. mature + *-ity*   = _____
18. *in-* + regular   = _____
19. involuntary + *-ly*   = _____
20. persuade + *-ion*   = _____

Number correct _____ (total 20)

Exercise B Three of the words in each row follow the same spelling pattern. Circle the word that does not follow that pattern.

1. irregular   immobile   imbecile   import
2. proceed   succeed   exceed   concede
3. heartiest   unified   mystifier   playful
4. admitting   abandoning   remitting   omitting

5. edition   evolve   elongate   expend

6. prediction   illusion   elevation   concentration

7. glamorize   advertise   specialize   symbolize

8. heritage   urge   plague   tragic

9. administration   navigation   direction   correlation

10. expansive   exposure   resembled   gravely

11. conceive   believe   shrieked   thief

12. compulsion   continue   constitution   convalesces

13. affection   attribute   acclaim   adhere

14. receipt   deceive   piece   perceive

15. movement   moderately   maturity   adventuresome

Number correct _____ (total 15)

Exercise C Find the misspelled words in these sentences and spell them correctly on the line after the sentence.

1. The teacher was concerned about John's inlegible handwriting.

_____

2. Dr. Washington's psychological approach to the problem was decieving.

_____

3. The espense of new uniforms forced many band members to reconsider wearing their old ones.

_____

4. Anna admitted her intention to get into mischeif.

_____

5. The new horror film promises to be terrifing.

_____

6. Greek tragedyes are usually part of the high-school English curriculum.

_____

7. The organization specialises in assisting the hearing impaired.

_____

8. Hannibal mobilised his troops in the Second Punic War.

_____

9. It is highly unnecessary to reserve a seat if one is returnning by train.

_____

10. The inregular behavior of the tides made swimming excedingly dangerous.

_____

11. Ida seized the opportunity to avoid an encounter with her old boyfreind.

_____

12. As the exspiration date neared, I became intensly nervous.

_____

13. Unity among the workers will help popularise their beliefs.

_____

14. My involvment in developing mechanicaly sound equipment has been constant.

_____

15. Let us try to adcumulate large quantities without hoardeing.

_____

Number correct _____ (total 20)

Exercise D Find the misspelled word in each group. Write the word correctly in the blank.

_____ 1. methodize
commercialize
surprise
specialise

_____ 2. deceive
efficient
mischeif
piece

_____ 3. intercede
proceed
secede
succede

_____ 4. advertise
afflict
acclaim
adcumulation

_____ 5. emigrateion
prediction
relation
conviction

_____ 6. communicate
compulsion
comvenience
combustion

_____ 7. incur
inspection
intrusion
inmobilize

_____ 8. advanceing
evolving
symbolizing
reclining

_____ 9. gravely
immoderately
involuntarily
heartyly

_____ 10. migration
discontinuation
expireation
restoration

Number correct _____ (total 10)

Number correct in unit _____ (total 460)

Commonly Misspelled Words

abbreviate
accidentally
achievement
all right
altogether
amateur
analyze
anonymous
answer
apologize
appearance
appreciate
appropriate
argument
arrangement
associate
awkward
bargain
beginning
believe
bicycle
bookkeeper
bulletin
bureau
business
calendar
campaign
candidate
certain
changeable
characteristic
column
committee
courageous
courteous
criticize
curiosity
cylinder
dealt
decision
definitely
dependent

description
desirable
despair
desperate
dictionary
different
disappear
disappoint
discipline
dissatisfied
efficient
eighth
eligible
eliminate
embarrass
emphasize
enthusiastic
environment
especially
exaggerate
exhaust
experience
familiar
fascinating
February
financial
foreign
fourth
fragile
generally
government
grammar
guarantee
guard
gymnasium
handkerchief
height
humorous
imaginary
immediately
incredible
influence

intelligence
knowledge
laboratory
lightning
literature
loneliness
marriage
mathematics
medicine
minimum
mischievous
missile
misspell
mortgage
municipal
necessary
nickel
ninety
noticeable
nuclear
nuisance
obstacle
occasionally
occur
opinion
opportunity
outrageous
parallel
particularly
permanent
permissible
persuade
pleasant
pneumonia
politics
possess
possibility
prejudice
privilege
probably
pronunciation
psychology

realize
recognize
recommend
reference
referred
rehearse
repetition
representative
restaurant
rhythm
ridiculous
sandwich
schedule
scissors
separate
sergeant
similar
sincerely
sophomore
souvenir
specifically
success
syllable
sympathy
symptom
temperature
thorough
throughout
together
tomorrow
traffic
tragedy
transferred
truly
Tuesday
twelfth
undoubtedly
unnecessary
vacuum
vicinity
village
weird

Commonly Confused Words

The following section lists words that are commonly confused and misused. Some of these words are homonyms, words that sound similar but have different meanings.   Study the words in this list and learn how to use them correctly.

accent (ak′ sent) n.—stress in speech or writing
ascent (ə sent′) n.—act of going up
assent (ə sent′) n.—consent; v.—to accept or agree

accept (ək sept′, ak-) v.—to agree to something or receive something willingly
except (ik sept′) v.—to omit or exclude; prep.—not including

adapt (ə dapt′) v.—to adjust, to make fitting or appropriate
adept (ə dept′) adj.—proficient
adopt (ə däpt′) v.—to choose as one's own, to accept

affect (ə fekt′) v.—to influence, to pretend
affect (af′ ekt) n.—feeling
effect (ə fekt′, i-) n.—result of an action
effect (ə fekt′, i-) v.—to accomplish or to produce a result

all ready adj.—completely prepared
already (ôl red′ ē) adv.—even now; before the given time

any way adj. (any) and n. (way)—in whatever manner
anyway (en′ ē wa′) adv.—regardless

appraise (ə prāz′) v.—to set a value on
apprise (ə prīz′) v.—to inform

bibliography (bib′ lē äg′ rə fē) n.—list of writings on a particular topic
biography (bī äg′ rə fē, bē-) n.—written history of a person's life

bizarre (bi zär′) adj.—odd
bazaar (bə zär′) n.—market, fair

coarse (kôrs) adj.—rough, crude
course (kôrs) n.—route, progression

costume (käs′ to͞om, -tyo͞om) n.—special way of dressing
custom (kus′ təm) n.—usual practice or habit

decent (dē′ s'nt) adj.—proper
descent (di sent′) n.—fall, coming down
dissent (di sent′) n.—disagreement; v.—to disagree

desert (dez′ ərt) n.—arid region
desert (di zʉrt′) v.—to abandon
dessert (di zʉrt′) n.—sweet course served at the end of a meal

device (di vīs′) n.—a contrivance
devise (di vīz′) v.—to plan

elusive (ə lōō′ siv) adj.—hard to catch or understand
illusive (i lōō′ siv) adj.—misleading, unreal

emigrate (em′ ə grāt′) v.—to leave a country and take up residence elsewhere
immigrate (im′ ə grāt′) v.—to enter a country to take up residence

farther (fär′ thər) adj.—more distant (refers to space)
further (fʉr′ thər) adj.—additional (refers to time, quantity, or degree)

flair (fler) n.—natural ability, knack for style
flare (fler) v.—to flame; to erupt; n.—a blaze of light

lay (lā) v.—to set something down or place something
lie (lī) v.—to recline; to tell untruths; n.—an untruth

moral (môr′ əl, mär′-) n.,—lesson; ethic; adj.—relating to right and wrong
morale (mə ral′, mô-) n.—mental state of confidence, enthusiasm

personal (pʉr′ s'n əl) adj.—private
personnel (pʉr sə nel′) n.—a body of people, usually employed in an organization

precede (pri sēd′) v.—to go before
proceed (prə sēd′, prō-) v.—to advance; to continue

profit (präf′ it) v. n.—to gain earnings; financial gain on investments
prophet (präf′ it) n.—predictor, fortuneteller

quiet (kwī′ ət) adj.—not noisy; n.—a sense of calm
quit (kwit) v.—to stop
quite (kwīt) adv.—very

step (step) n.—footfall; v.—to move the foot as in walking
steppe (step) n.—large, treeless plain

team (tēm) n.—group of people working together on a project
teem (tēm) v.—to swarm or abound

than (than, then; *unstressed* thən, thən) conj.—word used in comparison
then (then) adv.—at that time, next in order of time

thorough (thʉr′ ō, -ə) adj.—complete
through (thrōō) prep.—by means of, from beginning to end; adv.—in one side and out the other

Glossary

A

abundant (adj.) in plentiful supply; more than enough; p. 24. *Related word*: abundance; p. 31.

accessible (adj.) approachable; available; p. 148. *Related word*: access; p. 155.

acknowledge (v.) to admit the truth of something; to recognize (the authority or claims of); p. 137. *Related word*: acknowledgment; p. 144.

acute (adj.) serious; sharp; painful; p. 148.

adapt (v.) to change in order to meet certain needs or conditions; to adjust; p. 72. *Related word*: adaptation; p. 77.

advertise (v.) to announce publicly, especially a product or service; p. 63.

advocate (n.) person who pleads a cause, especially a lawyer; (v.) to support; to favor; p. 137.

affluent (adj.) wealthy; well-to-do; rich; p. 97. *Related word*: affluence; p. 104.

align (v.) to bring the parts of a whole into proper coordination with one another; p. 13. *Related word*: alignment; p. 20.

alternative (n.) choice between two things; other choice; option; p. 116. *Related word*: alternate; p. 122.

anticipate (v.) to expect; to foresee; to look forward to; p. 158. *Related word*: anticipation; p. 164.

aperture (n.) hole or opening; p. 13.

appraisal (n.) estimate of the value of something; p. 13. *Related word*: appraise; p. 20.

appreciate (v.) to value; to hold in high regard; to become more valuable; p. 148. *Related word*: appreciation; p. 155.

approximate (v.) to be very similar to; (adj.) near; about; p. 158. *Related word*: approximation; p. 164.

arid (adj.) dry; p. 148. *Related word*: aridity; p. 155.

array (n.) display; collection; arrangement; p. 97.

ascertain (v.) to discover; to determine; p. 158.

assemble (v.) to gather together; to congregate; to put together; p. 52. *Related word*: assembly; p. 59.

azure (adj.) clear blue; sky blue; p. 97.

B

barter (v.) exchange; trade; p. 116.

bazaar (n.) outdoor market; street filled with small shops; p. 97. *Commonly confused word*: bizarre; p. 102.

biosphere (n.) region on, above, and below earth where life can be supported; p. 148. *Related word*: sphere; p. 155

brilliant (adj.) shining brightly; sparkling; extremely intelligent or talented; p. 52. *Related word*: brilliance; p. 59.

C

careen (v.) to lurch; to sway sharply; p. 107.

catapult (v.) to move forcefully or quickly; to leap; p. 107.

circumstance (n.) condition or situation; p. 13. *Related words with the* circ *root*: circa, circuitous, circular, circulate, circulation, circumference, circumnavigate; p. 20.

clan (n.) group of people who are descended from a common ancestor; p. 34.

cleft (n.) opening; division; crevice; p. 34.

coarse (adj.) crude in speech or behavior; rough; cheap; p. 63. *Homonym*: course; p. 67.

coincide (v.) to happen at the same time; to intersect in time or space; p. 52. *Related word*: coincidence; p. 59.

comic (adj.) funny; (n.) comedian; p. 63. *Related word*: comedy; p. 70.

commerce (n.) business; trade; p. 116. *Related word*: commercial; p. 122.

comparable (adj.) equal; similar; like; p. 97. *Related word*: compare; p. 104.

complex (adj.) complicated; involved; intricate; (n.) system; group of related things that make a whole; p. 34. *Related word*: complexity; p. 39.

compose (v.) to make up; to put together; p. 148. *Related words with the* pos *root*: composer, composition, expose, dispose, impose; p. 155.

comprehension (n.) the ability to understand; understanding; grasp; p. 107. *Related words*: comprehend; comprehensible; comprehensive; p. 113.

compression (n.) applying of pressure; squeezing; p. 148. *Related word*: compress; p. 155.

compulsion (n.) irresistible driving force; p. 52. *Related word*: compulsive; p. 59.

confine (v.) to restrict; to keep in; p. 116.

confrontation (n.) face-to-face meeting, often in a spirit of hostility; p. 137. *Related word*: confront; p. 144.

conifer (n.) cone-bearing tree or shrub; p. 34. *Related word*: coniferous; p. 39.

constitution (n.) the way in which a thing is made up; structure; physical makeup of a person; p. 72.

contemplation (n.) deep thought; meditation; expectation; p. 158. *Related word*: contemplate; p. 164.

contemporary (n.) person about the same age as another; (adj.) living or happening in the same period of time; p. 158.

continuous (adj.) never-ending; proceeding without interruption or break; p. 158. *Related word*: continuity; p. 164.

contour (n.) outline (of land, a figure, etc.); p. 34.

convalescence (n.) period of recovery after illness or surgery; p. 72. *Related word*: convalesce; p. 77.

convey (v.) to communicate; to disclose; to reveal; p. 97. *Related word*: conveyance; p. 104.

corridor (n.) long hall or passageway, especially one onto which several rooms open; p. 24.

critically (adv.) carefully, with the purpose of judging for good or bad; p. 13. *Related word*: criticism; p. 20.

cubicle (n.) booth; small compartment; p. 97. *Related word*: cube; p. 104.

cumbersome (adj.) hard to handle because of size, weight, or shape; awkward; p. 24. *Related word*: encumbrance; p. 31.

curdle (v.) to thicken; p. 107. *Related word*: curd; p. 113.

D

deplete (v.) to use up gradually (resources, funds, strength, etc.); to empty completely or partly; p. 34. *Related word*: depletion; p. 39.

derision (n.) contempt; ridicule; mockery; p. 63. *Related words with the* de- *prefix*: decline, deride, derisive, p. 70.

determine (v.) to decide; to be the cause of an effect; p. 13. *Related word*: determination; p. 20.

development (n.) progression or growth; p. 52. *Related word*: develop; p. 59.

diagonally (adv.) on a slant, from corner to corner; p. 13.

disclose (v.) to reveal; to make known; p. 13. *Related word*: disclosure; p. 20.

disfigure (v.) to ruin the appearance of; to deform; p. 107. *Related word*: configuration; p. 113.

dissolve (v.) to melt from a solid into a liquid; to break apart; p. 13.

distill (v.) to heat a mixture in such a way that impurities are removed; p. 148.

distinguish (v.) to tell the difference between; p. 13.

document (v.) to provide a written record of; (n.) a written record; p. 148. *Related word*: documentary; p. 155.

E

effect (n.) result; p. 158. *Homonym*: affect; p. 165.

elusive (adj.) difficult to understand; puzzling; baffling; p. 97. *Related word*: elude; p. 104.

emotion (n.) feeling; p. 158. *Related word*: emotional; p. 164.

enact (v.) to put into action; p. 52. *Related word*: enactment; p. 59.

enclosure (n.) fenced-in area; p. 24.

envision (v.) to imagine; to expect; p. 24.

equality (n.) state of having the same significance, rights, benefits, etc.; p. 137. *Related words*: equalize, equation, equilibrium; p. 144.

essence (n.) extract; scent; perfume; p. 97.

evolve (v.) to develop, grow, or progress; p. 116.

exhaust (v.) to make or become tired; (n.) something given off, as fumes from a gasoline engine; p. 72. *Related word*: exhaustion; p. 77.

existence (n.) state of being; life; p. 97. *Related word*: exist; p. 104.

expand (v.) to increase in size; p. 116. *Related words*: expansion, expansive; p. 122.

expanse (n.) large, open area; p. 34. *Related words*: expand, expansive; p. 39.

expeditious (adj.) efficient; speedy; effective; p. 148. *Related word*: expedite; p. 155.

expire (v.) to end; to die; p. 116. *Related word*: expiration; p. 122.

exploit (v.) to make use of; to utilize; to profit by; p. 116. *Related word*: exploitation; p. 122.

expose (v.) to leave without protection; to make known; to reveal; p. 72. *Related word*: exposure; p. 77.

extinct (adj.) no longer living; nonexistent; p. 158. *Related word*: extinction; p. 164.

exultant (adj.) jubilant; triumphant; p. 107. *Related words*: exult, exultation; p. 113.

F

fierce (adj.) powerful; raging, violent; p. 34. *Related word*: ferocity; p. 39.

finery (n.) elegant or showy clothing; p. 34.

flank (n.) side; p. 107.

flare (n.) bright light used for signaling; p. 97. *Homonym*: flair; p. 105.

flounder (v.) to struggle clumsily; to stumble; p. 34.

formal (adj.) requiring a certain standard of dress; correct and orderly; official; p. 116. *Related word*: formality; p. 122.

foster (v.) to encourage; to promote; to nurture; p. 137.

froth (n.) foam; p. 52. *Related word*: frothy; p. 59.

G

glamorize (v.) to make charming or attractive; p. 63. *Related word*: glamorous; p. 70.

grace (v.) adorn; beautify; p. 107. *Related words*: disgrace, graceful, graceless, gracious; p. 113.

grave (adj.) serious; dignified; solemn; p. 13.

H

hazard (n.) danger; risk; p. 72. *Related word*: hazardous; p. 77.

heartily (adv.) strongly; with much feeling; p. 63. *Related word*: hearty; p. 70.

herald (v.) to usher in; to announce; p. 24.

horde (n.) large crowd; p. 24.

hurtle (v.) to race; to speed; to rush; p. 107.

I

image (n.) imitation of a person or thing, as in a mirror, photograph, painting, etc.; p. 13. *Related word*: imagination; p. 20.

immoderate (adj.) excessive; unreasonable; p. 72. *Related word*: moderation; p. 77.

incense (n.) substance that gives off a pleasant odor when burned; p. 97.

incrustation (n.) decorative layer; inlay; p. 97. *Related word*: incrust; p. 104.

indefinite (adj.) unclear; vague; p. 158.

indictment (n.) charge (often criminal) made against someone; p. 137. *Related word*: indict; p. 144.

inevitable (adj.) unavoidable; sure to happen; inescapable; p. 63.

inheritable (adj.) able to be received, especially from parents or ancestors; p. 116. *Related words*: heritage, inherit; p. 122.

innovative (adj.) recently introduced; new; original; p. 148. *Related word*: innovation; p. 155.

integral (adj.) necessary; essential to the whole; p. 116. *Related words*: integrate, integrity; p. 122.

intend (v.) to plan; to have as one's goal; p. 137. *Related word*: intention; p. 144.

intensity (n.) energy; emotion; passion; p. 97. *Related words*: intense, intensify; p. 104.

intent (adj.) thoroughly involved in something (n.) aim; goal; p. 13. *Related word*: intention; p. 20.

interior (n.) inside; (adj.) inner; of the inner nature of a person or thing; p. 52. *Related word*: exterior; p. 59.

intermingle (v.) to mix together; to blend; to combine; p. 97.

intermittently (adv.) from time to time; periodically; p. 13.

intruder (n.) unwanted person who forces his or her presence on someone else; p. 13. *Related word*: intrusion; p. 20.

inured (v.) to become accustomed to something unpleasant; p. 72.

involve (v.) to include by necessity; to require; p. 72. *Related word*: involvement; p. 77.

iridescent (adj.) showing changing colors; shiny; glowing; p. 97. *Related word*: iridescence; p. 104.

L

lawless (adj.) illegal; disorderly; not obeying the law; p. 63. *Related word*: lawful; p. 70.

level (v.) flatten; knock down; p. 107.

luminous (adj.) shining; glowing; radiant; p. 34. *Related words with the* lumen *root*: illuminate, illumination, illuminator, lumen, luminary; p. 39.

M

maelstrom (n.) powerful, often violent whirlpool sucking in objects within a given radius; turmoil; p. 52.

magnificent (adj.) beautiful; grand; rich or splendid; p. 24. *Related words with the* magn *root:* magnanimous, magnate, magnificence, magnitude; p. 31.

majestic (adj.) stately; magnificent; dignified; grand; p. 34. *Related word*: majesty; p. 39.

mar (v.) to ruin the beauty (of something); to spoil; p. 34.

mass (n.) large quantity or number; p. 24.

mature (adj.) fully developed or grown; p. 52. *Related word*: maturity; p. 59.

mechanism (n.) system of parts; machinery; p. 72. *Related words*: mechanical, mechanics; p. 77.

mentality (n.) capacity or power of one's mind; p. 137.

mere (adj.) only; nothing more than; p. 158.

migration (n.) act of moving from one region to another; p. 52. *Related words*: immigration, migrate; p. 59.

militant (adj.) eager to fight; aggressive in support of a cause; p. 137.

mobility (n.) capability of moving or being moved; p. 116. *Related words*: immobilize, mobile, mobilize; p. 122.

moderate (adj.) within reasonable limits; mild; not violent; (n.) person holding moderate views or opinions (as in politics or religion); (v.) to serve as an organizing authority (for a debate, meeting, assembly, etc.); p. 72. *Related word*: moderation; p. 77.

mottled (adj.) spotted; streaked; speckled; p. 107.

multitude (n.) crowd; p. 24. *Related words*: multiple, multiplicity; p. 31.

mysterious (adj.) difficult to explain; strange; p. 52. *Related words*: mystery, mystify; p. 59.

mythical (adj.) existing only in myths; imaginary; p. 34. *Related word*: myth; p. 39.

N

naive (adj.) simple; childlike; p. 137. *Related word*: naiveté; p. 144.

navigate (v.) to travel through or over (water, land, or air); p. 52. *Related word*: navigation; p. 59.

noxious (adj.) harmful to health; injurious; unwholesome; p. 72.

O

obstacle (n.) something in the way; obstruction; p. 148.

ominous (adj.) threatening; sinister; p. 24.

organism (n.) any plant or animal; any living thing; p. 72. *Related word*: organization; p. 77.

outcrop (n.) part of a rock or mineral formation that is exposed at the surface of the ground; p. 34.

overtake (v.) to catch up with; p. 13.

P

pent-up (adj.) kept or held in; shut; penned; p. 107.

perpendicular (adj.) at right angles to a line; p. 158.

perpetual (adj.) never-ending, everlasting; p. 158. *Related words*: perpetuate, perpetuity; p. 164.

persuade (v.) to convince someone to believe or do something; p. 63. *Related words*: persuasion, persuasive; p. 70.

pervade (v.) to spread throughout; p. 24. *Related word*: pervasive; p. 31.

pessimistic (adj.) expecting the worst; negative; p. 137. *Related word*: pessimism; p. 144.

phenomenon (n.) extremely unusual thing or occurrence; p. 52. *Related word*: phenomena; p. 59.

philosopher (n.) one who studies thought and the meaning of life; p. 158. *Related words*: philosophical, philosophy; p. 164.

picturesque (adj.) visually pleasing; striking; vivid; p. 63.

pious (adj.) having or showing religious devotion; p. 137. *Related word*: piety; p. 144.

plume (n.) large, showy feather; something that looks like a plume; p. 107. *Related word*: plumage; p. 113.

plunge (v.) to dive, especially into water (n.) a leap; p. 158.

potent (adj.) powerful; effective; influential; p. 72. *Related word*: potential; p. 77.

precede (v.) to come before or go ahead of in time or rank; p. 116. *Related word*: precedence; p. 122.

pristine (adj.) pure; unspoiled; p. 34.

proclaim (v.) to declare; to announce; p. 24. *Related word*: proclamation; p. 31.

prominence (n.) distinction; fame; state of being noticed or obvious; p. 137. *Related word*: prominent; p. 144.

propel (v.) to push or drive forward or outward; p. 137. *Related word*: propulsion; p. 144.

prophet (n.) one who predicts the future; p. 137. *Related words*: prophecy, prophetic; p. 144.

psychological (adj.) of the mind; mental; p. 72. *Related words*: psychologist, psychology; p. 77.

pulverize (v.) to completely destroy; to crush to dust or powder; p. 107.

puritanical (adj.) very strict; p. 137.

pyrotechnic (adj.) resembling fireworks; dazzling; brilliant; p. 107.

Q

quantity (n.) amount; p. 148.

R

recline (v.) to lie down; p. 63. *Related word*: incline; p. 70.

reel (v.) to sway; to stagger; to give way; p. 107.

reflection (n.) image in a mirror or water; deep thought; p. 158. *Related words*: reflect, reflective; p. 164.

repetition (n.) act of doing again; a repeating; p. 72. *Related word*: repetitious; p. 77.

reputation (n.) public opinion about a person's character; p. 63. *Related word*: reputable; p. 70.

resemblance (n.) likeness; similarity; p. 24. *Related word*: resemble; p. 31.

response (n.) answer or reaction; p. 72. *Related words*: respond, responsive; p. 77.

restorative (adj.) capable of returning something to its former state; p. 72. *Related word*: restore; p. 77.

restriction (n.) limitation; rule or law that limits; p. 116. *Related words with the strict root*: constrict; restrict; strict; stricture; p. 122.

retrieve (v.) to bring back; to recover; p. 13. *Related word*: retriever; p. 20.

rigid (adj.) stiff; inflexible; not open to change; p. 137. *Related word*: rigidity; p. 144.

romantic (adj.) characterized by love, adventure, excitement, or great feeling; p. 52. *Related word*: romanticize; p. 59

S

scuttle (v.) to run quickly; to scamper; p. 34.

seep (v.) to penetrate; to leak; to ooze; p. 97. *Related Word*: seepage; p. 104.

seldom (adv.) not very often; rarely; p. 63.

servitude (n.) slavery; enslavement; bondage; p. 116.

sheer (adj.) absolute; utter; unqualified; p. 24.

shrewd (adj.) clever; mentally sharp; p. 137. *Related word*: shrewdness; p. 144.

sophisticated (adj.) worldly-wise; refined; p. 137. *Related word*: sophistication; p. 144.

sordid (adj.) dirty; low; base; p. 116.

spacious (adj.) roomy; large; p. 97 *Related word*: spaciousness; p. 104.

spawn (v.) to reproduce; p. 52.

species (n.) class; kind; p. 158.

spectacle (n.) strange or remarkable sight; unusual display; p. 24. *Related word*: spectator; p. 31.

spontaneous (adj.) not planned ahead of time; impulsive; p. 34. *Related word*: spontaneity; p. 39.

status (n.) legal position; condition; state; p. 116.

statute (n.) law; formal regulation; p. 116.

steppe (n.) a vast plain having few trees; p. 34.

stockpile (n.) a supply of materials stored up for future use; p. 34.

strategist (n.) person who plans in a systematic way; p. 137. *Related word*: strategy; p. 144.

stratosphere (n.) layer of the atmosphere that stretches from about six to about thirty miles above the surface of the earth; p. 107.

stress (n.) physical or mental strain; pressure; p. 72.

strewn (v.) scattered; p. 107.

subtle (adj.) delicate; understated; p. 97. *Related word*: subtlety; p. 104.

suffice (v.) to be adequate; p. 13.

sufficient (adj.) enough; adequate; acceptable; p. 13.

suitable (adj.) appropriate; in keeping with; p. 52. *Related word*: suit; p. 59.

summit (n.) peak; highest point; p. 107.

supple (adj.) able to bend and move easily; flexible; p. 13.

surplus (n.) amount over and above what is needed or used; (adj.) excess; extra; p. 158.

symbolic (adj.) used to stand for something else; p. 97. *Related words*: symbol, symbolize; p. 104

system (n.) organized method; number of parts working as a whole; p. 116. *Related word*: systematic; p. 122.

T

tabular (adj.) flat like a table; p. 148.

taciturn (adj.) reluctant to talk; reserved; quiet; p. 63

technological (adj.) based on applied science, often related to use of machinery and automations; p. 148. *Related words*: technical, technology; p. 155.

tedious (adj.) boring; tiresome; p. 148.

teem (v.) to be full of; to swarm (with); p. 24.

testify (v.) to give evidence; p. 158. *Related word*: testimony; p. 164.

textile (n.) woven material; cloth; fabric; p. 116.

thrust (v.) to push suddenly; to stab; (n.) sudden, forceful push; lunge; p. 63.

trace (n.) very small amount; mark or sign; (v.) to track; to follow the course of; p. 148.

tragedy (n.) sad or disastrous event; serious play having a sad or unfortunate ending; p. 52 *Related word*: tragic; p. 59.

transitional (adj.) relating to a movement from one state or condition to another; p. 24. *Related words with the* trans- *prefix*: transcontinental, transcribe, transfer, transform, transfuse, transition, translate, transmission, transparent, transplant; p. 31.

treacherous (adj.) dangerous; p. 52. *Related word*: treachery; p. 59.

typical (adj.) usual; normal; characteristic; p. 63.

U

uncharted (adj.) unknown; not mapped; p. 24.

undoubtedly (adv.) certainly; unquestionably; without doubt; p. 63.

unerringly (adv.) exactly; without error or variation; p. 52. *Related word*: err; p. 59.

urge (v.) to encourage; to strongly suggest; (n.) basic inner drive or desire; p. 63. *Related words*: urgency, urgent; p. 70.

utilize (v.) to make use of something; p. 148. *Related words*: utility, utilization; p. 155.

V

vanity (n.) too much pride in oneself; egotism; self-admiration; p. 63. *Related word*: vain; p. 70.

vast (adj.) great in size, amount, etc.; p. 158. *Related word*: vastness; p. 164.

venture (v.) to take a risk; (n.) risky or dangerous undertaking; p. 24.

version (n.) one side or point of view of a story or incident; p. 63.

visionary (n.) person who sees into the future; (adj.) not realistic; impractical; p. 148. *Related word*: visualize; p. 155.

vista (n.) view; scene; p. 107.

volume (n.) loudness; the capacity of a container; p. 72. *Related word*: voluminous; p. 77.

Y

yield (v.) to give way to; to give up; to give or produce; (n.) amount produced; p. 148.

Pronunciation Key

Symbol	Key Words	Symbol	Key Words
a	ask, fat, parrot	b	bed, fable, dub
ā	ape, date, play	d	dip, beadle, had
ä	ah, car, father	f	fall, after, off
		g	get, haggle, dog
e	elf, ten, berry	h	he, ahead, hotel
ē	even, meet, money	j	joy, agile, badge
		k	kill, tackle, bake
i	is, hit, mirror	l	let, yellow, ball
ī	ice, bite, high	m	met, camel, trim
ō	open, tone, go	n	not, flannel, ton
ô	all, horn, law	p	put, apple, tap
o͞o	ooze, tool, crew	r	red, port, dear
oo	look, pull, moor	s	sell, castle, pass
yo͞o	use, cute, few	t	top, cattle, hat
yoo	united, cure, globule	v	vat, hovel, have
		w	will, always, swear
		y	yet, onion, yard
oi	oil, point, toy	z	zebra, dazzle, haze
ou	out, crowd, plow		
u	up, cut, color	ch	chin, catcher, arch
ʉr	urn, fur, deter	sh	she, cushion, dash
ə	a in ago	th	thin, nothing, truth
	e in agent		
	i in sanity	zh	azure, leisure
	o in comply	ŋ	ring, anger, drink
	u in focus	′	able (aʹ bʹl)
ər	perhaps, murder	″	expedition (ekʹ spə dishʹ ən)

Inventory Test

These are all the target words in the book. Why not see how many you think you already know . . . or don't know?
- If you're sure *you know the word, mark the* **Y** *("yes") circle.*
- If you think you *might know it, mark the* **?** *(question mark) circle.*
- If you have *no idea what it means, mark the* **N** *("no") circle.*

Y	?	N	
○	○	○	abundant
○	○	○	accessible
○	○	○	acknowledge
○	○	○	acute
○	○	○	adapt
○	○	○	advertise
○	○	○	advocate
○	○	○	affluent
○	○	○	align
○	○	○	alternative
○	○	○	anticipate
○	○	○	aperture
○	○	○	appraisal
○	○	○	appreciate
○	○	○	approximate
○	○	○	arid
○	○	○	array
○	○	○	ascertain
○	○	○	assemble
○	○	○	azure
○	○	○	barter
○	○	○	bazaar
○	○	○	biosphere
○	○	○	brilliant
○	○	○	careen
○	○	○	catapult
○	○	○	circumstance
○	○	○	clan
○	○	○	cleft
○	○	○	coarse
○	○	○	coincide
○	○	○	comic
○	○	○	commerce
○	○	○	comparable
○	○	○	complex
○	○	○	compose
○	○	○	comprehension
○	○	○	compression
○	○	○	compulsion
○	○	○	confine

That's the first 40.

Y	?	N	
○	○	○	confrontation
○	○	○	conifer
○	○	○	constitution
○	○	○	contemplation
○	○	○	contemporary
○	○	○	continuous
○	○	○	contour
○	○	○	convalescence
○	○	○	convey
○	○	○	corridor
○	○	○	critically
○	○	○	cubicle
○	○	○	cumbersome
○	○	○	curdle
○	○	○	deplete
○	○	○	derision
○	○	○	determine
○	○	○	development
○	○	○	diagonally
○	○	○	disclose

You're making progress.

Y	?	N	
○	○	○	disfigure
○	○	○	dissolve
○	○	○	distill
○	○	○	distinguish
○	○	○	document
○	○	○	effect
○	○	○	elusive
○	○	○	emotion
○	○	○	enact
○	○	○	enclosure
○	○	○	envision
○	○	○	equality
○	○	○	essence
○	○	○	evolve
○	○	○	exhaust
○	○	○	existence
○	○	○	expand
○	○	○	expanse
○	○	○	expeditious
○	○	○	expire

Y	?	N	
○	○	○	exploit
○	○	○	expose
○	○	○	extinct
○	○	○	exultant
○	○	○	fierce
○	○	○	finery
○	○	○	flank
○	○	○	flare
○	○	○	flounder
○	○	○	formal
○	○	○	foster
○	○	○	froth
○	○	○	glamorize
○	○	○	grace
○	○	○	grave
○	○	○	hazard
○	○	○	heartily
○	○	○	herald
○	○	○	horde
○	○	○	hurtle
○	○	○	image
○	○	○	immoderate
○	○	○	incense
○	○	○	incrustation
○	○	○	indefinite
○	○	○	indictment
○	○	○	inevitable
○	○	○	inheritable
○	○	○	innovative
○	○	○	integral
○	○	○	intend
○	○	○	intensity
○	○	○	intent
○	○	○	interior
○	○	○	intermingle
○	○	○	intermittently
○	○	○	intruder
○	○	○	inured
○	○	○	involve
○	○	○	iridescent

Take a break!

Y	?	N	
O	O	O	lawless
O	O	O	level
O	O	O	luminous
O	O	O	maelstrom
O	O	O	magnificent
O	O	O	majestic
O	O	O	mar
O	O	O	mass
O	O	O	mature
O	O	O	mechanism
O	O	O	mentality
O	O	O	mere
O	O	O	migration
O	O	O	militant
O	O	O	mobility
O	O	O	moderate
O	O	O	mottled
O	O	O	multitude
O	O	O	mysterious
O	O	O	mythical

Half the alphabet.

Y	?	N	
O	O	O	naive
O	O	O	navigate
O	O	O	noxious
O	O	O	obstacle
O	O	O	ominous
O	O	O	organism
O	O	O	outcrop
O	O	O	overtake
O	O	O	pent-up
O	O	O	perpendicular
O	O	O	perpetual
O	O	O	persuade
O	O	O	pervade
O	O	O	pessimistic
O	O	O	phenomenon
O	O	O	philosopher
O	O	O	picturesque
O	O	O	pious
O	O	O	plume
O	O	O	plunge

Y	?	N	
O	O	O	potent
O	O	O	precede
O	O	O	pristine
O	O	O	proclaim
O	O	O	prominence
O	O	O	propel
O	O	O	prophet
O	O	O	psychological
O	O	O	pulverize
O	O	O	puritanical
O	O	O	pyrotechnic
O	O	O	quantity
O	O	O	recline
O	O	O	reel
O	O	O	reflection
O	O	O	repetition
O	O	O	reputation
O	O	O	resemblance
O	O	O	response
O	O	O	restorative
O	O	O	restriction
O	O	O	retrieve
O	O	O	rigid
O	O	O	romantic
O	O	O	scuttle
O	O	O	seep
O	O	O	seldom
O	O	O	servitude
O	O	O	sheer
O	O	O	shrewd
O	O	O	sophisticated
O	O	O	sordid
O	O	O	spacious
O	O	O	spawn
O	O	O	species
O	O	O	spectacle
O	O	O	spontaneous

This list will end soon.

Y	?	N	
O	O	O	status
O	O	O	statute
O	O	O	steppe

Y	?	N	
O	O	O	stockpile
O	O	O	strategist
O	O	O	stratosphere
O	O	O	stress
O	O	O	strewn
O	O	O	subtle
O	O	O	suffice
O	O	O	sufficient
O	O	O	suitable
O	O	O	summit
O	O	O	supple
O	O	O	surplus
O	O	O	symbolic
O	O	O	system
O	O	O	tabular
O	O	O	taciturn
O	O	O	technological
O	O	O	tedious
O	O	O	teem
O	O	O	testify

Only 20 more.

Y	?	N	
O	O	O	textile
O	O	O	thrust
O	O	O	trace
O	O	O	tragedy
O	O	O	transitional
O	O	O	treacherous
O	O	O	typical
O	O	O	uncharted
O	O	O	undoubtedly
O	O	O	unerringly
O	O	O	urge
O	O	O	utilize
O	O	O	vanity
O	O	O	vast
O	O	O	venture
O	O	O	version
O	O	O	visionary
O	O	O	vista
O	O	O	volume
O	O	O	yield

Congratulations!

That was 240 words. How many of them *don't* you know? Highlight any words you marked **N**, and pay special attention to them as you work through the book. You'll soon know them all!

Acknowledgments

- Dell Publishing Co.: For an excerpt from "The Surround" by Stewart Edward White, from *Pioneers West: 14 Stories of the Old Frontier,* edited by Don Ward; copyright © 1966 by Dell Publishing Co., by permission of the Estate of Stewart Edward White.

- Wyoming Game and Fish Department: For "Trail of the Bison" by Larry Roop, from *Wyoming Wildlife,* July 1971.

- Crown Publishers, Inc.: For an excerpt from *Clan of the Cave Bear* by Jean M. Auel; copyright © 1980 by Jean M. Auel.

- Imperial Oil Ltd.: For "Salmon Run" by Linda Curtis, from *Imperial Oil Review;* copyright © 1968 by Imperial Oil Ltd.

- Harper & Row Publishers, Inc. (Thomas Y. Crowell): For "Cowhands," from *Frontier Living* by Edwin Tunis; copyright © 1961 by Edwin Tunis.

- International Creative Management: For an adapted and abridged excerpt from *The Tyranny of Noise* by Robert Alex Baron, pp. 85–86; copyright © 1970 by Robert Alex Baron.

- Harcourt Brace Jovanovich, Inc.: For an excerpt from "The Labyrinthine City of Fez," from *In Favor of the Sensitive Man and Other Essays;* copyright © 1973 by Anaïs Nin.

- The Daily News: For an excerpt from *Volcano: The Eruption of Mount St. Helens* in *The Daily News,* Longview, WA; copyright The Daily News, Longview, WA.

- U.S. Department of Labor: For an excerpt from *A Bicentennial Look at the Early Days of American Labor* by Richard B. Morris; courtesy of the *Monthly Labor Review* and the *U.S. Department of Labor Bicentennial History of the American Worker.*

- G.P. Putnam's Sons: For an excerpt from *The Days of Martin Luther King, Jr.* by Jim Bishop; copyright © 1971 by Jim Bishop.

- Science Service, Inc.: For "Is there an Iceberg in Your Future?" by Kendrick Frazier, from *Science News,* the weekly news magazine of science, copyright © 1977 by Science Service, Inc.

- For an adapted and abridged version of "Niagara Falls" by Abraham Lincoln, from *Sunshine and Smoke: American Writers and the American Environment,* edited by David D. Anderson.

Every effort has been made to trace the ownership of all copyrighted material and to obtain persmission.

Cover Art

Three Worlds (detail), 1955, M.C. Escher, Lithograph. National Gallery of Art, Washington, D.C.; gift of C.V.S. Roosevelt.

Photographs

FPG International: 36, 139; Culver Pictures, Inc.: 54; UPI Bettmann Newsphotos: 109; Sarkis Tatosian, Oscar Iberian Rugs, Evanston, Illinois: 122.

Illustrations

Suzanne Snider: 15, 65; Tom Dunnington: 26; Jack Wallen: 74; Diane McKnight: 79; George Suyeoka: 99, 118; David Cunningham: 150; Larry Frederick: 160.

Personal Vocabulary Log

Use the following pages to keep track of the unfamiliar words you encounter in your reading. Write brief definitions and pronunciations for each word. This will make the words part of your permanent vocabulary.

_____

_____

_____

_____

_____

_____

_____

_____

_____

_____

_____

_____

_____

_____

_____

_____

_____

_____

_____

_____

_____

_____

_____

_____

Personal Vocabulary Log

Personal Vocabulary Log

Personal Vocabulary Log

Personal Vocabulary Log